American Corporations and Peruvian Politics

American Corporations and Peruvian Politics

Charles T. Goodsell

Harvard University Press   Cambridge, Massachusetts   1974

For Liz

Preface

This book is intended to convey to an academic as well as general audience the results of several years' study of the political implications for Peru of the presence of sizable American business investments in that country. The author's normative inclination is to favor the interests, as perceived, of Peru. Atypically for a professor, perhaps, I am consciously neither sympathetic nor unsympathetic to the interests of American business. Regardless of my biases or the lack thereof, however, a sincere attempt has been made to arrive at sober, balanced judgments following a systematic sifting of available evidence.

Material support for the study came from four sources: Southern Illinois University, Carbondale; the Social Science Research Council, New York; the Council of the Americas, New York; and the American Philosophical Society, Philadelphia (Penrose Fund). In gratitude for this assistance I would like to thank personally Ronald G. Hanson, Bryce Wood, Enno Hobbing, and George W. Corner for their interest and cooperation.

I am deeply indebted to a number of people who assisted at various stages of research and writing. Dr. Arnoldo Rozenberg graciously introduced me to his native country of Peru in 1967. Seymour J. Schwartz and Ceferina C. Gayo served loyally as research assistants. Larry Hawse helped in the preparation of grant applications. My colleagues Orville Alexander, Willard Beaulac, Jack Van Der Slik, Samuel Long, and Samuel Pernacciaro offered valuable support and advice in selected aspects of the study. Professor David P. Werlich made numerous suggestions and caught many errors in regard to the book's content. M. Elizabeth Goodsell and Frances C. Goodsell reviewed the manuscript in its entirety for stylistic inadequacies. I hereby thank all of these individuals for their help.

By way of a substantive postscript added as this volume goes to press, I should like to note that in the final days of 1973 the Peruvian government expropriated the Cerro de Pasco Corporation. Nationalization of this American firm may appear to be a break with the past but is actually in accord with previous developments traced in this book. The military regime acted forthrightly, as it has in the past, when a foreign company was insufficiently cooperative or behaved contrary to standards of policy. Yet the takeover constitutes part of a contemplated larger bargain between Lima and Washington whereby substantial compensation to several expropriated concerns (including Cerro and Grace but not IPC) is being discussed in connection with augmented flows to Peru of American bank credits and investment funds. Meanwhile the huge Cuajone project, owned in part by Cerro, goes ahead. Thus what may seem to be a new turn of events is in reality in conformity with past events and is, possibly, a continuation of the delicate rapprochement between capitalists and generals that emerged in 1971.

Carbondale, Illinois   C.T.G.
1973

Contents

Tables

Figures

American Corporations and Peruvian Politics

Part I   Theory and Setting

One   Foreign Investment and Politics

Foreign investment is primarily an economic act with economic motivations lying behind it and economic consequences resulting from it. That economic acts can have *political* consequences as well is, of course, an ancient observation; a principal preoccupation of political thinkers down to the present day has been the extent to which economic power generates political power and those controlling money capital also control public decisions. When the capital is controlled by foreigners the issue takes on an added, crucial dimension. Questions are raised such as: To what extent is national independence compromised by foreign capital? Are there lasting effects on the political system? These questions would appear to be particularly important when the source of investments is a gigantic superpower, such as the United States, and the site of investments is a modest-sized, low-income country, such as Peru. The following pages are addressed to these questions as they relate to U.S. investment in Peru.

Two Gaps

The normative perspective of the writer is, quite frankly, the interests of Peru rather than those of American investors or the United States. Hence to him these questions are intrinsically of importance. To most Peruvians they will also be such.

To the disinterested observer the issues may also arouse interest because of certain intriguing features of existing comment on them. Two quite remarkable gaps characterize it—one of opinion and one of knowledge. The first gap separates widely divergent interpretations of foreign-investor political impact, and the second lies between confident assertions on the subject on the one hand and the amount of available empirical evidence on the other.

One school of thought answers the questions posed above by stating vehemently that national independence *is* compromised and even destroyed, and that a lasting effect on the political system is servility to the capitalists and their government. In short, "economic imperialism" is the consequence of foreign investment. Giant American-controlled multinational corporations, it is said, together with the U.S. government, are able to and do dominate the political systems of underdeveloped "Third World" countries. This position has many facets and will be spelled out in detail in a moment, but it can be illustrated by the following quotation from John Gerassi: "Private enterprise and especially the huge trusts coming into Latin America with millions or billions of dollars are perhaps not to blame for profiting from conditions that favor them. Of course, they perpetuate such conditions through bribes, boycotts, and the financing of political parties, *coups d'etat*, and even revolutions."[1]

Another school of thought entertains almost totally opposite opinions. It states that whatever the record of foreign investors in past decades, today they are politically weak and defensive in less developed areas such as Latin America. The local political environment is so hostile, according to this view, that the corporations steer clear of "politics," conscientiously obey local laws, and confine themselves to public relations and charitable good works in an effort to improve their image. The consequence is that they have little or no political "clout," but bring to the society the benefits of economic development and their charitable contributions. This "corporate good citizen" viewpoint is illustrated by the following excerpt from a dispatch sent from the Middle East by *New York Times* correspondent Dana Adams Schmidt:

Long gone are the days when oil companies made and unmade governments in Iran and Iraq. They have learned that in the politics of the Middle East as in the United States any enterprise backed by the oil companies is automatically discredited by a large segment of public opinion. They therefore confine themselves publicly to the most restrained support of philanthropic and scholarly works . . .

The companies as such are . . . political targets, mainly as symbols of the West, but in any case are politically impotent. Power is exerted, rather, by the [local] government, which is the beneficiary of the royalties and tax payments made by the companies.[2]

The second gap may help to explain this first one, but it by no means accounts for all of it. This is between opinion and knowledge. Broad generalizations are made about the political power of foreign companies with an air of confidence, even dogmatism. Yet precious few empirical studies have been made of the subject, and almost none systematically and in depth. Daniel J. Baum has said, in commenting on the concept of an "American challenge" in Europe à la Servan-Schreiber, "While study is pursued men and nations are acting as if the facts were clear."[3] The facts are not clear, leaving the way open to great divergence of opinion, based flimsily on the selected illustration and deducted conclusion. Yet, of course, those out to "prove" a case either against or for American business would probably indulge in hyperbole and propaganda regardless of the state of knowledge. Certainly in reviewing pertinent literature one senses that a number of writers are not particularly interested in facts.

A great many very good studies have been made of American foreign investment or the multinational corporations. But most of them concern primarily economic or managerial aspects rather than political consequences. This is understandable in that, as stated, foreign investment is first and foremost an economic and business act. A few overall analyses of international investment include excellent commentary on political aspects, but the comment is accordingly general rather than specific. Here one must cite in particular works by Jack N. Behrman, Charles P. Kindleberger, Raymond F. Mikesell, Louis Turner, and Raymond Vernon.[4] Other pertinent items of literature tend to be sketchy, or uninhibitedly biased, or both.[5] Similarly, writings on American companies in Peru either cover the subject in passing or are unrestrained in their praise or virulent attack.[6]

Others have noted the lack of detailed investigation of the political consequences of foreign investment. They offer a number of reasons. Gerassi, quoted above, believes it is because scholars "do not want to alienate their source of research funds, most of which comes from the government or from companies with assets in Latin America."[7] Miguel S. Wionczek suggests that opposition from "the actual holders of political power in Latin America" is the problem.[8] Former Congressman Thomas Curtis of Missouri perceives simply "a shocking decline of scholarship."[9] Merle Kling, in discussing the political role of international oil companies in Venezuela, concludes that precise details are unavailable and yet arrives at findings anyway: "While the exact techniques of the exercise of power are not easily demonstrated, obviously a substantial economic base of power in Venezuela is controlled by economic institutions beyond the geographical boundaries of the country. The control of mineral wealth, consequently, within the framework of colonial economies, introduces an external element of restraint on the exercise of power by domestic forces and movements with Latin America."[10]

Probably each of these explanations holds some validity. It was only with some difficulty that funds could be obtained to support the writing of this book, and as it turned out most of the money came from the author's own university. (See the preface for details of financing.) A definite and vexing problem encountered in conducting research for this book was gaining access to and cooperation from high-ranking Peruvian political and governmental leaders. However, over several years individuals at the congressional and ministerial level were interviewed, plus others including a past president. (See the appendex for information on respondents.) Certainly many of the details of power relationship are always unknowable in political research, and this study is not represented as having been based on an "insider" status. But an assumption of the undertaking has been that a persistent search for several forms of data could, over time, yield an improved understanding of the politics of foreign investment, at least as it obtains in Peru. In writing this book I

have no naive expectation that the gap of opinion will be closed. But the
gap of knowledge should be narrowed.

Foreign Investment

Before proceeding to the study proper I would like to comment on the
phenomenon of foreign investment.

It takes several forms. Foreign investment may consist of money capital
or other property, such as technology or organizational skills. It is usually
thought of as crossing national frontiers, although in such actions as
reinvestment of earnings acquired in the capital-importing or "host"
country the international transfer aspect is technically absent. "Portfolio"
investments normally consist of bonds or loans where managerial control
over the capital is not also transferred; "direct" investments involve
continuing managerial control over the use of capital. Ownership of the
property may be in either private or governmental hands and historically
has been in both. Here we are concerned with *private, direct* investment,
almost all of which consists of foreign operations of business firms—whether they be mines, oil fields, public utilities, factories, banks, retail stores,
or plantations. From the standpoint of legal organization, these operations
are usually subsidiaries of the parent corporation incorporated under the
laws of the host country, although they also consist of overseas branches.

Foreign investment is a very old phenomenon but has taken on greatly
increased significance in recent decades. Operations of the British East
India Company and loans by the great financial houses of Europe played a
profound role in world events of the seventeenth and eighteenth centuries.
British and French bond purchasers provided the capital for financing
much of the infrastructure built in the "new nations" of nineteenth-
century Latin America. After World War I portfolio capital from the
United States flowed by the hundreds of millions of dollars to war-ravaged
Europe and also to Latin America and other areas. Following World War II
the flow of private U.S. capital abroad took on new features and
dimensions and has since remained the world's greatest source of private
international financing.

Among the new, postwar features were the predominance of direct as
over against portfolio investments; an emphasis on local manufacturing
rather than extractive industries; and sales internally in the host country
rather than mainly abroad. As for amounts of capital involved, a tremendous increase has been registered in recent years. To illustrate, whereas
in 1943 the book value of U.S. private direct investments abroad was less
than $8 billion, by 1950 it had risen to nearly $12 billion. But by 1959
the figure was almost $30 billion, and by 1967 about $60 billion. The
1970 amount was $78 billion; of this about 40 percent was invested in
manufacturing, and about 30 percent each was placed in Europe and

Canada. The book value of U.S. direct investments in Latin America in 1970 amounted to $12.2 billion, of which $691 million was in Peru.[11]

Underlying this vast quantitative expansion, and probably the most significant qualitative change involved, is the growth of multinational corporations. These are business enterprises with operations located in often scores of countries around the globe (over 100 in some cases) and whose planning and decisions are integrated on a worldwide scale. Although a few international oil companies such as Standard Oil of New Jersey (now Exxon Corporation) pioneered in this approach long ago, today about 250 enterprises of various kinds fall into this category, according to Behrman. Although these firms operate under the laws and with the resources of numerous countries and are in these respects "multinational," their equity ownership is usually centralized with residents of one country. Behrman estimates that about 200 of the firms are American; most of the remaining are British, European, and Japanese.[12]

It should be stressed that these organizations are very big, both individually and collectively. This is a major reason why they inspire awe and fear in the hearts of many men, especially outside the United States. Companies like IBM and General Motors earn $500 to $600 million a year from overseas operations alone; this kind of figure compares favorably with the national budgets of many countries of the world. GM's annual sales at $25 billion is a figure greater than most national GNP's. It has been estimated that in 1967 the total world output of foreign subsidiaries of international companies was $240 billion, which is approximately an eighth of the entire free-world GNP.[13]

Governments of the free world have viewed these developments with considerable ambivalence. For its part, the U.S. government has both restricted and encouraged outflows of capital. To make short-term gains in the U.S. balance of payments, American banks and corporations are subject to limits on the amount of loans and new investment placed abroad, particularly in the industrialized countries. Yet on the other hand Washington promotes foreign investment in less developed countries as a means of fostering economic development in friendly nations without the heavy budgetary effects incurred by foreign aid. Assistance to U.S. business and promotion of private-enterprise ideology form elements of this policy. It is carried out by investment insurance and guaranties offered by the Overseas Private Investment Corporation, long-term loans made by the Export-Import Bank, and other activities.[14]

Governments of capital-importing nations have also exhibited ambivalence, both in the sense of somewhat contradictory policies of individual governments and of differences between governments. Great Britain and the West European powers have generally welcomed the multinational companies, with certain vivid exceptions. The investments are seen as providing needed capital and technology and improving the balance of payments position in a number of ways. Yet signficiant tensions have also arisen because of fears of economic concentration and dominance, technological dependence, the effects of U.S. laws, and disturbance to national economic plans.[15]

Governments of the less industrialized countries are deeply divided on the issue. Some of them actively seek and promote foreign investments in their economies with the hope that foreign firms will bolster national income by tax, wage, and other payments, contribute to economic development by closing enormous capital and technology gaps, and assist the balance of payments by export expansion and import substitution. The encouragements include tax holidays, depreciation allowances, profit-remittance guaranties, and other incentives. Several of the governments of Latin America do this, despite the increasingly bad reputation of that part of the world as being hostile to foreign business. It is of interest, for example, that the "Economic Survey of the Americas" published by the *New York Times* each January always contains numerous government-sponsored advertisements aimed at luring or at least calming foreign investors. Between 1959 and 1971 an average of eight Latin or Caribbean political units were represented by such advertisements, with no decline in number over the years. Brazil and Mexico advertise every year, with Argentina, Venezuela, and Peru often represented.

Yet great doubt, suspicion, and even hatred characterize responses to foreign business in the Third World countries. American companies are denounced daily in the strongest terms by the political Left and most intellectuals and students. Not infrequently acts of violence are carried out against American businesses and businessmen. In addition, of course, and also as an outgrowth of this political opinion and activity, official governmental policy is often hostile. In its milder forms this involves restrictions on foreign firms designed not to drive capital out but to condition its use. Examples are requirements of substantial and even majority participation by local capital, minima on numbers of foreign personnel, import restrictions, and foreign exchange controls. More radical policies are exclusion from certain basic industries, review of major managerial actions, and nationalization—with or without compensation.[16]

In Latin America we find a large variety of policies, but the general trend is an increasingly tough stance against foreign business. The three big countries of Brazil, Argentina, and Mexico still officially welcome most foreign capital, although conditions placed on it are often stringent. Venezuela, once the hemispheric showplace of foreign petroleum exploitation, has imposed increasingly higher rates of effective taxation and ever more restrictive control. Meanwhile all of the Andean governments, save Colombia, have taken drastic actions against foreign investors in recent years. Chile has nationalized the copper companies as a step in creating a socialist economy; Bolivia forced or frightened almost every sizable U.S.

firm out of the country; and Peru has, under the regime of Juan Velasco Alvarado, taken an entire range of radical steps designed to transform her economy and the role of foreign investment in it. Also to be considered in connection with this emergence of anti-investor policy along the Pacific coast is formation of the Andean Group, an economic integration effort begun in 1969 that includes Colombia, Ecuador, Peru, Bolivia, and Chile. This undertaking has developed surprisingly well and has included creation of an Andean Development Corporation and the signing of a common code on the treatment of foreign enterprise. The main outlines of the code resemble closely Peru's highly dirigistic approach to foreign capital, to be explained in the following chapter.

The explanation for what appears to be increasing moves against foreign enterprise in Latin America is complex and cannot be dealt with adequately here. But some of the elements are undoubtedly these: rising national pride; anti-Americanism and anticapitalism promoted by the political Left; opposition to perceived abuses by foreign companies, including huge profits, exploitation of labor, and removal of the national patrimony in the case of mining and petroleum; and fear of cultural erosion or subjugation.[17]

In addition there has emerged a sharp questioning of the highly touted economic benefits of foreign investment. Critics cite with a vengeance the fact that for most postwar years in Latin America the profit remittances, dividends, royalties, and other payments back to the United States from American subsidiaries have exceeded new capital brought to Latin America. This is interpreted as a "loss." Such a view ignores the fact that the yield is based on accumulated investments from the past and is accompanied by internal payment of taxes, wages, and purchases. Another factor is that sometimes operations of the companies may positively affect the country's balance of payments and levels of productivity. But under certain conditions the very opposite can be true, and moreover it is possible that unwise investments can actually retard economic growth or cause it to be skewed. No attempt is made here to assess these economic consequences; economists have done so in several places, and they are by no means in agreement. But in general it seems clear that the economic impact of foreign capital is multiple, complex, and varied.[18]

Scope and Hypotheses

Moving now to *political* impacts—in the specific case of American investment in Peru—the extraordinary gap between the economic-imperialism and corporate good-citizen schools of thought provides us with the stimulus for investigation along a number of fronts. These include the degree of local political involvement by the corporations, relationships between them and the U.S. government, the integrity of Peruvian polity vis-à-vis American business interests, and in general the ability of the companies to "get their way."

These matters all concern, at bottom, political *power*. Clearly this concept must play a central role in this book for it is the principal issue. It is the principal issue in politics generally but, unfortunately for the precision of political "science," the concept is a most elusive and multifaceted one. As John Champlin and others have pointed out, when the lay citizen employs the term "power" in ordinary conversation the meaning seems perfectly clear; but when political scientists or sociologists try to use it, they encounter such great semantic difficulties that dropping the term entirely is seriously considered.[19]

I shall use the word, but in doing so must draw attention to its ambiguities. To achieve "power," must sanctions be employed or need they only be available? Must the power-holder actually induce his subject to do something he would not otherwise do, or need the subject merely be aware of the power-holder's wishes and act "on his own" in accord with those wishes? Must the subject consciously want to do something else, or can he be induced unconsciously to desire what the power-holder wishes? Must the power-holder intentionally wield his influence, or may power be an unintentional consequence as well?[20]

Generally we answer "either one" to all these questions and hence employ a comprehensive and perhaps eclectic concept. But in so doing the task of measurement increases in degree of difficulty. Yet measuring power is very hard anyway unless one merely defines it as the configuration of bargaining outcomes, as some game theorists have done.

In tackling the problem of assessing degrees of power a multiple strategy is followed. Evaluation is attempted along three dimensions of power-related phenomena. First, an attempt is made to discern and evaluate the *capacity* of the corporations to wield power. This type of inquiry focuses primarily upon sanctions available to the companies for use against the Peruvians but also considers the companies' ability to shape Peruvian attitudes. (Since one aspect of the issue is *foreign* exercise of power, the actual degree to which the companies are "American" is also examined.) Second, the political *behavior* of the corporations and their allies is studied. Do investors at least *try* to exercise influence through various forms of political and public relations activity? In a sense power-seeking behavior also constitutes capacity for power, unless one is able to link it directly with political result, which is usually impossible. But if one can observe concrete and relevant political wishes, actions, and intentions, he can at least determine whether they are consistent with political outcomes. Third, the political *effects* themselves are examined, that is, the outcome of disputes in which the corporations are engaged or of decision-making processes in which they participate or have an interest. In assessing these effects we cannot tell precisely to what degree the companies were able to "get their way," but we can perceive roughly whether outcomes and decisions were substantially more favorable than unfavorable to their interests or vice versa.

Let us be very frank in saying that we are not establishing a direct causal chain between a capacity for power, power-seeking behavior, and political outcomes. Moreover we are unable to tell whether Peruvians (that is, their leaders) would have had different outcome desires in the total absence of American capital; laboratory experiments cannot be conducted on this question. Thus assessing "power" in this context must remain partially guesswork, but it can be made substantially "educated" guesswork by systematically exploring these three dimensions.

The scope of this book extends beyond the intriguing questions raised by the confrontation between the economic-imperialism and corporate good-citizen images. In conceiving and planning the study a wide conceptual net was thrown in that *any* important political consequences growing from American investments in Peru were sought out for identification and assessment. This took the focus of concern beyond the issue of corporate political power in the national (or, more accurately, capital-city) political arena of Peru. Significant effects were sought out for the Peruvian political system generally. By "system," reference is made not to the input-output or structural-functional paradigms but rather to power relationships and patterns of all kinds at all levels of the polity.

A number of hypothetical effects were not investigated in detail either because they appeared unimportant upon closer examination or because the linkages were simply too tenuous. An example of the latter is the relationship between corporate investments, economic development, and political participation or social mobilization. The literature offers numerous theories linking these variables but verification is very spotty and depends on rather dubious aggregative statistics.[21]

Three possible added consequences were identified, however. First, corporate bargaining with the Peruvian government over the terms of investments emerged as an area in which critical U.S. power may be exercised. Such power is not "political" in the partisan or lobbying sense, but it constitutes influence in a particular sphere of Peruvian public-policy formulation. Second, several of the corporations operate mines, oil fields, or plantations (or did so before expropriation) and at these sites relatively large communities have been established. The power structure of these communities is germane to this study, as the communities are parts of the larger Peruvian political system. Third, the corporations may unintentionally affect, over time, the extent to which the Peruvian polity is integrated. Here two activities of investors are hypothetically relevant: the construction and/or operation of transportation facilities, and the establishment and operation of remote industrial sites which "process" unassimilated Indians on their way to identification with the Hispanic national culture.

Admittedly, the difficulties of measurement are again very great. In analyzing bargaining one encounters the dual problem of secrecy with regard to objectives and secrecy with regard to behavior. But a rather surprising amount of openness characterizes some bargaining behavior. Even though true bargaining objectives are not known, the relative values (to the bargainers) of outcomes can be roughly assessed. As for examining community power structure, resources were not available for full reputational or decisional studies. But sufficient indicators of power-related capacity, behavior, and effect were available to support the level of generalization attempted. Measuring integrative effects was most difficult. Assessing the impact of transportation and assimilation activity depended on observing relevant behaviors and not measurement of the effects themselves. The evidence of some anthropologists with respect to cultural assimilation could, however, be introduced.

The propositions singled out for investigation are stated in the form of four hypotheses. This is not done in the belief that the statements can be scientifically confirmed or rejected, but rather as an attempt to sharpen the study's goals and conclusions.

The first hypothesis stems directly from the theories of economic imperialism. These theories are not only quite plausible in many instances but carry the weight of great conviction and widespread acceptance in certain quarters. They also must command the attention of anyone who places high value on the national integrity and independence of the developing countries of the Third World.

The basic position taken in the theory of economic imperialism is that the government and corporations of great "imperialist" or "metropolitan" countries such as the United States seek and achieve economic and political domination of smaller and weaker "satellite" or "peripheral" nations. This is perceived as a "neo-colonial" system in that outright military occupation or political annexation is replaced as the means of domination by foreign investment and various governmental activities such as military missions, counterinsurgency, and secret intelligence operations. The consequence is removal of vital national decisions from nationals of the subject country, a permanent freezing of oligarchic or "bourgeois" power in that country, and the "consolidation of an international ruling class constituted on the basis of ownership and control of the multinational corporations."[22]

This imperialism is "economic" simply because of the role of business investments in effecting it. True to the Marxist flavor of the theory, the explanation for the emergence of imperialism is also economic. The traditional explanation, which can be traced back to pre-Marxian classical economists, centers about the notion that mature capitalism tends to generate surplus capital and suffer a declining rate of profit. As a result pressures build up to invest the surpluses in nonindustrialized areas. This is not only profitable itself but has the added advantages of providing the basis for new markets for industrial exports and new sources of raw materials for the metropolitan economy. The capitalists, who supposedly control their home government anyway, are assured sufficient military, political, or diplomatic support to secure the investments, markets, and raw materials.[23]

This explanation finds general acceptance among modern-day theorists of the school but a number of embellishments have been made. One is that imperialist investors and governments approve of and actually promote mild forms of economic development so as to expand the neocolonial markets. Another stresses the role of the multinational corporations and concludes that their managements seek collectively to control world markets and production. This in turn requires making the entire globe safe for American capitalism. "But the reality of imperialism goes far beyond the immediate interest of this or that investor," argues Harry Magdoff; "the underlying purpose is nothing less than keeping as much as possible of the world open for trade and investment by the giant multinational corporations."[24]

The means by which domination is effected vary along a wide spectrum of imperialist tactics, according to the theory. One, essentially nonpolitical, is to make the satellite economically dependent on the metropolitan power. This is done by dominating the country's trade, controlling its export sector which earns foreign exchange, owning basic industries and the chief financial institutions (the latter control internal credit), providing directly or indirectly a large percentage of jobs, income, and tax revenues, and by encouraging an ever-increasing external debt obligation to imperialist financiers. These dependencies lay down the basis for external dictation of internal government policy by giving foreigners control of indispensable economic goods. These can be exchanged for favors. Perhaps more importantly, the implicit or explicit threat of withdrawal of these indispensable goods can inhibit governmental decision-making in those areas of concern to the foreigners. The economic "costs" of alienating the foreign interests may outweigh whatever preferences or benefits that may be associated with a particular policy move.[25]

A second tactic is alliance with conservative and reactionary political elements in the country. According to Sidney Lens, "It is to the interest of the U.S. corporations to ally themselves with conservative elements in the native country, because the conservatives are much more likely to give them favorable terms for conducting their business."[26] In the view of John Kautsky the foreign investors constitute a new political force separate from the "native aristocracy," but "a certain community of interest between these two political forces" exists because of shared profits and a common desire to maintain the status quo and prevent "any expropriation or redistribution of wealth."[27] That local bourgeois elites actually become the unconscious puppets of the foreigners is the opinion of Susanne Bodenheimer, who claims that imperialist penetration is so efficacious that it creates what amounts to a servile upperclass structure that develops a "clientele" outlook toward the foreigners.[28] Whether the relation between foreign and local elites is one of alliance or dominance, it becomes the local political base for American investors.

Another element of investor political activity is the "purchase" of desired governmental outcomes by the granting of various gifts or by the shrewd expenditure of money for political purposes. Specific actions perceived are large-scale bribery of government officials, campaign contributions to favored political parties, the financing of right-wing revolutions (as in Guatemala in 1954), the offering of company jobs to friends and relatives of officials, and the granting of other personal favors. Also, money can be spent in massive public relations campaigns that involve not only advertising but subsidized or controlled mass media. With its vast resources and communication skills the multinational corporation has "become the chief organizer and manufacturer of the international flow of communications," says Herbert Schiller. This leads not only to the shaping of mass opinion in favor of individual firms, but promulgation of the underlying values of U.S.-style capitalism through "imagery of technological gadgetry and consumer delights."[29]

Finally, the theory of economic imperialism contemplates that the metropolitan government will always stand ready to back the foreign enterprise with whatever interventions are needed to protect corporate welfare. In a classic work published in 1925, Scott Nearing and Joseph Freeman reasoned that the local representatives of American capital will first interfere on their own in internal politics, but "where United States investors do not receive satisfactory treatment from local authorities they apply to the United States government for support. In a number of such cases, the armed forces of the United States have intervened in the internal affairs of countries."[30] Other less obvious forms of intervention than landing the Marines (done numerous times in the Caribbean and Central America) are assisting rightist groups secretly, imposing trade embargoes, and offering or threatening to cut off trade privileges or lines of credit. Imperialist theory views Washington and Wall Street as being in the closest possible conspiracy to extend and preserve "the American empire."[31]

These four major elements of the theory of economic imperialism—economic dependence, alliance with conservatives, purchased influence, and metropolitan backing—have been intentionally discussed here in general terms, for the theory as proposed is believed to apply to almost any foreign investment situation in the Third World, particularly if the capital is American-owned. To show that the theory is also applied specifically to Peru is not difficult. Innumerable Peruvians and foreign writers on Peru fervently believe American investments in Peru constitute a clear case of economic imperialism. A few quotations illustrate.

José Matos Mar, a leading scholar associated with the Institute of Peruvian Studies in Lima, writes that Peru "forms part of the totality of Latin American societies which fall directly under the influence and domination of the United States of America." Internally Peru is ruled by a number of economic groups, he says, but their "existence, growth, and development acquire coherence and significance thanks to the umbilical cord of external domination. They are externally dependent and consequently their source of support is in the dominant metropolitan power."[32]

The Peruvian economist Virgilio Roel Pineda states that "our country is converted, in short, to a simple provider of raw materials, a subsidiary of the great foreign industrial enterprises."[33] Héctor Béjar, a former guerrilla and idol of the Peruvian Left, asserts that a "fundamental characteristic of the contemporary Peruvian economy is its dependence on U.S. imperialism, which is draining the country's capital and making its structural crisis more acute."[34] Augusto Salazar Bondy feels that economic domination has led to a "culture of domination" whereby Peruvians imitate foreign values and are alienated from their own country.[35]

The concept of investor alliance with reactionary forces is commonly espoused. Two non-Peruvian students of social stratification in Peru speak of the "subordination of the oligarchic groups to foreign interests" and give banking as an illustrative area.[36] Béjar, quoted above, writes that "foreign capital is linked to the large landholdings" and that "we observe in twentieth-century Peru a powerful oligarchy allied with foreign enterprise concentrating power at the apex of the system."[37]

In a book widely read in Peru, *Los dueños del Perú*, Carlos Malpica portrays the American corporations as subsidizing conservative political parties, bribing government officials, applying international pressures, and corrupting the body politic through control of the mass media. Parties initially "antiimperialist" in orientation (he means Aprista and Belaúnde's Popular Action) gradually succumb to a pro-American and anticommunist position as they make no headway in fighting the economic oligarchy, church, and army and are at the same time tempted by the opportunity of being bought off by U.S. enterprise. "In payment for its [the party's] surrender, the oligarchy and foreign consortia subsidize it generously." Having become safely transformed, the party is thereafter comfortably financed:

The great enterprises and the American government contribute money for sustaining the party bureaucrats and for payments to such recipients as local politicians, newspapers or magazines, and at the time of elections they are the major financiers, since money is essential to pay the expenses of propaganda. The millions spent by the parties, in each electoral campaign, come principally from the great foreign and national companies. The contributions of members are insignificant.[38]

These party contributions then become one of the means, Malpica says, "by which the foreign companies exercise influence over our congressmen and members of the executive." At the middle levels of government money and favors are frequently exchanged in a frank quid pro quo. But at the higher levels, according to Malpica, a more sophisticated bribery is used. International loans for public works are dangled before the government in exchange for favors to American companies:

If difficulties exist with some foreign enterprises, generally the financial entities condition approval of the requested credits on the solution of these problems. Such is the case, as everyone knows, and which has been denounced various times by President Belaúnde, when the Yankee government and the international organs of credit refused to grant loans to the country while no solution was forthcoming in the conflict with the International Petroleum Company.

He says, also, that the granting of commodity import quotas to Peru by the United States is used as a source of leverage.[39]

Malpica argues further that American control of Peruvian mass media leads to a gradual deterioration in the country's political health. The idea is suggestive of Salazar Bondy's "culture of domination" and Bodenheimer's concept of clientele societies. Malpica believes the penetration is slow and subtle, comparable to the ravages of Hansen's disease on the human body. No disability is noticed for years but eventually "the patient begins to lose sensibility." He goes on:

Having made the organism insensible, the bacillus attacks the skin and the muscles. In like manner, once newspapers, journals, chains of radio and television are controlled, Yankee citizens and businesses possess themselves of the most important sectors of our economy without letting the citizens' protest be heard.
    The process of decomposition of the muscles and organs becomes impossible to contain; over all the organism there appear pustules and ulcers. National institutions lose their authenticity and the corruption extends itself from the upper layers to the lower ones of executive, legislative and judicial powers. The body of the nation is sick and has started its putrefaction.[40]

I summarize the theory of economic imperialism as it applies to American investments in Peru in the form of Hypothesis I. It will be noted that the hypothesis is framed in terms of control of Peruvian public policy and not general societal domination. This is done for two reasons. First, this makes the hypothesis operationally more testable. Second, in view of the findings that will emerge regarding public policy and public opinion, I do not believe a plausible case can be made for general societal domination by the corporations. This does not mean, however, that they do not dominate on the community level.

Hypothesis I. American corporations in Peru participate actively and directly in Peruvian politics. By means of bribes and favors, control of the mass media, and intervention by the American government, the corporations are able to control Peruvian public policies pertinent to their interests. Basic to their influence is an alliance with conservative Peruvian elites and an economic dependence on the companies by Peru.

The corporate good-citizen viewpoint is obviously in very substantial disagreement with this hypothesis. It envisions foreign managements as defensively trying to protect themselves within hostile political environments by means of image-building and not direct political engagement. The corporations tend to be model citizens for their own good and are comparatively helpless politically. This point of view also tends to discount the importance of intervention from Washington. It does not, however, ignore the possibility of economic dependence in varying degrees and the implications this may have for economic bargaining and survival of the corporation. Indeed, some writers of this nonimperialist school are preoccupied with what they may interpret as "economic" power but what I consider political in nature since public policy outcomes can be affected.

Behrman writes that, despite the common fear that the enterprise has power over the "host" government, there are "no entities with such power, and no enterprise is able to achieve this stature among the advanced countries at least."[41] According to Turner, "In the advanced countries, government can normally resist the political pressures of multinational subsidiaries." He adds, "For the less-developed nations, the situation is obviously less happy, if only because it is still possible for single firms to dominate their national economy." He disclaims any notion of political domination, however, except in rare instances.[42]

Mikesell contends that "the foreign firm usually desires to stay clear of domestic politics," and "despite efforts to gain popularity by paying high wages, contributing to social projects, obeying the laws, and avoiding partisan politics," the investor is unable to live down the imperialism image of an earlier era.[43] Kindleberger takes a parallel position but emphasizes a desire for corporate invisibility: "Corporations want profits. They also want peace and quiet. As much as possible they want to become like citizens of the host country, invisible to the public eye, fading into the background, so long as it gives them peace and quiet at not too large a price in profits."[44] Stressing conformity to local laws, Vernon argues: "As a general rule, the subsidiaries of multinational corporate groups have a special sense of their 'foreignness' and of their vulnerability to criticism and hostility on the part of the local community. Partly for that reason, the subsidiaries of such groups ordinarily appear to be among the better behaved members of any local business community. Usually, they seem both sensitive and responsive to the formal requirements of national law, to a degree which national enterprises seldom match."[4][5]

Vernon is also dubious about theories of unflagging U.S. governmental support for American business abroad. Characterizing U.S. business-government relations on foreign problems as "exceedingly complex," he notes that "at times, there have been the overt signs of close coordination. . . . At least as often, however," he goes on, "there was indifference or even hostility on the part of the U.S. government to the foreign operations of U.S. firms." With respect to business requests for aid, Vernon finds that "U.S. enterprises have carried over into the international field the general style of their domestic relationships with government. That is to say, they have held the U.S. government at arm's length, neither soliciting nor receiving much guidance or advice."[4][6]

As economists and authorities on international business, these writers are well aware of foreign investor-host government bargaining. Kindleberger was one of the first to describe this as a nonzero-sum game, that is, bargaining in which payoffs can accrue to both sides and one party's gain does not necessarily constitute the other party's loss.[4][7] In what Carl Stevens calls "coercion" in his analysis of labor-management bargaining, one party can in a sense "force" another party to accept a concession if the first party has some thing the second wants and the first party possesses (or appears to) the ability to give or withhold that thing. Also the first party can attempt to affect the second party's preference function, which Stevens calls "persuasion."[4][8]

In the foreign-investment realm the "thing" is usually capital. If investors possess the capital and yet also possess the ability to withhold it, and if a host government wants or needs that capital, the investors are in a position to demand public-policy concessions, such as special tax regimes and currency-exchange guaranties. Depending on the host government's preference function and the availability of alternate sources of capital, the government is under pressure to yield. If the host economy is capital-poor and if the local political environment is forbidding to other investors, that pressure may be overwhelming. This type of "coercion" may be derived not only from the desirability of new capital but from the desirability of retaining existing capital or obtaining a revision of its terms. That is, a corporation can threaten to depart or it can offer more preferred terms than those existing to secure policy concessions.*

Mikesell has systematically considered the struggle over allocation of

---

*The host government can also, of course, "bargain back" by threatening to withhold its resources or markets. This leverage can become substantial under certain conditions, for example, when alliances have been formed among producer countries—as has occurred in petroleum.

economic "rents" or benefits between company and country, with emphasis upon the conditions arising in mining and petroleum. He sees a dynamic in the bargaining process. When a new investment is being contemplated the bargaining advantage is the company's—it can demand concessions prior to becoming committed. Furthermore it is initially taking only risks and is not removing profits from the country. After investment is in place, however, the firm's bargaining flexibility is reduced because of the commitment of fixed capital. At the same time the capital begins to yield earnings, thus the host country begins to feel "cheated." In short, at the very moment of investor inflexibility host-country demands begin to rise. The result is often an eventual reopening of negotiations on the terms of the investment, with the outcome favoring the country. The corporation can regain leverage only by offering added investments or reinvestment of profits. In Mikesell's words, "The moment of new investment is the moment of greatest bargaining strength for the company." Further, "Once investments have been made and the foreign investor is earning substantial profits the bargaining power shifts in favor of the host country."[49]

In framing a second hypothesis we apply the political-engagement and investment-bargaining theories of these writers. On political activities and general policy influence the first and second hypotheses must be almost diametrically opposed. On economic dependency they need not be, however, since the nonimperialist school envisages this as a possible source of investor bargaining leverage depending on the circumstances. As for economic bargaining itself, the imperialist interpretation would find this largely irrelevant because the subject peoples and leaders are controlled anyway, and the concept of bargaining includes a presumption that both parties have some freedom to negotiate. In view of these strong contradictions between the points of view, I shall state the second hypothesis as an *alternate* to the first.

Hypothesis IA. American corporations in Peru avoid active participation in Peruvian politics and do not seek important intervention from U.S. authorities. Instead they attempt to minimize their local visibility or improve their image. Public policies unfavorable to corporate interests are possible but, because of the economic importance of U.S. capital, the corporations are able to bargain effectively over investment terms. Corporate bargaining strength is greater with respect to new capital than existing capital.

A third hypothesis to be explored in this book concerns the communities in Peru in which U.S. corporations are the dominant employer. These are "company" towns in the economic sense. The issue to be examined is whether they are also "company" towns in the political sense. From a purely quantitative viewpoint the issue may not seem important.

Only about 160,000 persons lived in the eight sizable American company towns that existed in mid-1968 (the Velasco revolution caused three to be nationalized, but a new one was being built as this is written). Thus only 1 to 2 percent of the Peruvian population is directly involved.

Yet the question is more than peripheral. The Peruvians living in those towns are part of the economically active population, which is only about half the total. The communities are all important regional centers and affect their surrounding areas economically and in other ways. Considerable migration occurs into and out of some of the towns, with the result that over time they have an apparently spreading cultural impact—a subject to be addressed in the next hypothesis. Finally, it would manifestly be of concern to any Peruvian that even a small percent of his country's population might be under the political domination of foreigners—living in "states within a state," so to speak.

A writer employing the thought categories and vocabulary of economic imperialism who addresses himself specifically to the company town is C.H. Grant. He examines the sociological and political situations in two bauxite towns in Guyana, one owned by the Aluminum Company of Canada and the other by Reynolds Metals. The Reynolds town is "simply the prototype of a feudal industrial company town," he says, in which "almost every aspect of life is controlled by the company and benefits are handed down from on high by an alien corporate management to a subordinate group of Guyanese workers." In Alcan's community, Grant goes on, "the naked and pervasive company paternalism is giving way to subtler kinds of control." These are ostensibly antipaternalism actions such as the sale of houses to workers and creation of a supposedly independent local government authority to permit participative policy-making. But because of the company's continued control of employment relationships and various implementational difficulties, the "colonial situation" in the Alcan community is said to have remained. This situation, in Grant's words, revolves around "the monopoly of force or influence which an imported European oligarchy exerts upon a subject majority." Sociologically, Grant perceives "essentially a system of apartheid" in which the white managerial population is physically and socially segregated from the black workers. In fact, Grant reports, until 1954 white residential areas were out-of-bounds to Guyanese without a prior police permit.[50]

That these observations may describe company towns elsewhere in the world is suggested by other writings not from the economic-imperialism literature. From community power studies in American sociology comes the proposition that the degree of economic diversity found in a community should correlate directly with the degree of pluralism in the community power structure. Terry Clark hypothesizes, for example, "the more diverse the economic structures within a community, the more decentralized the decision-making structure." He furthermore proposes that "the more important any single function in a community, the more community members from the sector performing that particular function will be active in community decision-making, and the more community decisions will be oriented toward the values and interests of that sector of the community."[51] The empirical results of community power studies have not consistently verified these hypotheses, but they seem particularly plausible in the present context. Not only does *one* economic structure predominate in the American company town, but that structure is an appendage of a huge multinational corporation.

Grant's finding of strict social segregation in Guyanese company towns has been specifically noted in Peru. In 1959 the anthropologist Richard W. Patch visited Paramonga, one of the two American-owned sugar plantations (until it was nationalized in 1969) along the Peruvian coast. One of the features of the community reported was segregated living areas for managers, skilled white-collar employees, unskilled white-collar employees and skilled workers, and common laborers. The quality of housing declined in each successively lower class. Also Patch perceived that "for many years the prevailing philosophy of management-labor relations in Paramonga has been one of paternalism." Although he noted that "recently this has been tempered," the system has changed slowly, he says, in part because of resistance of the workers. To them withdrawal of a company service is a "dead loss" when they are without the "economic resources" with which to replace it.[52]

In a general treatise on American business behavior in Latin America published in 1956, William F. Whyte and Allan R. Holmberg addressed themselves to the company town. They noted that "the paternalistic relationship" that exists in such towns is often very expensive to management and, moreover, seems to yield dissatisfaction on the part of workers rather than loyalty. Residents take free services for granted and also make management the target of their everyday frustrations. As a result, Whyte and Holmberg point out, some companies have intentionally attempted to "de-paternalize" their camps by promoting home ownership and selling electricity and water to workers at cost. But, the authors agree, these experiments have not been overly successful, for "in general, people will not abandon paternalism when to do so requires substantial economic sacrifices from them."[53]

The anthropologist Solomon Miller comes to parallel conclusions when he examines the difference between the "traditional" hacienda of northern Peru and the "corporate" plantation that he says is now emerging. Although his study concerns Peruvian-owned agricultural enterprises, its findings would presumably apply also to the foreign-owned plantation. In the traditional organization the *patrón* personally and paternalistically cares for his workers in accord with reciprocal relationships not based on cash. Free services and debt bondage are used to attract and retain an

Indian labor force. The corporate hacienda, however, seeks profits rather than reciprocal maintenance of patrón and tenants, operates according to impersonal, contractual relationships, and pays workers at least partly in cash. Labor no longer needs to be "bound in" and paternalism is considered a burden by management.[54]

Both Grant and Whyte describe antipaternalism efforts involving projects that supposedly lead to wider participation in decision-making and worker ownership of housing. An attempt to cast these efforts in a different theoretical perspective can be made by reference to community-development theory. One of the most famous community-development "experiments" of recent decades was conducted in Peru under the leadership of Allan Holmberg. Beginning in 1952 Cornell University operated a hacienda, Vicos, in the Ancash Department of Peru, in which a deliberate attempt was made to replace the traditional patrón system with a self-reliant, participative community. The Indians were given representative government, land ownership, and technical assistance. Holmberg believes the results were "dramatic" in terms of agricultural production, health and social welfare, and a capacity for solidarity and self-rule.[55] This conclusion fits into the orthodox community-development viewpoint that an external "change agent" can, using flexible and subtle techniques, introduce into a local population a surge of cooperative, democratic, and self-reliant behavior.[56] In short, it is believed by this school of thought that not only can paternalism be ended but that it can be replaced by popular self-initiative and cooperation.

The community-development viewpoint has its strong skeptics, however. Charles Erasmus claims community development is merely an ideology rather than proven technique, and that instead of creating true self-reliance and "natural" solidarity, a new dependency is created. The change agent is, so to speak, the new patrón.[57] Gerrit Huizer adds the criticism that community-development schemes lead only to minor improvements and not to the radical and revolutionary steps needed to break through the "culture of repression."[58] Critics such as this, faced by the results at Vicos, dismiss the undertaking as not creating sufficient improvement in the Indians' material condition.

In constructing a hypothesis from this body of literature, we can start with the basic power relationship. From Grant and Clark, as well as through obvious plausibility perhaps, the prospect emerges of total political domination by company management. Clearly the issue extends beyond control of public policy outcomes; presumably the processes of policy debate, decision, and even agenda-selection are dominated. An enclave of "colonialism" is created, to use imperialist terminology.

Imperialist theory can be drawn upon to construct hypothetical mechanisms involved in this domination. Two elements that seem particularly relevant are economic dependency and the "purchase" of influence by bribes, favors, jobs, promotions, work assignments, and fringe benefits. If the company owns property such as housing, added resources are available to management for effective exchange relationships. If the company monopolizes mass communications in an isolated setting the possibility of controlling information and molding values also arises. Perhaps a psychology of dependence could be created in which conflict or criticism would be muted or at least limited to less significant matters.

Yet, too, the literature reviewed indicates that paternalism may be out-of-date and a burden to management. Furthermore it may be a source of some worker dissatisfaction and carping. Let us thus provide in the hypothesis given below for attempts by management to reduce paternalism and/or replace it with a self-help approach. These actions may very well have ambivalent effects from the power standpoint: on the one hand they reduce the resources available to management to effect exchanges, and on the other hand they may create a new, more subtle form of dependency or bonds of gratitude or feelings of reciprocal obligation. Attention is directed to both of these possibilities in the hypothesis.

Hypothesis II. In Peruvian communities where American corporations are the principal employer, company management dominates local political life. This is achieved by means of economic dependence, bribes and favors, worker benefits and services, and control of mass media. Attempts to reduce or replace paternalism are made, but they result in augmenting as well as reducing company political influence.

Just as this hypothesis concerns itself with parts of the Peruvian political system, the final hypothesis focuses upon the system as a whole. In fact the system's "integration" is the subject of interest.

Like the term "power," the term "political integration" has been troubled in its usefulness by elusive and varied meanings. Claude Ake identifies it with achievement of accepted legitimacy and normative consensus within the society.[59] To Lucian Pye it refers to systematic interrelationship within the polity.[60] Myron Weiner associates the term with a number of objectives, among which are reduction of elite-mass gaps, assimilation or accommodation of parochial subgroups, and establishment of exclusive internal jurisdiction by the central government.[61]

Philip Jacob and Henry Teune offer a broad articulation of the concept that subsumes most of these ideas: "Political integration generally implies a relationship of *community* among people within the same entity. That is, they are held together by mutual ties of one kind or another which give the group a feeling of identity and self-awareness. Integration, therefore, is based on strong cohesiveness within a social group and *political* integration is present when a *political*-governmental unit of some sort is cohesive."[62] Jacob and Teune then consider factors or variables that *may* be associated positively with political integration. They contend that the literature on the subject reveals ten potentially independent variables: geographical proximity, homogeneity, transactions (communication, trade, mobility), mutual knowledge, shared interest, "character," the power structure, the sovereignty-dependency status, governmental effectiveness, and previous integrative experience.[63]

Does foreign investment affect the extent of political integration in a host country? It may very well do so. If one expands the concept of foreign investment to include the economic outreach associated with historic instances of colonialism, it has been responsible for the very creation of "new" societies requiring "integration." Indeed, the super-imposition of Hispanic civilization upon the Incan empire in the sixteenth century established the cultural dimension of the present-day integration "problem" of Peru.

In the modern context, foreign capital could conceivably lead to impacts that run counter to political integration. For example, it could widen elite-mass gaps by intensifying the power and privileges of local elites. Also it could lead to the establishment of foreign enclaves around isolated industrial sites, at which national political jurisdiction would not be in effect. These possibilities are raised in Hypotheses I and II respectively, and a positive finding on either must be interpreted as revealing a potentially anti-integrative effect.

Yet prointegrative effects are also conceivable. Jacob and Teune's first and third variables, proximity and transactions, could be affected by the development of transportation linkages. With regard to the first, the authors note that others have employed as indicators of proximity such factors as contiguity, physical distance of separation, travel time by available transportation, costs of available transportation, and the number of "choice points" along a transportation route. They consider trans-actions in terms of the costs and benefits of movement of messages, goods and services, and persons through physical space.[64]

Hypothetically, foreign investment could contribute to transportation within the host country in two ways. First, generalized public benefit might accrue from transportation facilities built for the company's own use. This would obviously occur only if public or noncompany use were also permitted of the facilities. Eugene Staley has contended that this is feasible: "Materials development [by companies] generally requires the building of such facilities as ports, railroads, roads, and power stations. With proper planning, many such facilities can be so located and designed as also to serve general development." To illustrate, he cites the dredging of the Orinoco River in Venezuela by the U.S. Steel Corporation.[65]

Secondly, foreign capital could be involved in the construction of public transportation infrastructure or the operation of common-carrier transpor-tation enterprises as profit-seeking ventures. Some of the largest civil engineering and contract-construction organizations in the world are

American and they do work in numerous countries. Needless to say American capital has also been involved in civil aviation around the world.

But involvement by foreign capital in transportation does not automatically lead to true or significant additions to proximity and transactions. Not only might new facilities and services serve company interests only, they could also be irrationally designed; for example, David Chaplin has argued that Peruvian railroads, built mainly by foreigners, are deficient in that they tend to run east and west rather than north and south along the length of the country. Also, additions to the transportation system could be temporary, redundant, or fragmentary; it is of interest in this connection that Chaplin complains also that five different train-track gauges are in use in Peru. Activities of foreign capital might even conceivably have a negative effect, such as causing the squandering of local resources on unneeded transportation projects. Chaplin believes too that certain railroads have undesirably drained certain areas of population.[66] In assessing the impacts of transportation on integration we shall have to attempt to net out the pluses and minuses.

Jacob and Tuene's second variable, homogeneity, could also be affected by foreign investment. In the authors' words, it has been hypothesized that "social homogeneity will contribute strongly to the feasiblity of political integration and, conversely, that communities whose members are very different from one another will have a very hard time achieving or maintaining political integration." Indicators that have been used for homogeneity include wealth, income, education, status or class, religion, race, language, and ethnic identification.[67]

Conceivably a highly heterogeneous society, such as that of Peru, could be made less so through the cultural impact of remote industrial sites and the communities that grow up around them. A high percentage of the Peruvian population consists of unassimilated Indians living in the sierra. Mines, oil fields, and haciendas, operating in or adjacent to the sierra, could become, in effect, "assimilation centers" by attracting and transferring Indians to the Hispanic culture of coastal Peru. Again there are important "ifs." The sites would have to attract Indian labor in some way; work forces would have to be somewhat mobile, permitting in-migration and possibly out-migration as well; and the prevailing culture of the communities would have to be Hispanic. If the enterprises did not attract Indians and consisted of sealed, foreign enclaves they would obviously have no assimilationist or homogenizing effect. In fact their presence would stand as an obstacle to national integration.

On this subject a considerable body of relevant literature exists. Anthropologists studying Peru have long identified the Hispanization of the Indian with migration to the coastal towns and eventually Lima.[68] Richard Patch believes that Paramonga has served a particularly important assimilationist role because of its location on one of the major migratory routes.[69] Richard Adams has noted how a remote sierra village can be profoundly affected by the existence of nearby foreign-owned mines that attract village men for temporary employment.[70] In a study of another sierra town Paul Doughty reported that construction of a government hydroelectric project in the area affected social mobility; commuting workers gained status by achievement at the site rather than according to ascriptive village standards.[71] In all of these cases an industrial operation contributed to social change, and in the Patch and Adams data—to be reported more fully in Chapter Eight—one finds a specifically American enterprise having an assimilationist effect.

Two final comments are needed before proposing a hypothesis to cover these matters. First, the linkages that might connect transportation activity and remote enterprises on the one hand and political integration on the other must remain conjectural. They are patently impossible to "prove." The foreign actions may not, in fact, induce the Jacob-Teune variables of proximity, homogeneity, and transactions. Other forces may affect them more. Also these variables may not be associated with true political integration. To underscore the uncertainty, the anthropologist and Peruvian specialist William Mangin argues that new transportation channels, together with transistor radios, Quechua language broadcasts, military service, and other avenues of "assimilation" may actually lead to an aggressive Quechua or Indian nationalism that could profoundly influence the character of Peruvian politics.[72] If Mangin is right, the outcome could very well be *less* political integration rather than more.

Second, increased political integration is not held out as a normative "good." Integration is not being identified with the value-laden term "political development" even though not doing so flies in the face of much political science literature. If one looks upon nationalization and homogenization as a way of creating a unified, stronger Peru, integration is placed in a favorable light. If, however, one notes that assimilation and migration are accompanied by the cultural retreat of a distinct subgroup or the swelling of Lima slums, integration is seen as having a "bad" side. Although I am selecting integration as a topic of interest in this book I do not wish to imply normative approval of all its aspects.

Hypothesis III. The activity of some American entrepreneurs and corporations has had the unintended, long-term, net effect of adding to the political integration of Peru. This has resulted from contributions to the internal transportation network and the operation of remote or strategically located enterprises which accelerate assimilation of the Indian.

Methods and Evidence

"Testing" these four hypotheses in the strict scientific sense cannot be done. But the study assumes that by employing appropriate research methods enough evidence is obtainable to *estimate* the degree to which each is valid, at least to a closer extent than is presently possible.

The "universe" of data collection includes, from the temporal standpoint, the period 1967-1971 with respect to systematic investigation. Earlier periods are covered sporadically. As to subject matter, only the political consequences of *American*-owned investments in *Peru* are examined, and the reader who generalizes the findings to all foreign investors or all of Latin America does so at his own risk. Limiting the study this way has its advantages and disadvantages, but the scarce resources available to support it made a broader study impossible. Peru was chosen as the "case" country because of its intermediate size, the wide diversity of U.S. investments in its economy, and the fact that a reform-oriented, elected government was in power at the time (that of Belaúnde). The coming to power of a quite radical military government (the Velasco regime) while the study was in progress turned out to be an unexpected advantage in terms of longitudinal comparisons.

From the point of view of American corporations, the universe comprised all U.S. businesses in Peru for purposes of unsystematic data-gathering. That is, whenever any relevant information was obtained on any firm it was used. But systematic data-gathering was confined to twelve corporate subsidiaries. These were the largest twelve from the standpoint of total employment in Peru as of mid-1968. The criterion of size was used in the selection on grounds that if any American companies have significant implications for Peruvian politics it is the bigger ones. Certainly economic imperialism theory assumes that the large enterprises are the problem.

Although these twelve subsidiaries comprised only about 4 percent of the American companies in Peru in 1968, they employed 90 percent of the personnel that worked for U.S. firms and controlled well over 90 percent of U.S. direct investment in the country. This is due to disparity in the size of the firms; among the top twelve alone the employment range was 17,000 to 700.

These twelve enterprises were engaged in mining, oil drilling and refining, manufacturing, agriculture, communications, retail sales, and a wide variety of other activities. All nine of the Standard Industrial Classification divisions are represented except Services and Government, and if one includes company town operations these too are accounted for.

With respect to sources of data, by far the most significant was in-depth interviews conducted by the author. Some 220 interviews involving 182 respondents were conducted in the period 1966-1971, with about one-half conducted in 1968. Most interviewing occurred in Peru during the course of trips made to that country in 1967, 1968, and 1971. One-half the respondents were American and somewhat more than 40 percent were Peruvian. Eighty (or 44 percent) were U.S. business executives and the remainder held a variety of positions. Approximately one-half were decision-makers in business or government and thus communicated elite opinion and information available to elites. Nineteen individuals served as "informants" in that they were in a position to know significant information and were willing to talk with me at length about sensitive matters on an absolutely confidential basis. In 77 interviews (all conducted in 1968) a thirty-five page interview schedule was employed, containing questions ranging from the multiple-choice type to open-ended inquiry. In the remaining interviews a relatively unstructured format was followed. The appendix below furnishes further details on the interviews and respondents but does not list the latter by name; in footnotes I reveal some names when confidentiality is not at stake and when the identity of the source would assist the reader in evaluating my information.

The methodological strategy of the study is not to employ a single method consistently but rather to use a wide variety of methods. The topic is a difficult one to research and it was felt that any and all feasible means of generating reliable and relevant information should be brought to bear.

This multiple approach is particularly evident in the study of power relationships. The "capacity" for power was measured by indicators of both economic dependency and control of mass communications. Power-seeking "behavior" was analyzed in terms of the attitudes of U.S. businessmen, their avenues of access to Peruvian decision-makers, their employment of exchange relationships with Peruvian elites and groups, their use of bargaining and public relations techniques, their relationships with the U.S. government, and pertinent activities of components of the U.S. government. Power-related "effects" were sought by examining the outcome of disputes in which the companies were involved, the substance of Peruvian public policies affecting the corporations, the nature of bargains struck regarding investment, and the nature of public opinion toward the enterprises and foreign investment in general. In some instances (notably the company towns) the absence of significant disputes was also treated as evidence of "effects" in accord with "nondecision" or "standing decisions" theory.*[73]

The types of evidence and evidence-gathering varied also. Information came from direct observation (as in segregation in company towns), the opinions of respondents and authors (a principal source), and analysis of aggregative statistics (as in the degree of dependency). Data were gathered from samples of the universe (opinion polling), the universe in its entirety (for example, all twelve companies), and random sources which happened to come to my attention (such as reports of bribery). In analyzing the outcomes of disputes, policies, bargaining, and diplomatic intervention, an attempt was made to determine and generalize from all incidents within specific time-frames.

*This theory states that the effects of power may be hidden by the lack of ability or desire of the subjugated to raise significant questions for decision or even consideration.

Two   Peru and American Business

Understanding the relationships between American corporations and Peruvian politics obviously requires understanding something of Peru. Unfortunately no single chapter, and indeed no single book or even encyclopedia, can do justice to her rich complexity. The following pages should be accepted as only the barest minimum background needed for the reader unfamiliar with Peru. The footnoted literature will provide the interested reader with additional sources.

Peru and Its Politics

To appreciate Peru it is necessary first to cast aside any previous notion of a small, insignificant Latin American country. Its roughly half-million square miles make Peru the third largest South American state. Its Pacific coastline is about as long as that of the United States. The population of Peru is between 13 and 14 million, and in South America this level of magnitude ranks only behind Brazil, Argentina, and Colombia.

The country is definitely low-income by the standards of the highly industrialized countries. It is unquestionably "underdeveloped." As can be seen in Table 1, selected economic and social indicators place Peru on the intermediate level with regard to other Latin American countries, although

Table 1. Comparative Economic and Social Indicators of Development.

Indicators	19 Latin American republics				All areas of world (noncommunist)	
	Peru	Highest	Lowest	All	Less developed	More developed
GNP per capita ($US)	376	944	65	437	200	2620
Population growth rate	3.1	3.5	1.3	2.9	2.6	1.0
Life expectancy (years)	53	67	47	59	51	70
Percentage literate	61	91	10	68	40	96

Source: Agency for International Development, "Selected Economic Data for the Less Developed Countries" (May 1970). The figures are generally for 1968–1969.

its position is somewhat inferior to the aggregates for nineteen republics. As for comparison to underdeveloped areas generally, Peru's GNP per capita is substantially higher but so is its population growth rate.

Yet statistics such as these can have an inherently illusory quality. They may hide great differences within a country. Peru is a nation with enormous variations in the quality and way of life among sectors of its population, as is partially shown in Table 2. Those living in cities and towns are generally far better off than those not, although exceptions can be made to that statement. In particular, the *barriadas* (or *pueblos jovenes*—"young towns") of Lima contain masses of underprivileged humanity.

Similarly, great disparities exist between the three principal regions of the country, the coast, sierra, and selva. The coast, largely a desert punctuated here and there by fertile river deltas, constitutes only about a tenth of the country but is the locale of modern Peru in many respects. The great city of Lima lies at the approximate midpoint of the coast and in the Lima-Callao metropolitan area lives a quarter of the national population. This part of Peru, and especially Lima, is the center of monetized economic life and national political decision-making. As can be seen by Table 2, the coast's per capita income was almost double that of the nation as a whole in 1960.

The sierra is an awesome complex of Andean mountain ranges with

Table 2. Comparative Social and Economic Statistics for Peru.

Population and portions thereof	Percent served by piped water, 1970	Percent served by sewerage connection, 1970
Entire	35	27
Resident in places of more than 2000 persons	59	57
Resident in places of 2000 to 400 persons	33	0.5
Resident in places of less than 400 persons	1	0.0

Region	Population, 1960 (percent)	Income, 1960 (percent)	Income, 1960 (*Soles*) (per capita)
Coast	29.0	55.3	6908
Sierra	58.3	40.6	2523
Selva	12.7	4.1	1168
All regions	100.0	100.0	3626

Sources: Water and sewerage data: Inter American Development Bank, Social Progress Trust Fund annual report (1970). Population and income data: Banco Central de Reserva del Perú, *Plan nacional de desarrollo económico y social del Perú, 1962-1971* (1962).

peaks up to four miles high. The region's innumerable upland valleys and extensive plateaus contained 58 percent of the country's population in 1960, yet because of continuous migration to the coast this proportion is dropping. The bulk of the sierra population consists of Indians, many of whom have taken on few if any of the characteristics of Hispanic, coastal society. They speak Quechua and Aymara instead of Spanish and live for the most part under pitifully destitute conditions. Their world is completely different from that of coastal urbanites; it is said that many Indians are not even aware of the existence of "Peru."

The third region, the selva, is the vast territory east of the Andes. The bulk of its area forms part of the Amazon basin and except for a few centers it is very sparsely populated. Parts are totally unexplored and numerous primitive tribes remain within it. About 60 percent of Peru is classified as selva, yet the region contained only about 600,000 people in 1961. Iquitos, the most important outpost of the selva, is not connected by road to Lima. Before the days of aviation it was more easily reached via Cape Horn and Brazil than overland.*

In brief, the country is characterized by much cultural and spatial separateness. Some Peruvian writers depict their nation as a social and geographical archipelago and the analogy seems apt. Pozuzo, a town located at the eastern edge of the central sierra, is four days by muletrain to the nearest railhead. No television, telephone, or even telegraph penetrates from the outside world. Founded as a colony of German peasants in 1858, this community of 2000 still speaks German and its dress and architecture resemble nineteenth-century Europe.[1] When Irma Adelman and Cynthia Taft Morris ranked seventy-four countries of the world on their degree of "national integration and sense of national unity," Peru was graded "C+" on an A-D scale. Pakistan and the Philippines were graded equally with Peru; the only Latin American states rated lower were Guatemala ("C") and Bolivia ("D").[2]

Certainly the degree of fragmentation can be exaggerated. Even though Quechua, Aymara, and even German are spoken in numerous localities, visitors usually find at least a handful of Spanish speakers. Transistor radios and modern aviation have helped shrink the country greatly. Local government officials exercise at least nominal jurisdiction over the most remote villages and central government bureaucrats and civic action teams

---

*Fascinating historic anecdotes about the isolation of Iquitos can be told. In 1896 a small band staged an antigovernment revolt there, but Lima did not hear of the incident until a ship arrived via Cape Horn 16 days later carrying a Rio newspaper which mentioned it. Then more than a month was consumed getting an expeditionary force to the scene, by which time the revolt had ended. As late as 1925 the Lima-Iquitos trip via the "Pichis trail" took 15 to 17 days by rail, motor vehicle, muleback, canal, and river launch. The return trip was a little longer because of adverse river currents. Today, one can fly from Lima to Iquitos in approximately three and one-half hours.

roam the country. Even in communities inaccessible by road a connection
is often made with national political life. In investigating Mayobamba, a
village of 800 persons in Chancay Province that is not reachable by road,
Earl Morris and associates found: "The amount of interaction between
villagers and their national government is impressive. Though relatively
isolated in a geographic sense, Mayobamba is very much involved in
national political life. Residents know national ministries and organizations which Mayobamba can use for its own needs. Local leaders do not
hesitate to attempt to direct benefits at the disposal of national agencies
toward home. As a result, Mayobamba is subjected to the same faction-
alism and political machinations found in national Peruvian politics."[3]

The disparities and separateness that are Peru may be viewed also from
the perspective of social structure. As in many societies, racial, ethnic, and
class differentiations coincide and reinforce each other. At the bottom, of
course, is the unassimilated Indian. Partly because of a lack of data and
partly because it is impossible to define "Indian" precisely, one can only
estimate the proportion of the society so composed. Some have put it at
one-third, others as high as 45 percent. Indians of the sierra generally live
on haciendas, in indigenous communities, or on small plots of land; they
constitute a "peasantry" in that they are almost always engaged in
agriculture. Although generally passive and fatalistic, and politically
alienated and powerless, they occasionally in recent years have engaged in
violence and land invasions. Despite decades of governmental efforts to
upgrade their lot, Carlos Astiz concludes that "there have been no basic
improvements for the majority of the Peruvian peasants since independence, and perhaps since the Europeans arrived in Peru."[4]

Social classes rather than castes exist in Peru in that individuals are able
to move upward in the social scale. In fact much of the population consists
of persons in transition, either as individuals or by generation. The next
stage upward for the Indian is to abandon his ancestral dress, learn some
Spanish, and migrate to the coast for hacienda or urban employment. He is
then considered a "cholo" or "acriollado." A "mestizo" or "criollo" is
defined by some writers as a person who is even more fully acculturated
into the Hispanic world. Except for the fact that his skin will never be
white, the mestizo is forever removed from Indian status; in fact in the
sierra he is often depicted as exploitive of the Indian, and in urban areas he
constitutes the skilled and semiskilled working class.

Although observers of Latin American society are fond of commenting
on the supposed absence of a middle class, a socioeconomic stratum
definitely exists between the upper and lower classes in Peru. It consists of
white-collar employees, professionals, civilian bureaucrats, and much of
the military officer corps. Grant Hilliker estimates that the middle class
constitutes 15-20 percent of the population in the provinces and around
30 percent in Lima-Callao.[5] This group is urban sociologically and from a

psychological point of view is often seen as dependent on the upper class for its values. Some writers find a developing split between an "old" middle class that confines itself to unproductive paper-shuffling and a "new" middle class that is technologically oriented and dynamic. This latter group constitutes the technocrats and middle managers of Peruvian and foreign business enterprise and, under the Velasco regime, the governmental ministries.

The word "oligarchy" is used constantly to summarize the upper class of Peru. At one time the implications of this term were essentially valid; a small number of families dominated economic activity and the government, and the latter's primary function was to protect the oligarchy's interests. This elite was white and aristocratic and its power was based on feudalistically run haciendas in the sierra.

Today, however, this concept does not describe the pluralities and fluidities of the Peruvian upper class. More than a century ago the power of the sierra patróns began to erode in the face of rising coastal activity in mining and agriculture. The guano and nitrate mines and sugar and cotton plantations of the coast produced for export and were run as profit-seeking corporations, not personalistic feudalities. Thus a newer elite with a differing outlook emerged. Later, as Peru industrialized, an additional elite developed whose wealth and standing were based on industrial enterprise. This group was oftentimes composed of European and British immigrants who became Peruvian citizens. American entrepreneurs arrived also, but many remained as temporary residents and were not truly integrated into the industrial elite.[6]

Although these various elites often had common interests, and in fact sometimes merged through the extended family and interlocking financial structures, the Peruvian upper class was no longer monolithic. Moreover it was not unchallenged politically. Mass political parties, labor unions, students, and occasionally peasants introduced countervailing political forces. Governments came to power after World War II that were not exclusively handmaidens of the upper class—a rarity in the past. This erosion of the influence of economic elites reached its climax in 1968, when a military government came to power that was distinctly independent of upper-class control and which proceeded to undo many elitist bases of economic power by agrarian reform, nationalization, and government regulation.[7]

Hence the military, always significant in Peruvian politics but historically in a guarantor or buffer role rather than one of long-term rule, became the most powerful elite. Contrary to much Latin American practice, the regime of General Juan Velasco Alvarado was not one of personalistic *caudillo* leadership. The coup of 1968 was "institutional" in that it was undertaken collectively by the army, navy, and air force, and the succeeding government was one of corporate leadership rather than dictatorship by one man. Most signficantly, the military officer corps did not simply uphold the interests of the upper class. The army (more than the navy) has always been middle class, and in recent years even officers of darker skin and lower-class backgrounds have been coming to the fore. In this new situation the armed forces began actually to oppose the interests of the economic elites, probably not so much out of hatred or jealousy as out of insistence that Peru must be transformed. This feeling was the product of intense nationalism and the belief that socioeconomic development for Peru is possible and can be engineered. Although a developmentalist orientation had been evolving for some years, the generals experienced an eye-opening, antiguerrilla campaign in the sierra in 1965 which brought them to the realization that radical reforms were essential both for the peasants' sake and to avoid uncontrollable turmoil. The officers were furthermore certain that they, rather than bungling politicians, could bring about the changes. This self-confidence stemmed in part from the excellent military education system of Peru, which for years had been training officers at home and abroad and had stressed achievement and competence as criteria for promotion. Training in the service academies since 1950 had been supplemented by a course in the Center for Higher Military Studies (*Centro de Altos Estudios Militares* or CAEM) on social, economic, and political problems of Peru. Although allegations have been made that the Peruvian military is communist or under the influence of communists, its behavior is far more explainable in terms of pragmatic, technocratic planning than of political ideology.[8]

Meanwhile another key institution of the society, the church, also wavered in its traditional support of economic elites. The liberalized social doctrines of the church as reflected in Pope John's pronouncements created a new awareness on the part of some Peruvian clergy for the social miseries of their own country. Younger priests, many of whom were foreign, identified themselves with reformist and even radical currents in the society. The Peruvian church became split between extremists of left and right and those advocating political activism and those opposing it. Many clerics, both high and low in the church hierarchy, supported the Velasco regime.[9]

One might expect that organized labor would unanimously favor a populist transformation, but the complexities of Peruvian politics are such that here, too, is found political ambivalence. A substantial percentage of the nonagricultural working force is unionized (about 15 percent) and the workers of all important industrial and extractive corporations are organized. Thus the strike is a potent economic weapon in Peru. It is also a potent political weapon; as James Payne has pointed out, the unions can deliberately foster the type of unrest that sometimes brings down governments.[10] Prior to 1968 most unions were embraced within the Confederation of Workers of Peru (*Confederación de Trabajadores de Perú* or CTP), which since 1956 has been intimately tied to the Aprista party. This connection gave the Apristas a membership base but it never led to effective electoral performance, as was the case with the British Labour party. The army and apristas hate each other for historical reasons and the CTP was not a supporter of the Velasco regime. The Velasco government actively encouraged the growth of a radical counterpart to the CTP, the *Confederación General de Trabajadores de Perú* or CGTP, but this organization called such economically damaging strikes that the government itself eventually intervened.[11]

If labor's political role has been ambivalent, the role of organizations traditionally representative of the economic elites has been quite straightforward. In almost all cases they have brought a rearguard action that attempts desperately to forestall radical social change. The fact that their resistance and opposition were not followed by substantial modification of the policies of the Velasco regime speaks meaningfully to the deterioration of upper-class political influence.

Elitist organizations fall into various classes. One type is the exclusive social club, such as the *Club Nacional, Club de la Unión*, and *Jockey Club del Perú*. A luncheon club of secondary importance but of interest because it is frequented by the industrial elite is the *Club de la Banca*. Socially these organizations are the locale for business luncheons and evening parties, but from a political standpoint they are important as symbols of upper-class status and as means of inter- and intra-elite communication. It is said that at one time the president of Peru was informally chosen at the Club Nacional. Today, however, the clubs are more centers of antigovernment carping than of public decision-making. Although Carlos Astiz found that military men were numbered among Jockey Club members in 1963, it is said that after the 1968 revolution the generals refused to be seen there.[12]

As for business associations, the most important are the various "national societies" organized by economic sector. The most significant of these are the National Agrarian Society (*Sociedad Nacional Agraria*), National Society of Mining and Petroleum Companies (*Sociedad Nacional de Minería y Petróleo*), National Society of Industries (*Sociedad Nacional de Industrias*),* and National Society of Fisheries (*Sociedad Nacional de Pesquería*). Aside from the fact that the societies are concerned with different types of economic activity, they vary in sociopolitico complexion. The Agrarian Society primarily represents the coastal sugar elite and is probably the most conservative of the four societies named. It was instrumental in achieving a significant watering-down of the Agrarian Reform law of 1964, for example, including exemption from the law of the coastal sugar estates. The mining and petroleum group is dominated by

---

*In latter 1972 this organization lost much of its prior importance following a dispute with the regime.

American mining interests. The Society of Industries represents a wide variety of manufacturing and other activities and hence has a quite differentiated outlook, with emphasis on individual industry problems. Fisheries was for many years the personal instrument of the late Luis Banchero, a Peruvian fishmeal entrepreneur.

Prior to the 1968 revolution all of these groups had the reputation of exercising great influence over the formation of governmental policies affecting their respective areas. Pressure was mobilized and applied through commodity subgroups or committees within each society, such as for sugar, textiles, rubber, beer, and so on. Lobbying was carried on both before the national legislature and in the pertinent ministries. The groups frequently had formal links with government, such as seats on advisory boards and voting rights in official bodies. The Agrarian Society even received tax monies to conduct a type of extension service.[13]

Other business groups should also be named. The National Confederation of Businessmen (*Confederación Nacional de Comerciantes* or CONACO) represents retail firms and, unlike the other associations, has a reputation of alliance with rather than opposition to the military government. A great many chambers of commerce exist in Peru, including one for every sizable town as well as for Lima itself. These are organized in a loose federation called the Association of Chambers of Commerce of Peru (*Asociación de las Cámeras de Comercio del Perú*), which bears a resemblance to the Chamber of Commerce of the United States. Also each nationality of foreign enterprise possesses its group; there are, for example, German, Italian, Swiss, Japanese, and American chambers of commerce of Peru. The American Chamber, formed in 1960 as the *Comité Norteamericano Pro-Perú* (or CONOPROPE), sponsors monthly luncheons, arranges meetings among businessmen and Peruvian and U.S. Embassy officials, and undertakes various public relations activities such as plant tours and charitable good works.

We turn now to the governmental institutions proper of Peru. A feature of foremost significance is that the executive, particularly the presidency, is central. This is true regardless of whether the president is elected or not. The Constitution of 1933, operative until 1968, formally provided for an independent Congress and Supreme Court. Theoretically the national legislature, made up of a Senate and Chamber of Deputies, could bring a vote of no confidence against the government and force the resignation of the cabinet, formally known as the Council of Ministers. However this power was seldom used prior to the mid-1960's. As long as he remained in power the president usually dominated both the judiciary and legislature.[14]

With the advent of the Velasco government in 1968, the constitution was suspended and any pretense of tripartite government was abandoned. The Congress was disbanded entirely. All members of the Supreme Court were summarily dismissed and a new National Council of Justice was created to control the judiciary. The cabinet, however, became even more important than before, reflective of the corporate character of the Revolution's leadership. The president himself, the prime minister (also minister of war) and eighteen other ministers and top officials became the policy-making core. Decisions by this body generally reflected majority or unanimous opinion within it. Most statutory law was in the form of "decree-laws" signed by every minister. However, an Advisory Committee to the Presidency cleared all draft laws prior to their consideration by the cabinet, and thus this group enjoyed a special degree of influence.

But just as the president is traditionally paramount in Peruvian government, he is also traditionally very vulnerable. Under the 1933 constitution the president was elected for a term of six years. Legally he could be impeached by Congress but not forced to resign by a nonconfidence vote (unlike ministers). However the realities were that the concept of a fixed presidential tenure was never accepted by the political forces of the country, and in 150 years of independence at least twenty-two presidents were deposed by coups. Only twelve were permitted to serve out their terms. As a result a civilian president must not only govern but wage a continuous political battle to stay in office. Typically the coups are carried out by the military, occur shortly before or after elections and during times of economic stress, and are accompanied by little violence. The outgoing president is invariably permitted to leave the country unharmed. The October 3, 1968, coup d'etat fits these characteristics perfectly.[15]

Thus attainment of national political power is by two means, election and coup. The importance of the latter forces the former into a role of lesser consequence than is found in constitutional democracies of Europe and North America. Even when elections are held in Peru their "democratic" character can be questioned. Because of a Spanish literacy requirement that denied suffrage to the Indian, a small percentage of the population voted (about 16 percent in the 1963 election). Charges of electoral fraud were commonplace, and the Peruvian political parties were generally ineffective mobilizers of political opinion and action.

With one exception, Peru's political parties consist of splintered ideological factions or personalistic followings which are short-lived and without systematic organization. In the 1963 election four parties were of importance: Popular Action (*Acción Popular* or AP), the Christian Democrats (*Demócrata Cristiana* or DC), the Apristas (*Alianza Popular Revolucionaria Americana* or APRA), and the Odriistas (*Unión Nacional Odriísta* or UNO). AP had been formed a few years earlier by Fernando Belaúnde Terry and it was his vehicle to the presidency in 1963. The Christian Democrats, allied at least in spirit to parties of that name in Chile and Europe, attained their height of success in electing a mayor of Lima. The UNO consisted of supporters of former President Manuel Odría, identified with reactionary coastal and sierra elites. APRA is the only continuing party of the four, although it too had personalistic origins. The founder and nominal leader is Víctor Raúl Haya de la Torre, one of the most famous figures in Latin American revolutionary thought. Beginning in the 1920's Haya preached a nationalistic populism, economic planning, control of foreign investment, promotion of the Indian, and a pancontinentalism referred to as "Indo-America." Although Aprismo was originally conceived as international in scope, only the Peruvian branch prospered.* The party is highly institutionalized and, as mentioned, closely tied to the CTP. Its strength is primarily in the northern coast and sierra.[16]

Ostensibly this set of parties had the potentiality of creating the basis of a balanced political spectrum for the 1960's. The Christian Democrats called for drastic social changes and thus might have attracted the non-communist left. The UNO represented right-wing interests. In between were Belaúnde and Haya, both of whom preached social reform. A viable electoral system with effectively mandated governments failed to appear, however. In the first place, the constituencies were mixed; many of Lima's poor supported the UNO, for example. Second, the parties' formal positions were not reflective of their true positions; APRA had become conservative over time in the process of making numerous accommodations to win power. Third, the parties were unable to attain majorities or, usually, even sizable pluralities. None of them could obtain a majority of popular votes or a majority of seats in either legislative house in the national elections of 1962 and 1963. As a consequence coalitions were formed causing further compromises; the Belaúnde government was an AP-DC cabinet coalition, its opposition an APRA-UNO congressional coalition. The APRA-UNO group held a majority of seats in both houses and thus was in a position to block Belaúnde programs and censure his ministers. The executive and legislature became increasingly at loggerheads in the mid-1960's, creating vacillation and stalemate. Then the patchwork system itself began to fall apart. In 1967 and 1968 both coalitions dissolved and in addition the AP, DC, and UNO each broke into competing factions. Only the Apristas remained more or less intact, but their alliances with right-wing forces had destroyed their credibility as a reformist vehicle. The 1968 coup brought an abrupt end to the disintegrating party system, but in some measure it fell of its own weight.[17]

Foreign Capital in Peru

Foreign capital is inextricably bound up in the history of Peru. Pizarro's principal motivation in conquering that part of the Inca Empire now known as Peru was the promise of gold and other riches. Conceivably the

---

*Although commonly referred to as APRA, the technically correct name of the Peruvian party—the only one in existence—is *Partido Aprista Peruana* or PAP.

term "foreign" enterprise could be applied to the Spanish colonial mines opened in the sixteenth century at Huancavelica and Cerro de Pasco, where fabulous deposits of silver, mercury, and other metals were found. Moreover, the revolution against Spanish authority, fought between 1821 and 1824, was financed in considerable part by bond sales in London. In 1822 and 1824 British investors sympathetic with the independence movement lent almost £1.5 million to the patriots. And foreign loans were an essential element in the complex financial arrangements characterizing Peru's "Guano Age," lasting approximately from 1840 to 1875. Guano, a rich natural fertilizer formed from bird droppings built up on offshore islands, was sold through European consignees on a monopoly basis in return for sizable loans to the Peruvian government. The resulting capital financed extensive public works projects, including a series of spectacular railroad-building projects promoted and built by the American Henry Meiggs.[18]

As these comments suggest, British capital was particularly important to nineteenth-century Peru. Although much of this was in Peruvian government bonds, English investments also flowed into private ventures in mining, beer, telephones, and petroleum. At this time American capital was beginning to trickle in also, but slowly. By the 1850's at least one American-owned mine was in operation, and it was in this decade that an Irishman by the name of William Russell Grace founded the W.R. Grace & Company in Peru. According to a diplomatic dispatch sent to Washington in 1863 a "considerable amount" of American capital was present in Peru at that time, consisting for the most part of "business houses" in Lima and a "mill" at Callao.[19] Data compiled by Cleona Lewis indicate that by 1897 direct U.S. investment in Peru was on the order of $6 million, divided quite evenly among sugar plantations, public utilities, mining, and petroleum. But only after a group of American investors formed in 1902 what later became the Cerro de Pasco Copper Corporation did U.S. capital in Peru start to assume significant proportions; by 1915 it was an estimated $58 million, of which $39 million was in mining.[20]

British predominance ended in the 1920's, a decade that coincides with the second administration of President Augusto B. Leguía (1919-1930). This period, known as the *Oncenio* because of its length of eleven years, is the longest presidential tenure in Peruvian history. Although historical judgments of the Oncenio still bitterly disagree, Leguía presided over a period of considerable economic prosperity in Peru. He undertook many public works; during his administration more than 1100 miles of roads, over 800 primary schools, and numerous municipal plazas, public buildings, and waterworks were constructed. It was at that time that the contemporary physical appearance of Lima began to take shape.[21]

The Oncenio was the original golden age for American business in Peru. Leguía hated the landowning aristocracy but was devoted to American capitalism. He was himself a businessman and at one time in his career served as general manager of the Peruvian-Ecuadorian-Bolivian branches of the New York Life Insurance Company. Speaking fluent English and at home with the American business mentality, Leguía developed personal friendships with all executives in Peru and actively encouraged them to expand their operations. This sometimes involved what were later judged to be sellouts of the national patrimony, as in the case of the International Petroleum Company (IPC). In any case U.S. capital began to pour in and by 1929 it surpassed British investments in value, as is shown in Table 3.

In addition to direct investments, Americans bought the Peruvian government bonds needed to finance the dictator's public works projects. From 1919 to 1929 American portfolio holdings in Peru increased from almost zero to over $75 million.[22] Leguía's son, Juan, collected huge commissions on the bond sales and accepted bribes from the Electric Boat Company for arranging submarine purchases for the Peruvian navy. This corruption has since formed part of the Oncenio's controversial reputation and it has had a residual effect on the reputation of American business in Peru as well.[23]

Leguía was overthrown in 1930, and another truly favorable period for foreign investors in Peru did not come for almost twenty years. The Great

Table 3. Value of Private Direct Investments in Peru ($ millions).

Year	Historical estimates	
	Great Britain	United States
1915	121	58
1925	125	90
1929	141	151

Year	Book values computed by U.S. Department of Commerce
	United States
1929	124
1936	96
1943	71
1950	145
1955	304
1960	446
1965	515
1970	691

Sources: Robert W. Dunn, American Foreign Investments (New York, B. W. Heubsch, 1926), p. 82; Max Winkler, Investments of United States Capital in Latin America (Boston, World Peace Foundation, 1928), pp. 284–285; UN Economic Commission for Latin America, External Financing in Latin America (1965), p. 17; U.S. Department of Commerce, U.S. Business Investments in Foreign Countries (1960), p. 92, and Survey of Current Business, various issues.

Depression dried up all international capital flows temporarily and then World War II delayed them for several additional years. During the 1930's and early 1940's the book value of U.S. private direct investments in Peru actually dropped as depreciated capital was not replaced (see Table 3). Investments began to rise finally after 1945 but the growth did not continue, probably because of political uncertainties in Lima. Between 1945 and 1948 the Peruvian presidency was occupied by José Luis Bustamante y Rivero, elected to office with the support of APRA. Far from being perceived as a friend of foreign investors, the Bustamante regime introduced controls over foreign exchange for the first time in the country's history and imposed nontariff import restrictions and price controls.[24]

In 1948 Bustamante was overthrown by General Manuel Odría. Backed by conservative landowning interests, Odría outlawed APRA, forced Haya into exile in the Colombian Embassy, and dismantled the economic controls. With all opposition suppressed he permitted elections in 1950 with himself as the only candidate. The dictator then filled out this term, thus retaining the presidency from 1948 to 1956; this eight-year regime is known as the *Ochenio*.

From the standpoint of American business the Ochenio of the fifties bore considerable resemblance to the Oncenio of the twenties. Both were characterized by personal dictatorial rule, laissez-faire economic policies, and general prosperity. As Leguía benefited from economic conditions of the bullish twenties, Odría benefited from the Korean war and its high metal prices.

In one sense Odría went beyond Leguía in creating a favorable investment climate, however. The latter had encouraged the foreign capitalists informally and personally. Odría did this as well, but he also had formal laws passed that provided tangibly stable conditions. Three investment promotion laws were significant: the Mining Code of 1950, the Petroleum Law of 1952, and the Electricity Law of 1955. Each act enhanced greatly the advantages of investing in the industry covered, by domestic Peruvian investors as well as foreigners. But it was primarily the foreigners that responded. The Petroleum Law's liberal rules on exploration and concessions attracted several new foreign oil companies to Peru and benefited IPC as well. The Electricity Law, which guaranteed utility consumer rates sufficient to assure adequate investor profits, brought additional European capital to the Lima Light and Power Company (Empresas Eléctricas Asociadas). The Mining Code simplified and reduced mining company taxes, provided a generous depletion allowance modeled on U.S. tax laws, and established low canon payments on mining concessions and gave them indefinite life even if unworked. Article 56 of the Code was particularly attractive to the investors for it permitted special investment contracts whose terms could be individually bargained.[25]

Thus a second golden age for American business in Peru had come. During the Ochenio American business investments more than doubled in value. Business publications in the United States praised enthusiastically the Peruvian investment climate (see, for example, "Dollars Flock to Peru," *Business Week*, October 11, 1952, and "Why Peru Pulls Dollars," *Fortune*, November 1956). No government since Odría's has been so distinctly favorable to foreign investor interests. The next regime, that of a previous president, Manuel Prado, was by no means opposed to foreign capital, but it did represent other interests and was, in fact, helped to power by APRA. During the Prado administration (1956-1962), additional investment promotion laws were written, namely the Industrial Promotion Law of 1959 and an automobile assembly decree. At the same time steps were taken, however feeble, toward assisting nonelite portions of the population. In 1962, ten days before Prado's term was to end, the armed forces took control of the government in the face of an electoral impasse in which Haya had won a plurality of votes but not enough to become president. The military ruled for the following year and in 1963 it scheduled the election by which Belaúnde achieved the presidency.[26]

The Belaúnde government (1963-1968) came to power with great reformist momentum and announced objectives, including tax reform, agrarian reform, community development in the sierra (*Cooperación Popular*), ambitious road building in the selva (*Carretera Marginal de la Selva*), and a "final solution" to the IPC issue. The program presented no direct threat to the foreign investment community generally, but of course IPC's fate was of interest, and properties of Cerro de Pasco, Grace, and other foreign enterprises could have been affected by agrarian reform. But as the Belaúnde period unfolded, any dangers of expropriation were at least temporarily removed. Procrastination and vacillation marked the IPC negotiations. The APRA-UNO coalition in Congress weakened reform laws and failed to raise and appropriate sufficient funds to carry out development projects. To obtain resources Belaúnde permitted high levels of deficit financing and a steep rise in the debt owed to foreign banks and governments. A serious inflation and balance of payments problem broke out in 1967, with a currency devaluation in September of that year. Now the investors faced not nationalization but a runaway economy. For a time the congressional opposition cooperated in establishing an emergency fiscal program, but improvements in finance were overshadowed by two political events of 1968: the exposure of smuggling operations involving high officials and a bitter cause célébre over IPC. Meanwhile the political parties, except for APRA, were disintegrating. In this atmosphere of ineptitude and near-chaos the military physically removed Belaúnde from the presidential palace on October 3 and General Velasco came to power.[27]

The Velasco government was drastically different from its predecessors.

Unlike previous military regimes, the generals ruled over the long term (unlike in 1962-1963) and on behalf of no other elites. They were not blatantly repressive of the political opposition or individual freedoms, although the press was muffled by several retaliatory acts. Political parties were not outlawed and political prisoners were few.[28]

The regime was different from previous civilian as well as military governments in that it set out to transform radically the entire Peruvian social order. A revolution in the deepest sense was contemplated and the government referred to its actions collectively as the "Revolution." Its principal values were uncompromising nationalism and economic populism; by systematic changes throughout the society and economy the aim was to reduce social and economic inequalities, foster economic growth, and terminate dependence on the United States. In foreign affairs the government took a decisively independent line, augmenting diplomatic and trade contacts with communist countries, defending a 200-mile fishing jurisdiction, and rejecting belligerently efforts by Washington to employ threats or sanctions against Peru. At the same time this independence was accompanied by moves toward regional cooperation; the regime actively promoted development of the Andean common market composed of Colombia, Ecuador, Peru, Bolivia, and Chile.

In economic policy the government's avowed intention was to avoid both capitalism and communism as models and to push pragmatically along a unique path of state-directed development. Generally this was accomplished. Expropriations of several enterprises were undertaken, particularly in oil, banking, communications, and sugar. The marketing of some commodities was nationalized, including fishmeal, some minerals, and precious stones. A supermarket chain was government-operated following bankruptcy. Unworked mining concessions and eventually railroads were taken over and the state engaged in metal refining. An ambitious agrarian reform program was pushed; many lands were expropriated and redistributed, but the social results were not always what was desired.

Supplementing these traditionally socialist actions were policies not inconsistent with private ownership. The bulk of the economy was left in private hands although a formal goal of the Industrial Law of 1970 was that eventually all "basic" industry is to be state-owned. Expropriated lands under agrarian reform were given over to cooperatives or individuals rather than retained by the government itself. In fostering economic development, public investments were emphasized in infrastructure and heavy industry, but in many other areas the main economic instruments were regulatory controls and differentiated incentives designed to direct a continuingly significant private sector.

Foreign exchange transactions were completely controlled. Advance government approval was needed whenever a business planned new moves with regard to imports, production changes, and the formation, liquidation, or merger of business entities. It was required that 2 percent of gross profits be invested in approved industrial research. Attractive exemptions and reductions were given on income taxes and import duties if prescribed behavior was followed in plant location and reinvestment. Credit and even government subsidies were available for new industry established under specified conditions. A government development corporation was created along the lines of the *Nacional Financiera* in Mexico.

A particularly interesting innovation was the *"comunidad."* This is an organization composed of all workers employed in a firm (or occasionally an installation or industry). Required by law in manufacturing, mining, fishmeal, and many other sectors, the comunidad elects its own officers (separate from union heads) and receives automatically a fixed percentage of net profits. In "industrial" comunidades, the proportion is 25 percent; 10 percent is given to workers as income and 15 as equity in the enterprise. The organization is represented on the firm's board of directors by at least one member, and its number of seats increases with its equity share to an eventual level of half.*

With regard to foreign capital the Velasco government's policies can be summarized as follows. It (1) generally imposed on existing investments the comunidad concept and the various dirigistic techniques mentioned. At the same time, however, it (2) recognized the validity of existing investor arrangements with certain prominent exceptions, such as IPC, the mining concessions, and the automobile assembly industry. In accord with plans for a socialized basic sector of industry, (3) foreign capital was eventually prohibited from certain sectors; in some it was automatically limited (as example, banking). Yet the regime (4) actively encouraged new foreign investments, including American but more particularly European and Japanese. Eventually (5) a majority of the assets of all wholly foreign-owned firms were required to be purchased locally (such as by the comunidades) except under specified conditions. This so-called "fade-out" concept is in accord with Andean Pact policy toward foreign investment as embodied in "Decision 24" of the Common Market's commission. The time schedule for the divestment was somewhat ambiguous, but (6) in any event foreign investors were guaranteed the right to repatriate foreign exchange equivalent to the original investment plus a "reasonable" profit margin above this. In short, the Revolution's approach to foreign investment was ambivalent, complex, and varied. New external private capital was encouraged at the same time that foreign business was subject to unprecedented restrictions. As one might expect, this lack of adherence to

---

*In 1972 plans were being laid for another innovative concept, a type of collective enterprise in which the notion of owned assets is omitted in favor of rental payments to the state for nonlabor factors of production. Workers would manage the enterprises on democratic principles and would receive all net income.

traditional ideologies earned vehement criticism for the military regime from both ends of the political spectrum.[29]

Major American Corporations

Aggregate data on the total dimensions of the American business community in Peru come from the U.S. Department of Commerce. For 1957 the department estimates that American companies employed 50,000 persons in Peru.[30] In a "trade list" for Peru compiled by the department in August 1965, 337 firms are mentioned as being partially or totally owned by Americans. The department report on investments in Peru for 1971 puts the total book value of direct investments at $688 million. Of this, $415 million was in mining and smelting and $92 million in manufacturing.[31]

The Commerce Department's investment figures have a tendency to err on the low side, however. When one inquires of the companies themselves the value of their investments in Peru, figures are given which are not reconcilable with the published totals. The department's figure for total U.S. direct investment in Peru in 1967, for example, is $660 million.[32] Yet my own survey of the twelve largest firms alone yields a total of $930 million for that year, as shown in Table 4. Total employment of these firms in mid-1968 was 45,650.

Although the firms given in Table 4 were the "top twelve" as of mid-1968, they are not so at this writing. As can be seen by the far-right column, six of the twelve experienced major reductions or alterations in the scope of their operations between 1968 and 1971. Properties of Grace and IPC were expropriated (as well as marginal properties of Cerro); the telephone company and Anderson Clayton were affected by forced or pressured sale; and General Motors and Emkay were essentially forced to cease operations. Thus one generalization that can be drawn from the table is that substantial withdrawal of American business from Peru has coincided with the Velasco Revolution. At the same time, however, three companies made substantial new investments, namely Southern Peru Copper Corporation (SPCC), Marcona, and Goodyear.

A second general feature thrown into relief by the table is the wide disparity in size among the firms, as measured both by employment and investment. In 1967-1968 five corporations overshadowed the rest; these were Cerro, Grace, IPC, SPCC, and Marcona. Together they accounted for 84 percent of the personnel and 94 percent of the investment of the top twelve at that time.

Third, it can readily be seen that the parent corporations involved are big and famous. In fact they are among the largest enterprises in the world. Almost all of them rank in *Fortune*'s list of top 500 industrial corporations; in the 1968 list, General Motors placed number 1 in sales; Standard

Table 4. Twelve Largest U.S. Business Firms in Peru (in Terms of Total Employment in Peru in Mid-1968).

Peruvian affiliate(s)	Parent company(ies)	Principal activity(ies)	Number personnel in Peru, mid-1968	Value of investment as given by company, end of 1967 ($millions)	Status as of end of 1971
Cerro de Pasco Corp.	Cerro Corp.	Metal mining and refining	17,000	253	Approximately the same, except that 247,000 hectares of sierra sheeplands were expropriated in 1969
Grace y Cía. (Peru); Soc. Paramonga Ltda.; Cartavio S.A.; and others	W. R. Grace & Co.	Sugar, paper, chemicals, textiles, fishmeal, candy, mining, importing	10,150	80	Because of sugar expropriations and the sale of several properties, only about 2,000 were still employed / Agreement signed for sale to government of most of remaining properties
International Petroleum Co. (IPC)	Standard Oil Co. (N.J.)[a]	Oil drilling & refining; gasoline distribution	4,750	188	No operations whatever in Peru because of expropriations of 1968 & 1969
Southern Peru Copper Corp. (SPCC)	American Smelting & Refining Co.; Cerro Corp.; Phelps Dodge Corp.; Newmont Mining Corp.	Copper mining & smelting	3,850	240	An additional $15 million invested in an existing open-pit mine (Toquepala) & $90 million committed to developing a new one (Cuajone)
Marcona Mining Co.	Utah International, Inc.; Cyprus Mines Corp.	Iron ore mining & benefaction, shipping	2,700	110	$65 million more invested in or committed to added treatment & related facilities

Company	U.S. parent	Activity	Value	No.	Remarks
Cía. Peruana de Teléfonos S.A.	International Telephone & Telegraph Corp.	Lima telephone system	1,700	19	ITT interest sold to the Peruvian government in 1969; ITT reinvested proceeds in a new Sheraton hotel & telephone equipment manufacturing plant
Constructora Emkay S.A.	Morrison-Knudsen Co.	Contract construction	1,500	7	All operations suspended by 1969 as a result of completion of projects and allegations of wrongdoing by Peruvian government
Sears Roebuck del Perú S.A.	Sears Roebuck & Co.	Department stores	950	3	Essentially no change
International Basic Economy Corp. (IBEC)	International Basic Economy Corp.	Supermarkets, poultry insurance, housing	800	7	Essentially no change
General Motors del Perú S.A.	General Motors Corp.	Assembly of cars & trucks	800	6	All operations suspended in 1970 because of failure to win bid to produce under new regulations
Cía. Goodyear del Perú	Goodyear Tire & Rubber Co.	Manufacture of tires & tubes	700	12	Expansion & modernization increased investment by $4 million and employment by 30
Anderson, Clayton & Co. S.A.	Anderson, Clayton & Co.	Cotton, coffee fats, & oils	700	5	Coffee export company & cotton farm sold to government, reducing investment by $1.5 million and employment by 200
Totals			45,650	930	

[a] Exxon Corporation after 1972.

Oil (New Jersey), number 2; ITT, 11; Goodyear, 22; Grace, 45; American Smelting, 160; Phelps Dodge, 181; and Cerro, 232. In addition, Sears was number 1 in *Fortune*'s top 50 retailing companies. Furthermore, *Fortune* claims that if it had classified Anderson Clayton, the International Basic Economy Corporation (IBEC), and Morrison-Knudsen as "industrial" corporations, these firms would have ranked 162, 358, and 400, respectively, in the top 500 for 1968.[33] In consequence, this leaves, among the corporations listed in the table, only Marcona with relatively small parents, Utah International, Inc., of San Francisco, and the Cyprus Mines Corporation of Los Angeles.

The Peruvian Andes have long been recognized as one of the great mineral storehouses of the world and it is not surprising to find mining as the largest single activity of American business in Peru. More than 75 mining companies exist in the country, but the industry is completely dominated by Cerro de Pasco, SPCC, and Marcona. These three constitute in fact a class by themselves in Peruvian mining law: the *gran minería*. Together they produce between 80 and 90 percent of the mineral output of the country. SPCC mines and processes about two-thirds of the copper and Cerro almost all of the remaining one-third. About two-thirds of the lead and 60 percent of the zinc and silver output are Cerro's. Cerro also produces a number of minor metals such as antimony, cadmium, and bismuth (of which it is the world's largest producer). Since late 1968 Marcona has been the sole producer of iron ore.[34]

Of the three gran minería, Cerro is by far the oldest. In fact, for half a century it alone dominated the Peruvian mining scene. The corporation's history goes back to 1900 when the American mining engineer James B. Haggin conceived of mining the ancient and isolated Cerro de Pasco silver district for copper, an operation made potentially profitable by substituting railway transportation for llama-back or muletrain in carrying ore to the sea. Together with financiers A.W. McCune, J.P. Morgan, and others, he formed a syndicate in 1902 to further the plan. With the help of the U.S. State Department rival claimants to the necessary concessions were fought off. In two years the "Cerro de Pasco Copper Corporation"—as it was soon called—had reopened the mine and had built a smelter, coal mine, and connecting railroad. In the 1920's a new smelter complex was begun at La Oroya, eighty-three miles south of Cerro de Pasco, and this locality eventually became operational headquarters. Smoke from the La Oroya smelter contained so much sulphur that it killed all vegetation for miles around, with the result that wealthy landowners in the area were happy to sell their pastures to the corporation. Some years later a taller smokestack was built and still later a precipitator was installed in it (after the Cottrell type was invented). These actions permitted grass to grow in the area once again, and Cerro responded by going into the sheep-raising business. In this way it supplied its own company stores with fresh meat.

During the 1960's the Cerro haciendas became a political issue of some importance and they were expropriated at the end of the decade.[35]

Even aside from this venture into ranching, elaboration of operations and diversification of interests were the hallmarks of Cerro's post-World War II history. As a result of expanded mining, concentrating, and smelting activities, the tonnage output of lead and zinc surpassed that of copper by 1948. This prompted the removal of "Copper" from the firm's name in 1951. Operations continued to grow until they encompassed six metal mines, six concentrating mills, several different smelting processes, four hydroelectric power plants, and 160 miles of railroad. Outside of mining itself, the enterprise achieved vertical integration in Peru by acquiring minority or majority shares in both mining supplier firms (explosives, welding rods, steel castings, and refractory brick) and metal manufacturing plants (copper rod rolling, wire and cable mill, lead alloys, and extruded products). Oil and gas concessions in the selva were also obtained. At the same time that this expansion was going on in Peru acquisitions were made elsewhere: metal fabrication, cement, oil, and real estate interests in the United States and iron ore deposits in Australia and a copper mine in Chile (expropriated in 1971). Cerro was no longer a Peruvian mining company but a multinational conglomerate; in recognition of this a parent company was created and given the still more generic name "Cerro Corporation." By 1971 its business was about equally split between South American mining and other activities.[36]

In Peru, the place of its birth, Cerro remains that country's most important private enterprise, however. With 17,000 on its payroll (19,000 if contractual personnel are included), the company is Peru's largest employer outside of the government. It is also the largest private investor. Although by 1971 the investments of SPCC had slightly exceeded those over which Cerro de Pasco had direct control, Cerro Corporation owns about 22 percent of Southern Peru. Thus, directly or indirectly, the enterprise controlled from the Colgate Palmolive Building on Park Avenue in New York is still the largest industrial capitalist in Peru.

The majority stockholder (51.5 percent) in the Southern Peru Copper Corporation is the American Smelting & Refining Company (ASARCO). Two minority stockholders other than Cerro are the Phelps Dodge Corporation (16 percent) and Newmont Mining Corporation (about 10 percent). The SPCC joint venture was put together in 1952 for the purpose of developing an open-pit copper mine in southern Peru called Toquepala. Although the presence of copper ore bodies had been known at Toquepala for decades, they had not been exploited because of the enormous cost involved in extracting and refining 1 percent ore located 8500 feet up in the Andes and transporting it some 50 air miles to the sea. The job eventually cost over $240 million, the largest single private investment in the history of Peru. Involved was not only the removal of vast quantities of overburden, but the construction of a town and mill near the pit, a port and smelter near the fishing town of Ilo (plus additional housing), and a 114-mile railroad connecting the two. The project was in part financed by a $100 million loan from the U.S. Export-Import Bank and went into production in 1959.[37]

A great success economically (because of the high world copper prices of the 1960's), Toquepala was not without its political troubles. Shortly after Odría left power the Apristas began to question the contract signed with SPCC under Article 56 of the Mining Code. The upper tax limit of 30 percent of net profits was denounced as too low, and for the next several years a subject of national debate was renegotiation of the contract. Finally in 1968 the corporation reluctantly yielded to the pressure and a new contract was signed, shortly before Velasco came to power.

But a regional political squabble remained unresolved. Reminiscent of Cerro's smelter-smoke episode, the smokestack at the Ilo smelter emitted significant quantities of sulphur despite certain antipollution precautions. The company could have done more to clear the smoke but did not wish to because a resulting by-product of further antipollution efforts, sulphuric acid, was unneeded and unprofitable. The emissions clearly damaged crops in the nearby Osmora valley, and SPCC made continuing damage payments to its farmers. The landowners of a more distant valley, the Tambo, claimed that their crops were also being damaged, which SPCC insisted was impossible because of the distance—about thirty-five miles. The Tambo farmers mounted a publicity campaign against SPCC and tried to get action from the central government. Various independent bodies investigated the situation but the controversy remained unresolved. Finally the corporation arranged for some test plots in the Tambo to support its case and claimed the true problem there was excessive boron in the soil and not the smoke. The fight was muted but still underway in 1971.

The third of the gran minería, Marcona, in some ways resembles SPCC. It is a joint venture involving more than one U.S. parent and was also originally created in Peru, for open-pit mining, and in 1952 under Article 56. But, unlike Southern, the product sought was iron rather than copper, and the deposits were conveniently located only nine miles from the coast. The ore was crushed at the mine, transported by conveyor to benefaction and pelletizing plants, and then moved again by conveyor or slurry pipeline (the "Marconaflo" method) directly to Marcona ships in the company's harbor. Increasingly Marcona became involved in iron-ore shipping itself and its executives began to describe it as a "natural resources transportation company."

From a political standpoint Marcona is distinct among the mining companies in the degree to which it has avoided nationalist attacks and battles with successive Peruvian governments. This may be explainable in terms of an almost symbiotic relationship with a Peruvian government agency, Corporación Peruana del Santa, plus an ability to renegotiate contracts willingly before it is too late. Santa was created in 1943 for, among other purposes, establishing a Peruvian steel-producing capacity. To this end it built an integrated steel mill at Chimbote, a fishing village 220 miles up the coast from Lima. The Marcona iron deposits, known to exist a similar distance down the coast from Lima, were anticipated as the source of ore. However, analysis of the costs involved in relation to the size of the Peruvian market led Santa to seek out Utah International (then Utah Construction), which at that time was interested in diversification. In 1952 a contract was signed by Santa and the newly created Marcona Mining Company whereby the latter would obtain a thirty-year lease on the deposits, mine them, supply Santa's ore needs, and export the remainder.[38]

As the years went by, successive Lima governments demanded increasingly favorable terms from the company. Instead of resisting the revision of unsatisfactory contracts as SPCC had done, Marcona willingly entered into negotiations prior to expiration of existing terms. The corporation did this no less than four times, with the last contract at this writing signed in 1970. In addition to paying regular taxes, Marcona gives Santa a 25 percent royalty; moreover Santa will own half-interest in all production facilities by 1982. In return the company is guaranteed availability of foreign exchange and an unchanging tax structure while its investment is being recovered.[39]

Turning now to investments in other fields than mining, W.R. Grace is the oldest American enterprise in Peru to my knowledge. Its history reaches back to the 1850's when William Russell Grace emigrated to Peru from Ireland at the age of nineteen. He obtained employment in Callao with Bryce & Company, a supplier to guano ships. The young Irishman was so energetic and full of ideas that he soon became a partner with Bryce and later founded his own firm. Grace transformed it from a ship chandler to an international trading and shipping company. Later when Grace moved to New York he became prominent to the extent that twice he was elected mayor in the 1880's.[40] During the twentieth century the corporation gradually grew into a leading conglomerate, involved in chemicals, plastics, paper, mining, petroleum, foods, consumer products, and—until recently—shipping and aviation.

In its heyday in Peru, Grace was second only to Cerro de Pasco as the leading American enterprise in the country. From a banklike commercial structure in central Lima referred to as "Casa Grace," a far-flung empire was run. This included four textile mills; two sugar plantations; various importing, trading, shipping, and lighterage services; trucking and aviation; real estate; manufacture of liquors, chemicals, paints, plastics, paper, boxes, candy, crackers, and flour; and (quite recently) mining and fishmeal. A grossly flattering study of the company published in 1954 concluded, "There is hardly a Peruvian participating in the money economy of the country who does not eat, wear, or use something processed, manufactured, or imported by Casa Grace."[41]

Those days are now over. No longer does Peru constitute a sentimental "home" for Grace executives as it once did. The corporation is urgently attempting to sell everything it owns in the country and much was already disposed of as of mid-1971. All that remained were the industrial plants associated with the two haciendas, Paramonga and Cartavio, plus investments in a box factory, mine, and mineral trading company. Even the old Casa Grace building had been sold, symbolically ending an era.

The Peruvian divestiture program took place in the context of internal management shakeups within Grace plus the arrival of the Revolution. In 1969 the lands, sugar mills, and worker housing associated with Paramonga and Cartavio were taken by the government as part of its agrarian reform program. Not seized, however, were two paper plants (one brand new, the other with a new machine) and various chemical plants, all of whose operations depended on supplies of bagasse, molasses, and other by-products of sugar. The corporation was promised compensation for the expropriations, but after more than two years none was forthcoming. Grace attempted to get along with the military government by offering it consultative services or a partnership arrangement in connection with the industries, but this strategy failed. Overtly abandoning it, the company formally asked the U.S. Congress to withhold part of the U.S. sugar quota payment to Peru for the purpose of compensating expropriated American companies. In late 1971 an agreement was reached on the general outlines of a settlement but not the financial details, including the amount of compensation.

If Cerro was the largest American investor in Peru and Grace the oldest, Standard Oil of New Jersey was the most controversial. Its subsidiary, the International Petroleum Company, Ltd., operated the La Brea y Pariñas oil field and an adjoining petroleum concession in northern Peru until the Velasco government expropriated all Peruvian properties of IPC in 1968 and 1969. By far the largest petroleum enterprise in the country, prior to its seizure IPC produced 64 percent of Peruvian crude oil, and its refinery at Talara accounted for two-thirds of the national refining capacity. Almost all output was sold to the Peruvian market via "Esso" service stations. Technically IPC is incorporated in Canada because at the time of its creation (1913) affiliation with Standard's Canadian subsidiary, the Imperial Oil Company, was considered politically expedient. Imperial's control ended after World War II, and in recent years IPC has been managed by Esso Inter America, whose central offices are at Coral Gables, Florida. Although IPC is now totally excluded from Peru, it continues to own and operate properties in Colombia and Venezuela.[42]

The bitter and long-standing dispute with IPC sprang originally from questions surrounding the ownership and taxation of the La Brea y Pariñas oil field, one of the oldest in South America. In 1826 title to a tar pit at the site of the present field was granted to a Peruvian aristocrat by the revolutionary Peruvian government. In 1888 another Peruvian oligarch who had earlier acquired the title was able, through personal influence, to get this title confirmed in relation to the surrounding area. He also was able to secure an extremely light and irregular tax on the property. A few days after this attractive investment package had been put together the property was sold to British oil investors who later sold it again to the London & Pacific Petroleum Company. This organization worked the fields unprofitably for more than two decades.

In 1913 Standard Oil bought controlling interest in London & Pacific and took over management of La Brea y Pariñas. By this time doubts were beginning to be voiced in Peruvian political circles over the legitimacy of the field's ownership and tax status. In 1914 the government began to demand tax payments in accord with regular Peruvian law. For the next eight years Standard fought an unremitting battle—employing almost every conceivable form of pressure, propaganda, and external intervention—to preserve the highly favorable status it had purchased. This struggle was won in 1922 when the Leguía government acceded to a highly pro-Standard Oil settlement which was embodied in an arbitration award handed down by the International Court of Justice. In 1924 ownership of the field was acquired outright by IPC and this company proceeded to develop and exploit the field at great profit over the next quarter-century.

In 1932, following the ouster of Leguía, the Peruvian government demanded that the arbitration settlement be reopened, but to no avail. Periodically thereafter sporadic political outbursts were heard against IPC, but not until the late 1940's did they intensify into a continuing campaign. The issue that crystallized opposition was the price of gasoline. Because of postwar price control, IPC was unable to raise its revenues to meet rising costs and as a result its profits turned into losses. The company aggressively sought a price increase and finally in 1959 this was granted. The storm of protest signaled the beginning of the end for IPC in Peru, exactly one decade later.

When Belaúnde came to power in 1963, he promised to solve the IPC question permanently and quickly. But, even though negotiations with the company seemed close to fruition in the ensuing months, continuing vacillation and postponement at the presidential palace kept a settlement from being reached. Impatient, the Peruvian Congress took action on its own; in 1963 it declared the arbitration award void and in 1967 it stated that La Brea was part of "national reserves." Meanwhile in 1964-1966 the U.S. Department of State withheld development loans from Peru in an apparent effort to bring pressure for a settlement. As talk of expropriation of IPC intensified, a theory was evolved in Lima that the company owed the Peruvian government large debts for back taxes. The claimed amounts, ranging from $50 to $690 million, were based on the argument that IPC's title and tax regime were technically illegal (rather than morally illegitimate because of past pressures brought to secure them). These "debts" gradually assumed such political importance that forgiveness of them became a bargaining point for the Peruvians and eventually a rationalization for payment of no compensation to Standard Oil.

The controversy was brought to a head in 1968. The Belaúnde regime authorized the state oil company, Empresa Petrolera Fiscal (EPF), to negotiate a final settlement. Suddenly in July the talks were quickened by an unprecedented offer by IPC to give up all of its properties and rights in return for refining and distribution concessions and certain exploration rights. The basic offer was accepted and on August 13 an "Act of Talara" was signed which incorporated these terms. But twenty-eight days later Loret de Mola, the politically ambitious head of EPF, charged that IPC had deceitfully suppressed a page of an ancillary, crude oil contract it had signed with EPF which contained a statement of profits due the state enterprise. The "missing page 11," which IPC insists never existed, became the trigger for a massive withdrawal of political support for Belaúnde. The military coup of October 3 followed. The next day the new government declared all contracts with IPC void and on October 9 it took possession of the Talara complex.

Apparently the Revolutionary regime intended originally not to confiscate all of IPC's properties. For some three months the company's headquarters in Lima remained intact and it continued to operate the service stations and an oil field adjacent to La Brea y Pariñas. But additional trouble arose when IPC refused to pay EPF (now operating Talara) for delivered gasoline on grounds that its price had not been negotiated and that no compensation had been arranged for the expropriations. This led the military government to seize all remaining IPC properties on January 28, 1969. Soon EPF was converted to a new organizational form, Petróleos del Perú ("Petroperú"), which has since operated the former Standard Oil assets.

Public utilities have traditionally been a popular field for foreign investment in Latin America, but in Peru the only major examples are the Lima Light and Power Company, largely Swiss-owned, and Cía. Peruana de Teléfonos, 69 percent American-owned until 1969. The telephone company, serving the Lima metropolitan area, had been created in 1920 with controlling interest purchased by International Telephone and Telegraph in 1930. During its early years under American mangement the Lima phone system improved gradually and when the Odría government provided rate increases and a generous telephone law, modernizing investments were stepped up. But after the Ochenio was over, the company experienced a chronic inability to get rate increases; this prompted it to halt successive expansion programs, and as a consequence the rapidly growing city of Lima developed a severe telephone inadequacy in the 1960's. The terrible service made rate increases politically almost impossible and eventually led to a 1967 law providing for progressive nationalization of the company. But in 1969, before this process was complete, the military government decided that nationalization must be immediate. Following amicable negotiations with ITT an arrangement was worked out whereby its stock was exchanged for properties and rights valued at $17.3 million. As part of the settlement ITT constructed a Sheraton hotel in Lima (Sheraton Corporation of America being an ITT subsidiary) and established a telephone equipment factory jointly owned with the government.

According to Commerce Department computations, about 13 percent of American direct investments in Peru are in manufacturing. The two companies among the top twelve that are exclusively manufacturers are General Motors del Perú and Goodyear del Perú. Although GM began assembling trucks in Peru on a very small scale in 1942, the commencement of significant operations awaited industrial promotion measures by the government, namely the tax exonerations decreed in 1961 and 1963 to firms which imported CKD ("completely knocked down") automotive kits and then assembled vehicles in Peru. On the strength of this encouragement a large, modern plant was put up on the outskirts of Lima.

By the end of 1970, however, the new plant had ceased operations as a result of the military government's reorganization of the automotive assembly industry. No less than thirteen assemblers had entered the small Peruvian market, and most of the units they produced were too expensive to sell in quantity. The Velasco regime ordered a bidding process and as a result narrowed the field to five assemblers, eliminating GM as well as Ford. Among the requirements for the winning companies were 51 percent Peruvian ownership, 70 percent Peruvian-made components within three years, and government control of price.

The Goodyear plant in Peru, also located in Lima, manufactures most of the country's automobile and truck tires and tubes. The firm was founded in 1943 at the urging of a local Goodyear dealer, Eduardo Dibos Dammert, a distinguished Peruvian who twice served as mayor of Lima. Unlike GM, the corporation has prospered under the Revolution. It is the only producer in Latin America of the mammoth tires used on mining-industry vehicles and it has exported automotible tires to the United States and other countries.

In retail trade the most obvious U.S. corporation is Sears Roebuck del Perú. Sears opened its first Peruvian outlet in 1955 and by 1970 had four stores in the Lima area. It, too, survived the Revolution intact. Whether or not pertinent, the company has traditionally followed what it considered an "enlightened" policy in its foreign operations. This has included replacement of U.S. executives with nationals up to a certain level, worker profit-sharing plans, and the cultivation of local suppliers of nationally produced merchandise for sale in its stores. When Sears opened in Peru in 1955 80 percent of its merchandise was imported; by 1969 90 percent was Peruvian-made.[43]

Sears pioneered in the formation of Lima's first suburban shopping center by building its first store in San Isidro, away from central Lima. The "Americanization" of Lima retailing was then furthered by the International Basic Economy Corporation, which established a "Todos" supermarket next to Sears. Founded by Nelson Rockefeller in 1947, IBEC was established "to promote the economic development of various parts of the world" and to make a profit while so doing. After several years of poor performance it became a successful conglomerate with 119 subsidiaries in thirty-three countries. A considerable amount of Rockefeller money is in the firm, and Governor Rockefeller's son Rodman is its president. In Peru IBEC operates a chain of Todos stores and also has investments in residential middle-class housing, poultry breeding, insurance, bread-baking, trucking, and flavorings.[44]

The two remaining enterprises in the 1967 top twelve did not endure the Revolution happily. Anderson Clayton, a grower, processor, and seller of cotton and coffee, was pressured by the Velasco government into selling its cotton farms and coffee export organization to employee cooperatives. In 1971 the enterprise was trying to dispose of all its Peruvian properties, in the manner of Grace. Constructora Emkay, a subsidiary of the huge Morrison-Knudsen contract-construction empire, had essentially left Peru by 1970 after several years of work for the government and mining companies. In the 1950's it had received public works contracts for irrigation projects and had helped build Toquepala. In the 1960's it did work for Cerro de Pasco and headed a consortium of contractors that built a link in Belaúnde's Marginal Highway. However, when charges of misuse of funds, inadequate performance, and conspiracy were made against Emkay and another U.S. firm (Brown & Root, Inc.), work on the road ceased. Soon both companies were out of Peru, badly discredited and defendants in civil and criminal litigation.[45]

American Company Towns

The eight principal Peruvian towns that have been economically dominated by American corporations are listed in Table 5. Of these, three are no longer under the control of U.S. enterprise as a result of the expropriations of the Velasco government. In October 1968 Talara was expropriated, and since then the city has been operated under the auspices of Petroperú. In August 1969 the two W.R. Grace sugar plantations, Cartavio and Paramonga, were in effect expropriated, as has been noted.

Table 5. Present and Past American Company Towns in Peru.

Company town	Location	Population (1968)	Company	Description
Talara	North coast, 120 road miles from Ecuadorian frontier	35,000	IPC	Center for IPC oil drilling and refining operations until 1968 expropriation
Cartavio	Near coast, 25 road miles north of Trujillo	17,000	Grace	Grace sugar plantation until expropriated in 1969; Grace paper mill nearby
Paramonga	Near coast, 120 road miles north of Lima	22,000	Grace	Sugar plantation and paper-chemical complex; the former expropriated in 1969
La Oroya	In sierra at 12,000 feet, 117 road miles upland from Lima	25,000	Cerro	Cerro–Peru's operational HQ and a principal smelting-refining center
Cerro de Pasco	In sierra at 14,200 feet, 83 road miles north of La Oroya	25,000	Cerro	Site of underground and open-pit mining of nonferrous metals
San Juan	On coast, 250 air miles south of Lima	15,000	Marcona	Supports Marcona's iron ore mining, processing, and shipping activities
Pueblo Nuevo[a] (at Ilo)	On southern coast, 90 air miles south of Arequipa	4,000	SPCC	Location of SPCC's copper smelter and port facilities
Toquepala	At 8200 feet, 80 road miles inland from Ilo	17,000	SPCC	SPCC operational HQ and site of Toquepala open-pit copper mine

[a]Known until recently as "Ciudad Nueva."

One new major town was under construction in 1971-1972 on behalf of SPCC for servicing the Cuajone mine.*

The eight towns are of modest size, but for Peru each is a very significant community—particularly from an economic standpoint. Talara, San Juan, and Ilo are among Peru's most important seaports. Cartavio is the second largest sugar hacienda in the country (17,287 acres) and Paramonga is the center of Peru's paper and chemicals industry. La Oroya and Cerro de Pasco are key locales with respect to nonferrous metal mining and Toquepala is the site of the largest single mining operation in Peru.

Even though these eight towns are being grouped together for analysis much diversity exists among them. The towns are located in the northern, central, and southern portions of Peru (see Figure 1). They are situated at altitudes from sea level to 14,200 feet. The physical environments include arid desert (Talara), fertile valley (Cartavio and Paramonga), barren, treeless coastline (San Juan and Pueblo Nuevo at Ilo), and varying heights of harsh sierra (La Oroya, Cerro de Pasco, Toquepala). Town industries include not just sugar growing, oil drilling, and mineral mining but a great variety of processing, manufacturing, and transportation activities. Furthermore, some towns are the site of operational headquarters (Talara, La Oroya, San Juan, Toquepala) while others are not.

The physical appearance of the towns also varies greatly. The author has visited all of them one or more times and can testify from direct experience. Half of them make a quite good impression if one values such features as decent housing and an attractive physical environment. These are found in the company-controlled portions of Talara, San Juan, Pueblo Nuevo, and Toquepala. Here most construction is recent and sound, streets and plazas are quite pleasing, and public facilities such as schools, hospitals, and theaters seem reasonably good. In the remaining four towns, however, the physical milieu—with some exceptions—is inferior in quality. I found the worker sections of Cartavio and Paramonga depressingly dirty and crowded. Much of the housing is small, multiple, unpainted, and without running water. The streets alternate between mud and dust and contain debris and the leavings of freely running animals. The stench of Cartavio's public toilets (the only ones for many residents) is quite unbelievable.[46]

The sierra towns of La Oroya and Cerro de Pasco are worse. La Oroya lies in a deep canyon created by the Mantaro River; naked rock walls surround the community like a prison. Cerro de Pasco is situated in an open upland valley, but the extreme altitude creates so much cold, mist, snow, and rain that the atmosphere is forbidding. The quality of housing in both towns varies but the worst in each is atrocious—either monotonous, dirty rowhouses without running water or tumbledown adobe and

*This consists of Villa Cuajone, for staff, and Villa Botiflaca, for workers.

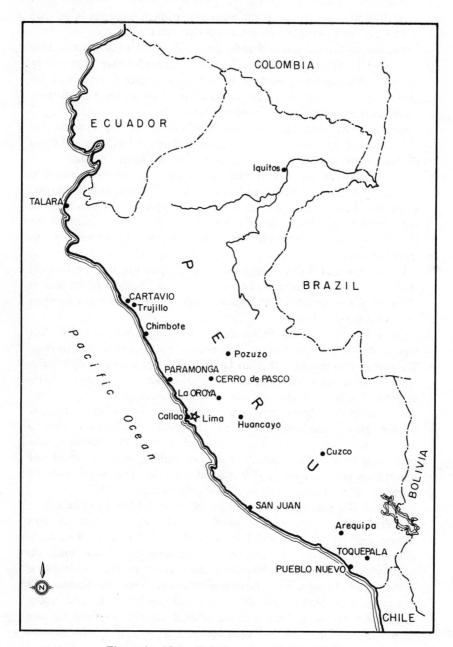

Figure 1. Major U.S. Company Towns, 1968

wooden huts. Yet, in all fairness, both towns also contain some very good living accommodations: plain but modern apartment buildings in the case of La Oroya and an entire new town near Cerro de Pasco.[47]

A glance at Table 5 shows that the physically inferior towns are or were controlled by Grace and Cerro. The moralistic reader may immediately conclude that the management of these two companies is responsible for permitting unacceptable conditions to occur. This writer himself must condemn them for not having done much more.

An informed judgment will not ignore some of the complicating variables involved, however. For instance, residents of La Oroya and Cerro de Pasco are culturally the most Indian of the eight towns. Another factor is that the Grace and Cerro communities are very old—settlements at Cartavio and Cerro de Pasco can be traced back to the sixteenth century. When the oldest U.S. company housing was built—sixty years or more ago—concepts of human decency were very different. By contrast the Marcona and SPCC towns built de novo in the 1950's were much better from the start.

The oil town of Talara is an interesting exception to the rule that old towns are physically inferior. For this reason and because of the light it sheds on the evolution of IPC, space is taken here to trace the development of that community.

Oil drilling took place at La Brea y Pariñas as early as 1868. Yet modern-day Talara is one of the most attractive and healthy cities of Peru. The explanation for this is that the La Brea oil camps were entirely rebuilt, in fact, twice. When IPC assumed control of London & Pacific in 1913 its managers found quite adequate executive staff housing but "unspeakable" conditions in the laborer camps scattered through the oil field. Smallpox, bubonic plague, and beriberi were rife. The English company had failed to provide the workers with treated water, access to fresh vegetables, and protection from rat invasions. As indices of health care, the company had one six-bed clinic for the 12,000 residents of Talara and two doctors for the entire oil field community of 25,000 persons.[48]

The new IPC managers were sufficiently concerned to take some action, including the construction of small hospitals at the other La Brea communities of Negritos and Lagunitos. But the Americans were more interested in oil than welfare, and no concerted attack was made on sanitary and nutritional problems for many years. In 1925, when extraordinary rains brought on a devastating malaria epidemic, the Standard Oil management in New York—which had had conditions in Peru under surveillance for some time—sent its medical director to Peru. He was deeply shocked by what he found and as a result several reforms were instituted. These included building a water plant, establishment of inoculation programs, and the destruction and subsequent rebuilding of all worker quarters.

In the early 1940's the New York and Canadian parent companies of IPC sent a three-man team to Talara to conduct an in-depth study of social conditions. The committee's report, completed in September 1945, was strongly critical. It concluded that "present housing standards in the Talara area must be improved to conform to current national concepts." In addition to photographic evidence a detailed description of conditions was given:

Out of 578 Peruvian employees earning between 200 and 275 soles per month, 47% are living in houses without lights and water and with community bath and toilet facilities. The majority of skilled and unskilled workmen live in wooden housing units designed for 6 and 8 families. Of this group 82% are without lights and have community bath and toilet facilities. Some married workmen, with their families, are living in bachelor units which has created a greatly over-crowded condition. The staff employees, generally speaking, are comfortably housed, although about 75% of the houses are between 15 and 25 years old.

Street lighting, where installed around workmen quarters, is the bare minimum to permit pedestrian travel. Many of the workman's quarters are painted a dull brown color, which, coupled with nature's drab, sandy surroundings, present a very unpleasing aspect.[49]

Proposed reforms were explicit. Living arrangements for all IPC workers were to be consolidated in Talara, which was to be totally rebuilt. A complete city plan calling for an investment of more than $11 million was appended. All new residences were to consist of brick, detached homes in place of the flimsy wooden multiple-dwelling units.

The report was not immediately implemented. But when control of IPC was later taken from the conservative Imperial Oil management, work could begin. The new American leadership appointed H.A. Grimes, one of the report's authors, as manager of Talara, and he was given ample authority to rebuild the town. A Peruvian architectural firm was retained to make detailed plans; it is a historical curiosity that one of the architects assigned to the job was Fernando Belaúnde Terry. Between 1952 and 1954 new homes, schools, recreation facilities, and a shopping mall were built. At the same time a systematic public health effort was launched that included programs of immunization, sanitary education, prenatal and baby care, and TB and VD control. New hospitals and clinics raised the number of hospital beds per thousand population to a level (4.4) almost double the national Peruvian figure and just short that of Lima. By 1967 Talara's mortality rate from infectious diseases was one of the lowest in the world.[50]

If the physical nature of the eight towns varies widely, the social arrangements within them have notable features in common. One such attribute is sharply defined class distinctions and physical segregation.

Roughly four classes exist in the towns as defined by status in relation to the company. These are "staff," composed of managers and important technicians (many Peruvian); *empleados*, the monthly salaried supervisors and white-collar workers; *obreros*, or day-paid laborers; and the *población flotante* (floating population), or hangers-on not employed by the firm or legitimate supporting businesses. The empleado-obrero distinction is universal in Peruvian industry, with separate labor laws for each. Each group usually has its own trade unions and wage contracts. The picture was somewhat more complicated at the Cerro towns in that a further distinction was made between empleados paid in dollars and those paid in soles; the former were of a definitely superior status. The term "población flotante" is not employed in all towns, but in all of them this lowest class exists.

Status differences are reinforced not just by pay differentials but also by living arrangements, for the quality of housing and services is directly correlative with class. Staff personnel and their families enjoy detached, spacious houses with all of the modern conveniences of the average middle-class home in the United States. Empleado and obrero housing varies greatly in quality, but within the range available in each town the more commodious and spacious is given to empleados, especially if they are dollar-paid. Most of the población flotante subsists in miserable slum huts; the companies bear (or at least accept) no responsibility for their welfare. As for recreational facilities, the staff, empleados, and obreros are typically each provided a separate social club. This generally consists of a restaurant, meeting rooms, and various other facilities. The staff clubs are, of course, the best; they usually boast a swimming pool, elaborate bar, and perhaps bowling alley and golf course. The other clubs are generally plain and unequipped, by comparison. Since many Peruvians now are staff the best facilities are no longer reserved for foreigners only, as was largely the case in decades past.

Part II   **The Challenge to National
          Independence**

Three   Control, Dependence, Attitudes

This chapter is the first of four to present evidence bearing on Hypotheses I and IA. Both hypotheses assume implicitly that the ostensibly "American" corporations in Peru—such as those described in the last chapter—are truly foreign in all crucial aspects. This basic matter has more facets than initially meet the eye and needs checking.

Both hypotheses assume that economic dependency by Peru on the corporations and/or the United States is a variable affecting power relationships between corporate managers and Peruvian decision-makers. The extent and nature of such dependency must be examined.

Hypothesis I predicts that the corporations are allied with conservative Peruvian elites. Study of this critical question begins by looking at political attitudes within the corporation managements as they pertain to Peru. If these are conservative within the Peruvian context, at least an attitudinal affinity with the elites can be assumed.

Extent of American Control

Widely different degrees of "foreignness" can exist in foreign investment. For example, a hypothetical Subsidiary A which is 100 percent owned and managed by American citizens and is under close supervision from New York is substantially different from a Subsidiary B which is 49 percent Peruvian-owned, staffed entirely by Peruvians, and largely autonomous from the U.S. parent. We are dealing here with the linkage between, so to speak, the Colgate Palmolive Building in New York and the Cerro de Pasco Building in Lima and also with the "Peruvianness" of staff and activity in the latter. Subsidiary B is not necessarily "national" in any complete sense, but its prevalence as a model would shed a different light on our subject.

Turning first to nationality of ownership, the vast majority of "U.S." companies in Peru are totally or almost totally owned by U.S. citizens. Of 337 firms on the 1965 Department of Commerce trade list, 80 percent were 95 to 100 percent American-owned, 15 percent were 50 to 94 percent, and 5 percent were 5 to 49 percent.[1] Of the companies in the 1968 top twelve only four had any Peruvian capital invested in them to my knowledge. Cía. Peruana de Teléfonos was for decades 31 percent Peruvian-owned and its Peruvian stockholders were represented on the board of directors. That enterprise became entirely Peruvian in 1969. Sears Roebuck, because of its profit-sharing plan, was 15 percent owned by its local employees by 1969.* Grace had several partnerships with local capital, especially before it began its Peruvian divestment program; in mining and banking enterprises the company had both majority and minority status. Cerro was in partnership with Peruvian capital in no less than eight mining, supplier, and fabricating firms in the late 1960's; in two of these it had a majority position, in five, a minority position (29 to 49 percent), and in one, a half interest. On at least two occasions Cerro attempted to interest Peruvian investors in financing 60 percent of the equity of new ventures but without success. These were Cía. Minera Raura S.A., formed in 1960 with 40 percent national capital, and the Cobriza copper mine, opened in 1968 with none.[2]

As for the nationality of personnel rather than capital, the great majority of persons working for U.S. companies in Peru are, not surprisingly, Peruvians. It is costly to bring Americans to Peru and companies have a direct economic incentive to minimize their number. The upper part of Table 6 shows that no company among the 1968 top twelve employed more than 5 percent of foreigners of all nationalities, including American. In most instances the proportion of foreigners was 1 to 2 percent, with the aggregative percentage 1.76. Thus the enterprises are usually in no danger of violating the Peruvian law which limits the proportion of foreigners to 20 percent (although it has been said that in its early years SPCC paid more than 20 percent of its payroll to foreigners, also a violation of Peruvian law).[3] The figures for these companies are not too different from previous calculations for U.S. investment in Latin America as a whole; a 1956 study showed 2.1 percent American employees and a 1957 survey indicated 1.6 percent.[4]

What is of greater interest, however, is the relative frequency of foreigners versus nationals in managerial positions. Each of the twelve firms was asked to indicate the number of positions on the level of "plant superintendent or department head or similar post and above" and how many of these were filled by Americans, other foreigners, and Peruvians at that time (mid-1968). The results are given in the lower half of Table 6. Perhaps the outstanding feature of the figures is that much variation in the degree of "Peruvianization" of management exists. Whereas Sears had 92 percent Peruvians at the upper echelons, Constructora Emkay had none. Five companies were more than half Peruvianized in this sense and seven less than half. The mangements of all firms in the aggregate consisted of about 30 percent Americans, 14 percent other foreigners, and 56 percent Peruvians.

On its face this finding may seem quite impressive in terms of Peruvian

*As stated above, under the comunidad concept of the Velasco government the workers gradually accrue equity and elect at least one director in all enterprises.

control of American enterprise in Peru. This is especially true if comparison is made with a study conducted in 1958 of 39 U.S. companies in Brazil and Mexico. There it was found that of 185 persons in executive positions, 122 were Americans, 16 other foreigners, and 47 nationals.[5] Also the finding is put in a favorable light if present practice is compared with that in past years. Several of the companies produced figures showing how they had had many more foreign executives in the past: when Sears

Table 6. Nationality of Personnel in Twelve Largest U.S. Companies, 1968.

| | Foreign only, all levels | | | |
| | Number | | | Percentage |
Company	U.S.	Other	Total	Foreign
Sears	3	0	3	0.3
Teléfonos	3	7	10	.6
GM	6	0	6	.8
IPC	53	0	53	1.1
Anderson	3	6	9	1.3
Goodyear	9	0	9	1.3
IBEC	5	6	11	1.4
Cerro	50	190	240	1.4
Grace	42	117	159	1.6
Marcona	53	32	85	3.1
SPCC	120	21	141	3.7
Emkay	76	2	78	5.0
Totals	423	381	804	1.76

| | Upper management only | | | | | |
| | Number | | | Percentage | | |
	U.S.	Other foreign	Peruvian	U.S.	Other foreign	Peruvian
Sears	3	0	34	8	0	92
Goodyear	6	0	23	21	0	79
IBEC	5	6	37	10	13	77
IPC	15	0	39	28	0	72
GM	6	0	11	35	0	65
Teléfonos	3	4	6	23	31	46
Anderson	2	4	4	20	40	40
Marcona	8	1	6	53	7	40
Cerro	13	20	12	29	44	27
Grace	12	9	7	43	32	25
SPCC	14	2	1	82	12	6
Emkay	9	0	0	100	0	0
Totals	96	46	180	29.8	14.3	55.9
Grand total		322			100.0	

opened in Peru in 1954, for example, 21 Americans were brought in; by 1969 the number had shrunk to 2. Over the course of the 1960's SPCC's total foreign staff was approximately halved, and between 1966 and 1968 the number of Americans in Anderson Clayton dropped from 7 to 2.

If, however, the nature of the positions occupied by foreigners is noted, a much different picture emerges. Business organizations are, of course, hierarchical in nature and what really matters is who occupies the very highest jobs. Of the twelve companies all but two had Americans as president or general manager of the Peruvian subsidiary in mid-1968. The exceptions were Cerro de Pasco, whose president was Alberto Benavides Q., a Peruvian, and the telephone company, headed at that time by a Canadian. As of mid-1971 all but three of the eight enterprises still active and American-owned were headed by Americans. Benavides had resigned as president of Cerro and had been replaced by an American; but a Peruvian had been installed as managing director of Marcona Mining, namely, Dr. Enrique R. East Alvarez Calderón. Meanwhile IBEC had promoted a Peruvian to the top slot and Anderson Clayton had replaced an American with an Argentine. Thus over the three-year period the proportion of American top managers had dropped slightly but was still high.

It should additionally be pointed out that when Peruvians enter top management they are usually placed in areas of secondary importance and where a national is of particular value, such as legal counsel and assistant general manager. Frequently they head the departments of personnel, public relations, industrial relations, sales, and medicine. Rarely does a Peruvian have high responsibility in operations or finance.[6]

If American businesses in Peru are generally American-owned and run, it perhaps becomes academic to consider the degree of parent-company supervision. Yet the issue may have a residual importance if American businessmen abroad experience the supposed tendency of diplomats to become advocates of the country in which they are located (which some observers argue is true).

Secondary literature on this point offers varying evidence. A study of U.S. companies in Brazil found that two-thirds of the Brazilian managements felt they were "less closely supervised than were their management counterparts in branches of their parent firm within the United States." Another survey of American companies in Brazil and Mexico concluded that home offices determined organizational structure in detail, maintained overall financial control, particularly with regard to capital expenditures, approved products sold and often monitored quality, controlled prices at times, designed new plants, and determined the selection, promotion, and salaries of executives at high levels. Vernon hypothesizes a cycle in the evolution of central financial control in the multinational corporations whereby the stages are decentralization, centralization, and decentralization again.[7]

Although systematic data were not obtained from all twelve companies on this matter, information obtained from some presents a picture of quite close supervision. In the Grace organization, for example, New York reviews an operating budget prepared in Lima, passes on all capital expenditures to occur in Peru, approves new products prior to marketing, and makes all top appointments.[8] Much the same is true for Cerro; all capital expenditures above $5,000 must be approved by the parent's Board of Directors as well as all salary increases for employees receiving more than $15,000 compensation. Appointments down to and including department head are reviewed in New York.[9]

In the realm of governmental relations Peruvian subsidiaries appear to have slightly more autonomy. In dealing with the bureaucracy on largely routine matters, the general managers operate quite freely within policy limits laid down at headquarters. Mild initiatives can even be taken provided reports are sent home. But when a political "flap" occurs the U.S. headquarters does not hesitate to intervene. During IPC's controversial last few years, for example, its general manager conducted continuing negotiations himself but at crucial points he received telephoned instructions from Coral Gables daily or even hourly. As another illustration, when the Agrarian Reform Law was announced in 1969 and it became clear that Paramonga and Cartavio would be affected, Grace's vice-president for Latin America was immediately dispatched to Lima. Although some high jobs in Grace's Peruvian operations are occupied by Peruvians, Americans were always on hand for the key negotiations with government.

Thus American control of U.S. capital in Peru is very great. Most enterprises are almost totally American-owned; although many Peruvians are at the upper-management level, the top positions are usually held by Americans; and parental supervision is very close on important business matters and reasonably close, at least after the fact, on political questions. The model followed corresponds more with Subsidiary A than Subsidiary B.

Extent of Economic Dependence

In a major policy pronouncement of the Revolutionary government, reference is made to "dependence of the Peruvian economy upon foreign decision-making centers."[10] Is this true? If so, to what extent—especially when those centers are American?

In a *wholly aggregate sense* American direct investments do not appear overridingly important to the Peruvian economy. One economist has estimated that for the year 1955 only 5.4 percent of Peru's net national product originated in U.S. firms. The proportion calculated for Chile, by comparison, was 8.7 percent; for Cuba it was 11.8 percent; and for Venezuela, 16.4 percent.[11] That Peru is somewhat below the Latin American norm in this regard is suggested by Galo Plaza's statement in

1969 that U.S. firms account for about a tenth of Latin America's gross product.[12]

As for employment, a rough guess would be that about 2 percent of the economically active population was employed by American companies in the late 1960's, and about 4 percent of salary and wage employees. With respect to investment the proportions are a little higher. A Peruvian economist has estimated that in 1955 7.15 percent of private investment in Peru (accumulated value, apparently) was American.[13] A planning document published by the Peruvian government in 1962 says that during the 1950-1960 decade 18.5 percent of all private investment financing was foreign; of this, 14.4 percent was direct investment.[14] The planners of the Velasco regime maintain that over two decades (apparently 1950-1970) the foreign flow of capital "represented as an average only 8% of the Gross Total Investment."[15] These figures for all foreign capital include, of course, other than American investments. In 1966, according to one estimate, accumulated private foreign investments in Peru were 67.5 percent American;[16] if one takes roughly two-thirds of the above 14.4 and 8 percent figures, the proportions are in the neighborhood of 10 and 5 percent, respectively.

The payment of government tax revenues by American corporations can be a particularly sensitive source of economic dependence. Public decision-makers are affected very close to home, so to speak. As for the aggregate tax contribution of U.S. companies, the U.S. Department of Commerce estimates that in 1955 all American firms paid a total of $23 million in income and other taxes to Peru. This amounted to 10.8 percent of total Peruvian government revenues for that year.[17] A similar figure results from my own calculations of the total tax contribution of the top twelve American corporations, which undoubtedly account for the bulk of taxes paid by all U.S. business. As indicated in Table 7, in 1966 the top twelve paid a total of 10.1 percent of government revenues. A one-tenth contribution is relatively small compared to many other countries; foreign

Table 7. Tax Payments of Twelve Largest U.S. Companies, 1966.

Company	Payment amounts ($ millions)	Government revenues (percent)
IPC	26.1	2.9
SPCC	25.1	2.8
Cerro	12.8	1.4
Marcona	12.5	1.4
Other[a]	14.2	1.6
Totals	90.7	10.1

Sources: The companies and Banco Central de Reserva del Perú.
[a]Estimated and individually much less.

extractive firms provide 60-70 percent of Venezuela's revenue and 85 percent of Saudi Arabia's. For Latin America as a whole, U.S. affiliates account for about 15 percent of revenues.[18]

But, as Table 7 shows, four corporations carried a large part of the burden. IPC, SPCC, Cerro, and Marcona paid about 85 percent of the top twelve's contribution and 8.5 percent of Peruvian revenues in 1966. The taxes paid by IPC and SPCC together were more than $50 million, a sum greater than the average annual U.S. Government assistance of all forms to Peru from 1963 to 1968. In short, tax dependency must be understood in terms of individual corporations as well as the aggregate of U.S. business.

The large American corporations' tax role can be seen in the context of contributions by other enterprises with the aid of Table 8. Here the top ten entities are ranked in order of taxable income (not total taxes paid, the basis of Table 7) for the years 1966-1970. SPCC, IPC, Cerro, and Marcona are obviously prominent; in fact Southern Peru Copper Corporation is continuously in first place. Other U.S. firms present in the rankings are the telephone company, Sociedad Paramonga (Grace), IBM del Perú, the Northern Peru Mining Company (a subsidiary of American Smelting & Refining Company), and Pesquera Meilan, a fishmeal producer. Of the fifty entries in the table, twenty-six represent American business. The other enterprises in the rankings are Peruvian, with the exception of Cía. Petrolera Lobitos (British) and Marubeni Iida (a Japanese trading company).

The period covered by Table 8 encompasses the Revolution and is of interest from the standpoint of contrasts over time. It should be noted that the Revolution did not disturb SPCC's foremost position; the fundamental importance of this point will become increasingly clear in the pages below. The 1968 upheaval did, of course, cause IPC to be replaced by Petróleos del Perú, and it is of interest to note that by 1970 Petroperú occupied the same place formerly held by Standard Oil. The Revolution's nationalization of the sugar haciendas resulted in the conversion of these enterprises to workers' cooperatives. This step coincided with a fall in Tuman's tax ranking but a rise in Pucala's standing and the appearance of Casa Grande for the first time. As far as overall U.S. occupancy of the top ten places is concerned, by 1970 the former solid block of three top American positions was no more. Yet the total number of U.S. companies in the top ten remained about the same.

American corporations abroad have the reputation in some circles of being careful to pay all taxes owed in order to avoid public charges of cheating host governments.[19] U.S. managers in Peru claim they are more careful on this score than other local businessmen, not only for business taxes but for personal taxes as well. In this connection it is of interest to note that top U.S. corporate managers often place high in published lists of individual taxable income. A list for the Lima area for 1967 contained

Table 8. Top Ten Taxpaying Enterprises in Peru, 1966–1970 (In Terms of Taxable Income).

Rank	1966	1967	1968	1969	1970
1.	*SPCC*	*SPCC*	*SPCC*	*SPCC*	*SPCC*
2.	*IPC*	*IPC*	*Cerro*	*Cerro*	Petróleos del Perú
3.	*Cerro*	*Cerro*	*Marcona*	Petróleos del Perú	*Cerro*
4.	Cía. Petrolera Lobitos	Cía. Petrolera Lobitos	Neg. Tuman	*Marcona*	Cooperativa Casa Grande
5.	Cevercería Backus & Johnston	Cía Nacional de Cerveza	*Cía. Peruana de Teléfonos*	Neg. Tuman	*Marcona*
6.	*Marcona*	Banco de Crédito	Cervecería Backus & Johnston	Cía. Petrolera Lobitos	Pesquera Meilan
7.	Neg. Tuman	Marubeni Iida	Soc. Agrícola Pucala	*Northern Peru Mining Co.*	Cooperativa Tuman
8.	Cía. Nacional de Cerveza	Cía. Explotadora Milotingo	*IBM del Perú*	*IBM del Perú*	Cervecería Backus & Johnston
9.	*Soc. Paramonga*	*Cía. Peruana de Teléfonos*	*Northern Peru Mining Co.*	*Cía. Peruana de Teléfonos*	Cooperativa Pucala
10.	Banco de Crédito	Soc. Agrícola Pucala	Corp. Minera Castrovirreyna	Cervecería Backus & Johnston	*IBM del Perú*

Note: Names in italics are those of U.S. interests.

Sources: El Peruano, May 5, 1967; *Peruvian Times,* May 17, 1968, June 13, 1969, June 26, 1970, July 30, 1971. It should be kept in mind that many large companies are taxed as several affiliates and hence do not appear here.

nine identifiable U.S. managers among the top 100 taxpayers. The highest was Fernando J. Espinosa, general manager of IPC, who ranked 19th. The chief executives of SPCC, Cerro, Sears, Grace, and Marcona were respectively numbers 29, 30, 40, 44, and 71. Many well-known Peruvian "oligarchs" were far down the list.[20]

Another source, and a classic one, of economic dependence is foreign trade. Here the crucial issues include the degree to which foreign production and markets are depended upon generally and the extent to which foreign trade is diversified. In the latter matter a particularly important question is whether exports are concentrated in a few raw material commodities whose prices are subject to external fluctuation or manipulation. From the standpoint of dependence on direct investors an issue is the concentration of export earnings emanating from the production of a few foreign-owned companies.

Foreign trade is important to Peru. In 1968 the value of imports was 12.9 percent of GNP and of exports 17.6 percent. The United States is Peru's foremost trading partner, providing 30.9 percent of imports in 1969 and absorbing 34.5 percent of exports. The bulk of Peru's exports is primary commodities, principally minerals, fishmeal, sugar, cotton, and coffee. Yet the commodities are diverse and only two comprise more than a fourth of total export values—copper and fish products (30.0 and 25.5 percent, respectively, in 1969). Thus Peru is not in the position of a Venezuela with enormous dependence on oil or a Chile with heavy reliance on copper. Moreover exports of manufactured goods from Peru have increased in recent years, for example, canned fish, paper goods, cement, zinc ferrite, automobile tires, cotton textiles, and covered cable.[21]

Aggregatively, U.S. firms produce somewhat over half of Peru's top ten exported commodities by value, as is shown in Table 9. In 1968 the top twelve corporations produced or were crucial in the production of 53.8 percent of the value of the top ten exports. Expropriation actions of the Velasco government eliminated Grace's sugar and IPC's oil from this list, but the loss in aggregate terms was more than made up by the growing importance of U.S. capital in the fishmeal industry. Whereas in 1968 only about 13 percent of fishmeal output was from American firms, by 1970 it was in the neighborhood of 28 percent.*[22] Thus the aggregate proportions shown in the table were probably somewhat higher by 1971. In a comparison with Latin America as a whole, this 50-60 percent range is quite high; a regional estimate for 1966 is that about 35 percent of total Latin exports originated in American firms.[23]

As in the case of tax dependency, the situation is particularly acute when one examines the big mining companies individually. Table 9 indicates that about 19 percent of export values was generated by the

---

*In May 1973 this industry was expropriated also, at which time American capital comprised about one-third of total investments.

Table 9. Top Ten Peruvian Exports and Involvement of U.S. Business, 1968.

Top ten export commodities of Peru	Total value ($millions)	U.S. firms involved in production	Portion of commodity accounted for	
			Percent[a]	Value ($millions)
1. Fish products	234.3	Grace	1.7	3.9
		Other	11.0	25.8
2. Copper	233.9	SPCC	67.0	156.7
		Cerro	31.3	73.2
3. Silver	68.4	Cerro	60.9	41.7
4. Iron ore	63.3	Marcona	97.3	61.6
5. Sugar	62.3	Grace	20.0	12.5
6. Cotton	55.7	Anderson	83.3	46.4
7. Coffee	35.7	Anderson	10.0	3.6
8. Zinc	33.1	Cerro	58.6	19.4
9. Lead	29.4	Cerro	67.4	19.8
10. Petroleum products	10.8	IPC	56.5	6.1
		Other	19.4	2.1
Total:	826.9			Total: 472.8

U.S. firms	Percent[a] of all top ten exports accounted for
SPCC	19.0
Cerro	18.6
Marcona	7.4
Anderson	6.0
Totals: four firms above	51.0
Top twelve firms	53.8
All U.S. firms	57.2

Sources: Export figures: Banco Central Reserva del Perú, as reported in the *Peruvian Times*, September 19, 1969. Company percentages of fish and mineral commodities are derived from total production shares on a tonnage basis, as reported in the *Peruvian Times*, March 28 and September 5, 1969. Sugar and coffee percentages are estimates furnished by the companies. The cotton percentage is derived from the fact that Anderson Clayton owned 5 out of 6 cotton compressing machines in Peru. Petroleum percentages are based on shares of crude production in 1968, derived from *Ingeniero Andino*, May–June 1969
[a] Of value.

output of both SPCC and Cerro; thus together they accounted for more than a third of export earnings. Just four companies were associated with slightly more than half.

As the primary source of foreign exchange, these earnings are essential to Peru in order to buy imports and meet innumerable other external financial obligations.*

One such obligation is repayment of Peru's quite massive external public debt, which is, in and of itself, a potential source of economic dependency. During the Belaúnde administration this debt was tripled, largely owing to ambitious public works projects unfunded by taxes or local savings. By 1969 the debt amounted to $1112 million (including unspent credits), of which 18.5 percent was owed to international organizations, 17.5 percent to U.S. private banks, 16.7 percent to the Italian government, and 10.2 percent each to the American and West German governments. The remaining 26.9 percent consisted of obligations to ten other governments plus a small amount to Canadian banks. The Velasco regime, which had not contracted the debt, was naturally unhappy with being obligated to spend what amounted to $150 to $223 million annually for principal and interest in 1970-1975. Several times it attempted to get the debt rescheduled to a longer period. This was achieved in 1969, but on other occasions it was told "no" by international agencies, New York banks, and the so-called "Paris Club" of European governments.[24]

A final potential mechanism of dependency that must be examined is foreign monopoly or dominance in crucial industries. As was observed in the last chapter, U.S. capital is involved in many Peruvian agricultural and industrial sectors; in this context the question arises as to its relative position in these.

In certain industries American participation is significant, but no one U.S. firm occupies more than a minority share of the market. This is the case in fishmeal, automobile assembly, chemicals, textiles, foodstuffs, and retailing. In sugar Grace produced 21 percent of the output from Cartavio and Paramonga prior to expropriation.[25]

In at least three industries, however, American monopolies or oligopolies existed in 1971. One of these was metal mining; as explained above, SPCC produces two-thirds of Peru's copper, Marcona mines all iron ore, and Cerro is responsible for well over half of the output of lead, zinc, silver, and many other metals. Cerro's importance is extended by the fact that it refines the ores of many independent mining companies. This corporation's importance even reaches to railroading; one of the main roads is owned by Cerro and another receives two-thirds of its revenues by shipping Cerro ores to Callao.

The other two U.S.-dominated sectors are in manufacturing. Goodyear

*I do not consider here a vital related point, namely the extent to which the corporations that earn foreign exchange for Peru also spend it. I will leave it to the economists to calculate such net effects.

makes two-thirds of Peru's vehicle tires and tubes under its own label and an additional 14 percent under the Dunlop label. Thus it is the source of 80 percent of total production. Grace, at its paper mills at Paramonga and Santiago de Cao (near Cartavio), produces almost all of Peru's paper and cardboard with the exception of newsprint. Three other small mills operate, but they produce 10,000 to 15,000 tons per day compared to Grace's capacity of more than 200,000 tons. Grace's paper is made largely from bagasse, the fibrous residue left from ground sugarcane, employing a technology developed by Grace in Peru in the 1940's.[26]

In three other industries American and other foreign capital was dominant prior to the 1968 revolution, but in each case the situation was radically changed by actions of the Velasco regime. As already mentioned, prior to its expropriation IPC had controlled about two-thirds of Peru's petroleum industry. That situation was of course wiped out by the Revolution. The government's purchase of ITT's stock in Cía. Peruana de Teléfonos similarly ended U.S. domination of Peruvian telecommunications. A third field invaded by the Revolution was commercial banking. Prior to Velasco this critical industry was in the hands of either foreigners or traditionalist oligarchs. The most important bank by far was Banco de Crédito, controlled by Italian interests. Three other banks were at a second level of importance: one owned by the Prado family (Banco Popular), another majority-owned by the Chase Manhattan Bank (Banco Continental), and a third with minority American participation (Banco Internacional). Several branches of foreign banks also operated, including the First National City Bank of New York.[27]

In its closing days, the Belaúnde administration took steps to require that the nationality of ownership and boards of directors of all national banks be two-thirds Peruvian. The Velasco regime upped this to three-fourths ownership and four-fifths directorships. In 1970 it went one step further and had a government bank, Banco de la Nación, purchase majority ownership in the three second-level institutions. This ended the financial power of more than one upper-class Peruvian family and also reduced the extent of American participation in banking. Banco de Crédito met significant competition for the first time; in 1971 the government began purchasing shares in that institution as well. In short, foreign domination of Peruvian finance had been radically challenged if not ended.

To summarize findings on Peru's economic dependence, it can first be noted that no generalized, overwhelming dependency exists. Not more than a tenth, and often a much lesser proportion, of output, jobs, investment, and taxes are traceable to American investments. Moreover, exports are diverse and most domestic industries are not U.S.-dominated. And the Velasco government had reduced if not ended foreign domination in several sectors.

The other side of the picture is that three areas of vulnerability appear.

First, the large external public debt creates a dependency on foreign financiers. Conceivably they could demand policy concessions from the Peruvians in return for debt rescheduling or new credits. Second, two important domestic industries are completely dominated by U.S. corporations, namely, heavy rubber and paper. Although this output could always be imported, the costs would be heavy in foreign exchange. Finally, and most importantly, the three gran minería occupy a profoundly important place in the Peruvian economy. SPCC, Cerro, and Marcona dominate one of the country's most important industries, pay very substantial taxes, and provide the basis for almost half of foreign exchange earnings. Obviously it is greatly to Peru's economic interests that these enterprises are kept producing, profitable, and growing. Economic dependence may not be great in a generalized way, but *in relation to a handful of individual U.S. corporations* it is significantly present.

Political Attitudes in U.S. Business

The remainder of this chapter considers attitudes within U.S. business managements as they pertain to Peruvian politics. This topic is germane for at least two reasons: It leads us to any tendencies that might exist on the part of businessmen to desire one kind of public policy over another, and it suggests any tendencies that may exist to ally with one group or another in Peruvian politics.

Three means are used in the attempt to appraise such attitudes. None is fully satisfactory from the methodological standpoint. Yet for the modest level of generalization that is attempted each seems far superior to intuitive conjecture, the usual procedure in this realm. Moreover the findings of the three methods are consistent and reinforce each other.

The first approach is to compare rates of foreign investment flow with the character of the regime in power. This method permits some quantification in measurement. Its disadvantage is that many factors other than the nature of the current regime in a host country influence foreign investment decisions; these include the presence of raw materials, world prices of commodities, the size of internal markets, tax laws in the home country, and such intangibles as the fashionableness of multinational expansion among businessmen. Although one cannot assume these variables as constant, sharp contrasts in flows over time may give us political insights.[28]

The relevant data are presented in Table 10. U.S. Department of Commerce book values for U.S. private, direct investments in Peru are converted to 1958 dollars to avoid the distortions of inflation. When these accumulated, net values are examined for trends, the periods 1945-1950, 1958-1963, and 1969-1971 stand out as marked by decline, stagnation, or uneven movement. Definite upward trends are visible in the periods

1951-1958 (a 10.1 percent annual rate) and 1964-1968 (a 6.6 percent rate).

To a substantial degree these trend periods coincide with Peruvian regimes in power following World War II, as seen in the far-right column of the table. (In this regard it should be kept in mind that a time lag exists between planning and making investments.) Leaving aside the uneven movement of 1959-1963, the periods of decline correspond roughly with the Bustamante and Velasco administrations. The periods of steady expansion coincide with the Odría and Belaúnde governments. The net rates of change during each tenure underscore regime differences: declines

Table 10. U.S. Private Direct Investments in Peru and Peruvian Regimes.

Year	Current dollars	1958 dollars	Nature of fluctuation (1958 dollars)	Regime in power
1945	127	213		Bustamante
1946	131	196		(3.1% rate
1947	149	200	Decline and	of decline)
1948	149	187	stagnation	
1949	148	187		
1950	145	181		
1951	203	237		Odría
1952	242	277		(11.9% rate
1953	268	303		of increase)
1954	283	316	Steady, rapid	
1955	305	336	expansion (10.1%	
1956	343	365	rate)	
1957	400	410		
1958	429	429		Prado
1959	427	420		(0.7% rate
1960	446	432	Uneven	of increase)
1961	437	418	movement	
1962	451	426		
1963	448	418		Military
1964	464	426		Belaúnde
1965	515	465	Moderate	(6.6% rate of
1966	548	481	expansion	increase)
1967	660	561	(6.6% rate)	
1968	692	566		
1969	721	563	Decline	Velasco
1970	688	509	(4.6% rate)	(4.6% rate of
1971	688[a]	486[a]		decline)

Sources: U.S. Department of Commerce, *Survey of Current Business,* various issues, 1955–1971, and *U.S. Investments in the Latin American Economy* (1957), p. 112. Estimates for 1945, 1947, and 1948 were calculated from the net effect of capital outflows and reinvested earnings in those years. Book values in 1958 dollars calculated by means of the implicit price deflator for the U.S. GNP.

[a]Preliminary.

of 3.1 and 4.6 percent, respectively, under Bustamante and Velasco, and growth of 11.9 and 6.6 percent under Odría and Belaúnde, in that order.

The *form* of rule seems to have no relationship to investor behavior. Of the two regimes named which came to power via coup d'etat, one shows the most rapid expansion (Odría) and the other the sharpest decline (Velasco). These were also the most authoritarian long-term regimes of the group. As for *policy* differences, a critical fact is that the heaviest rates of new investment occurred during the most conservative regime (Odría's) while the heaviest rates of disinvestment took place under the most radical (Velasco's). Businessmen found the Ochenio comparatively safe and the Revolution comparatively unsafe, a not surprising conclusion. Quite consistent with this is the decline under Bustamante, an administration identified with economic controls and uncertainty.

One might have expected more growth under the moderately conservative Prado. Even more unexpected, perhaps, is the very substantial growth rate under Belaúnde, who came to power bearing the image of an activist reformer and liberal; although his expansion rate is about half of Odría's, it is the otherwise highest rate of change of any government in the table. This suggests that, although investors are generally happier under conservative, noninterventionist, and pro-status quo regimes, they are not dogmatic on this point; attempts at socioeconomic reform do not in themselves halt the flow of dollars.

The second method used to assess U.S. business attitudes was opinion polling. This approach is direct but involves difficult problems of sampling and the eliciting of sincere answers. Of the 322 upper-management personnel in the top twelve U.S. companies in Peru at mid-1968 (see Table 6), it was possible to request and secure the full cooperation of only 9—a sample of somewhat under 3 percent—in the filling out of a structured, multiple-choice, survey questionnaire. (Great resistance to this endeavor was encountered, probably because of both the time involved and the sensitive nature of the questions.) The 9 respondents were not randomly selected but represented a cross section of executives: 4 general managers or the equivalent and 5 department heads; 6 located in Lima and 3 elsewhere; 5 Americans, 3 Peruvians, and 1 European; and associations with GM, Goodyear, Grace, IBEC, IPC, Marcona, and Sears.

One question in the survey concerned the three civilian presidential administrations in power between 1948 and 1968, those of Odría, Prado, and Belaúnde. The executives were asked to rank these regimes (1st, 2nd, 3rd) "in terms of (a) their being best for Peru and (b) their being best for U.S. business in Peru." Another question used identical language in asking the respondents to rank the four most important political parties operative in 1968, AP (Belaúnde's party), APRA, DC (Christian Democrats), and UNO (Odría's party). It was fortunate for the survey that these choices represented a fairly wide political spectrum, with Odría and UNO on the far right, Prado and APRA right-of-center, Belaúnde and AP left-of-center, and DC on the far left.

The results are displayed in Table 11. Both the frequency distribution of choices and a weighted total score are given, the latter computed in the regime analysis by multiplying first choices by four, second by two, and third by one. In the party analysis first choices were multiplied by four, second choices by three, and so on.

It should first be noted that the "best for Peru" answers differ substantially from the "best for U.S. business" answers. In the regime question a preference is shown for Belaúnde with regard to Peru and for

Table 11. Political Attitudes of Nine U.S. Business Managers, Mid-1968.

I. Rankings of Regimes

	A. "Best for Peru"					B. "Best for U.S. Business in Peru"			
	Frequency distribution			Weighted[a] score		Frequency distribution			Weighted[a] score
Regime	1st	2nd	3rd		Regime	1st	2nd	3rd	
Belaúnde	5	3	2	23	Prado	3	6	0	21
Prado	4	3	1	19	Odría	4	2	3	19
Odría	0	3	6	12	Belaúnde	2	1	6	14

II. Rankings of Political Parties

A. "Best for Peru"

	Frequency distribution				Weighted[a] score	Party grouping	Frequency distribution				Weighted[a] score
Party	1st	2nd	3rd	4th			1st	2nd	3rd	4th	
AP	3	4	2	0	28	AP–DC					
APRA	4	2	2	1	27	(left)	12		6		49
DC	2	3	0	4	21	APRA–UNO					
UNO	0	0	5	4	14	(right)	6		12		41

B. "Best for U.S. Business in Peru"

	Frequency distribution				Weighted[a] score	Party grouping	Frequency distribution				Weighted[a] score
Party	1st	2nd	3rd	4th			1st	2nd	3rd	4th	
APRA	4	2	2	1	27	APRA–UNO					
UNO	2	3	2	2	23	(right)	11		7		50
AP	0	4	5	0	22	AP–DC					
DC	3	0	0	6	18	(left)	7		11		40

[a]Weights are inverse of choice number. Hence the higher the weighted score, the higher the aggregative ranking.

Prado with regard to U.S. business in Peru. Odría, the symbol of conservatism, ranked comparatively high as a servant of investors but low as a servant of Peru's overall interests. A parallel bifurcation is shown in the party results. AP ranks high for Peru but comparatively low in connection with U.S. business interests. UNO is not perceived as best for Peruvian interests but has a high standing in regard to business needs. This phenomenon is even more striking with regard to parties when the distribution matrixes are collapsed to 2x2 tables that group the first-second and third-fourth choices and the left-leaning and right-leaning party groupings. The AP-DC alliance was preferred for Peru, the APRA-UNO coalition for U.S. business in Peru.

One cannot be sure what this means. One explanation may be that the respondents perceived a difference between the interests of their companies and those of Peru, or at least they wanted me to believe this. If the distinction was genuine, a less than blindly selfish or probusiness orientation is suggested; at least they were aware of conflicting nonbusiness interests. Another explanation may be that the "best for Peru" answers tapped the respondents' private opinions as over against views they hold as corporate executives. If so, they were not so much personally conservative as organizationally so. Yet the differences are not extreme.

More important, perhaps, is the fact that a generally conservative political orientation is indicated. The moderately conservative Prado and moderately conservative (by 1968) APRA did very well in all rankings. Conversely, the Christian Democrats did comparatively poorly. Yet the fact that in the "best for Peru" answers Belaúnde and his party scored highest and Odría and his party scored lowest suggests that the conservatism is not extreme.

One added insight suggested by the data is a wide divergence of viewpoints among the executives. In the "best for U.S. business in Peru" answers the most ideologically divergent regimes and parties *all* received *both* first and last choices. Obvious differences of opinion were also evident from ancillary comments made by respondents during interviewing. Whereas some executives looked back fondly to the days of Odría or even Leguía as the zenith of Peruvian history and perceived recent social change as the mere consequence of communist agitation, others declared emphatically that Peru must revise its socioeconomic order drastically in the direction of mass welfare in order to avoid chaos.

The respondents were also questioned in mid-1968 in a less structured way with regard to their views of "agrarian reform" and "economic planning" in Peru. The responses could not be tabulated, but a common pattern did emerge. It was felt that the ideas in abstraction were acceptable, while concrete performance was criticized. This may have been an effort to appear "liberal" to the interviewer or it may have reflected a businessman's distrust with the irrationalities of the political process. For example, agrarian reform would be described as "the only solution" but that "breaking up efficient estates will greatly lessen productivity." Economic planning was accepted as necessary to economic development, but, "planning is fine in theory; however there are no coordinated objectives." Time and time again the "aims" of reform would be saluted, but the "means" denigrated. "Radical changes" are essential, but they "must not be too fast." The government's "intentions" are fine, but it constantly "makes errors" and is "incompetent" and "doesn't understand economics."

The third method used to assess political attitudes was to rely on reports from informants developed in the Lima and New York business communities. Most of my information concerning opinion in the 1968-1971 period was generated in this unsystematic but sometimes enlightening way.

Tradition has it that foreign investors in Latin America are favorably disposed to military governments. When the military regime of Bolivia expropriated the U.S.-owned Gulf Oil Company in 1969, *New York Times* correspondent H.J. Maidenberg wrote, "The initial reaction of the petroleum industry to Bolivia's takeover of the Gulf Oil Company's operation in that country was to shatter an article of faith that has long sustained foreign businessmen in Latin America. The belief was that 'You can always do better with a military government than a civilian one because Latin American countries can only function under a strong hand.' "[29]

Information I was able to obtain during the first few months of Peru's Revolution supported this long-standing image. A letter from an informant high in U.S. business circles in Lima dated November 26, 1968 (seven weeks after the Velasco coup), said in part: "The American businessmen have varied opinions but for the most part they were all in agreement with the action taken (aside from the fact that the democratic process took a punch in the nose). Business is as usual and so nobody is very upset about anything." A letter from another informant received later but referring to the period immediately after the coup contained this paragraph: "The reaction of the business community in general was that perhaps the revolution would be a good thing. 'Yo creo que nos conviene'* was a common expression at the time. Traditionally military governments have always been right of center and 'no-nonsense' in their orientation. The business community, Americans included, generally looked towards the revolution hoping that it would stabilize the economy."**

*Roughly, "I believe it suits us."

**A *New York Times* dispatch filed from Lima three weeks after the coup confirms these views. Published October 25, 1968, and headlined "Foreigners' Investment Fears in Peru Have Largely Subsided," it said: "North American and European businessmen with major investments here seem generally confident now they will be able to get along at least as well with the new military dictatorship as with the democratically elected government it ousted."

It should be kept in mind that this apparent early calmness within the foreign investment community prevailed despite the expropriation of all IPC's Talara assets. This action was the biggest and practically only business expropriation ever executed by any Peruvian government in modern history. Yet most executives did not seem to identify themselves with IPC or expect its fate to be their own. In fact in my conversations with businessmen prior to the Revolution they often spoke of IPC as "a special case" and not relevant to them. Some had long hoped that Standard Oil would be more flexible in its negotiations so that the vexatious La Brea y Pariñas issue could be disposed of once and for all.

After about six months, however, the viewpoint of U.S. investors drastically changed. The Velasco regime had by that time taken a number of steps which collectively were an anathema to most businessmen. Announcements had been made of various far-reaching governmental moves against the private sector, including meaningful agrarian reforms and the nationalization of communications. Rumors circulated that the fishmeal and mining industries would also be expropriated. At the same time relations between the U.S. and Peruvian governments deteriorated to the lowest point in a century as a result of continued seizure of American tuna clippers inside the 200-mile limit, the unwillingness of the Peruvians to consider compensation to IPC, and the establishment of new trade and diplomatic ties with communist countries. The situation was not helped by the nationalistic outpouring in Peru following President Nixon's decision not to adhere (officially) to the April 9 deadline for application of the Hickenlooper Amendment in the IPC case.

On April 23, 1969, one of my informants in Lima business circles wrote, "The business community—and I make no distinction between Peruvians, Americans, Germans or anyone else, is plainly concerned. The IPC problem has created a big international question mark which has effectively shut off foreign credits and foreign investments. The government is apparently willing to make whatever sacrifices are necesssary to get along without these items which in my opinion are essential for the development of the country. We are in a depression. The auto plants are now producing at a fraction of their capacity. There is considerable unemployment. . . . No one is investing. It is 'wait and see.' "

Subsequent interviews, both with informants and other respondents, confirmed this anxiety. For at least the following two years foreign investors were exceedingly hostile to the Velasco regime. Opposition seemed to grow to a new high when in 1970 the Industrial Law, the comunidad concept, and the fade-out doctrine for foreign investment were all announced. Every executive with whom I spoke in 1969 and 1970 had grave reservations about the new policies and almost none thought the revolution was doing any "good." The vast majority of businessmen were outspokenly antagonistic to the regime and some bitterly so.

By mid-1971, however, three years after Velasco came to power, at least some contrary opinion was beginning to surface. The general manager of Goodyear described himself as "cautiously optimistic."[30] The former general manager of another company declared the generals to be "definitely more capable" than the previous leadership. Dr. East of Marcona characterized the generals as "reasonable" and "open to communication."[31] These scattered comments cannot be taken as evidence of a systematic trend toward acceptance of the Revolution, but they seem to indicate either some softening of earlier opposition or the emergence of individual departures from the general antagonism.

In conclusion, the available evidence with regard to the political attitudes of U.S. business executives is that these men tend toward conservatism within the Peruvian context but not radically or consistently so. Attitudinally the businessmen are usually more "at home" with rightist regimes, parties, and policies but do not identify with them totally. Our evidence so far suggests that rather than being in a conspiratorial alliance with oligarchic elites, the businessmen share with them a certain number of common goals and values.

Conservatism is evident in the following: Over a twenty-five-year period new investments came to Peru at the fastest rate under a definite rightest regime and disinvestment occurred during leftist administrations. A limited degree of polling revealed a general preference for moderate or rightest presidents and political parties and also a general suspicion of activities such as agrarian reform and economic planning. Informant reports since 1968 reveal that once the Revolution started in earnest it was strongly opposed by almost all executives, at least for a time.

That the conservatism is, however, qualified is indicated by this evidence: Capital came to Peru during the reformist Belaúnde period as well as the Ochenio. When polled, the businessmen seemed to differentiate between the interests of Peru and those of foreign capital in Peru. Wide disagreements existed among individuals with respect to the value of past chapters of Peru's history and where the country should head in the future. The Velasco government was by no means liked by the businessmen, but the confiscation of IPC alone was not generally upsetting and after three years of Revolution at least some executives were beginning to adjust to it—or else the Revolution was beginning to adjust to them, a possibility that must be investigated in subsequent chapters.

Four   Corporate Political Behavior '

The previous chapter dealt with the issue of a foreign challenge to Peru's national independence from the standpoint of control capacities and political attitudes. The latter constitute aspects of political behavior. The present chapter continues the inquiry into corporate political behavior by examining managerial lobbying before Peruvian decision-makers and business attempts to cultivate support within Peruvian public opinion. When evidence of the effects of such activity is available that also is presented.

These matters bear directly upon the first two hypotheses presented earlier. Hypothesis I predicts that the companies participate actively and directly in political decision-making. They are perceived as employing bribery, favors, and mass-media penetration with the end effect of controlling relevant public policy outcomes. Alternatively, Hypothesis IA postulates that the enterprises avoid active participation and attempt merely to minimize their visibility or improve their image. This hypothesis nevertheless envisions a degree of political influence on the part of the corporations, but it is attained through investment bargaining.

Avenues of Access

With respect to direct exertions of pressure on Peruvian decision-makers, the various channels that are potentially open for corporate lobbying will be considered first. Concerns at this stage will be primarily two: To what extent does lobbying take place? To what extent does it occur in association with Peru's traditional economic elites? The answer to the latter question should shed further light on corporate relationships with these elites.

One can conceive of perhaps five potential avenues of lobbying access to the Peruvian government on the part of American corporations. These are (1) the professional, for-hire lobbyist, (2) the legislature, (3) political parties, (4) interest groups, and (5) direct contact by the companies themselves.

The American affiliate in Peru, unlike its parent in the United States, seldom hires professional lobbyists. In fact it would appear that this type of service is little used generally in Lima. Innumerable firms specialize in law and public relations but not governmental relations as such. Of the top twelve U.S. companies in 1968 only two indicated any dealings with lobbyists not employed full-time by the enterprise itself. Goodyear retained one of the old law firms of Lima, but this was done because of its members' contacts in elite Lima society rather than a technical lobbying expertise. In connection with its work on the Marginal Highway, Constructora Emkay and other members of a construction consortium hired a Lima law firm to conduct business with the Peruvian authorities. This was convenient in that Emkay had not built up a large permanent staff in Peru. With respect to Emkay's construction projects undertaken for Cerro de Pasco, the contractor relied on Cerro itself to deal with the government.[1]

Legislative representatives are probably of somewhat greater importance than retained lobbyists as avenues of access but their overall significance is still comparatively small. An underlying factor is that the Peruvian Congress has been traditionally weak in the policy-making process vis-à-vis the executive. The Belaúnde administration was unusual in the degree to which the legislature assumed influence over decisions, at least in the negative sense of blocking action. Under Velasco, of course, the Congress did not sit. Moreover, even when Congress is in session pressures are not easily brought to bear by means of a constituent's own geographical representative. Deputies and senators do not hold their seats over long periods in most cases. A constituent's social position or political connections normally assume more importance in pressure politics than mere physical residence. As for corporate constituents, almost no legislator can afford to be identified with an American company—to do so would be a political kiss of death. Thus Cerro de Pasco, for example, has no overt "friends" among the senators and deputies from the Departments of Junín and Pasco where most of its operations are located. Although some covert legislative relationships with the company have existed in the past, the typical sierra politician must publicly portray himself as an outspoken enemy of Peru's largest private employer. This is not to say that the corporations do not carefully nurture friendships in the legislature (when it is not suspended), but they do so as quietly as possible.

The leading political parties are a third potential avenue of access. One American executive told me that he systematically developed personal contacts in all major parties, as well as in all important ministries and all services of the armed forces. As we shall see shortly, U.S. firms are known to contribute campaign funds to the parties on occasion at least, and this in itself constitutes a kind of political relationship. Yet close ties with the parties may not have much significance apart from the general network of personal and congressional acquaintanceships. Much party activity, such as the issuance of manifestoes and the rendering of services to members, has no importance whatever to the corporations. In fact they are disdainful of it. Moreover it should be kept in mind that, except for APRA, Peruvian political parties are poorly organized and have significance mainly as followings of individual personalities. If the companies can obtain direct contacts with the leaders themselves relationships with the lower party organization are superfluous. A further consideration is that many American businessmen are alienated from Peruvian parties in general, not just because of ideological differences but because they perceive them as empty institutions engaged in hyperbole and squabbling rather than any serious wielding of power.

If lobbyists, legislators, and parties are comparatively unimportant as avenues of access, the same cannot be said with regard to business interest groups. The national societies and chambers of commerce and other business associations described in Chapter Two all lobby on behalf of their memberships. This is done on all levels, from the presidency and cabinet on down through the ministries, bureaucracy, and legislature. Like business groups everywhere, these organizations are useful to the companies in that a united front is presented to the government, which not only implies unity within the industry but safeguards individual corporations from being singled out for counterattack.

The U.S. corporations normally join the groups relevant to their industry regardless of the associations' ideological orientations. Thus, for example, Anderson Clayton, General Motors, and Goodyear were members of the National Society of Industries in 1968; IBEC and Sears participated in CONOCO; and Cerro, SPCC, Marcona, and IPC belonged to the National Society of Mining and Petroleum Companies. Most of the firms were in one or more chambers of commerce as well. All of the top twelve U.S. corporations belonged to the American Chamber except SPCC and Marcona.

In the national societies voting power is not equal among members but is based on relative size in the industry. Hence the role of American corporations in the various societies differs. In the National Society of Fisheries, for instance, American fishmeal producers take a secondary position; the late king of Peruvian fishmeal, Luis Banchero, completely dominated the group during his career. In the National Agrarian Society, where voting power is based on the amount of land owned, U.S. influence (that is, that of Grace) was also secondary; the great Peruvian sugar families of the coast such as Gildemeister and de la Piedra predominated. In the mining society, dues are based on ore output and voting power in turn is based on dues. Thus this group has been dominated by American capital for decades. Following IPC's expropriation the gran minería alone controlled it even though Cerro, Marcona, and SPCC had only a fifth of the seats on the board of directors. For its part, the National Society of Industries is somewhat different in that many separate manufacturing industries are embraced; thus the focus of lobbying activity is individual industry committees. Some forty-seven of these exist: one for textiles, one for rubber, another for beer, and so on.[2] For many years the chairmanship of the rubber committee was held by the late George B. Olbert, the president of Goodyear del Perú, a logical choice in view of Goodyear's near-monopoly position in the heavy-rubber industry.

As indicated in Chapter Two, the influence of these groups over public policies affecting them was reputed to be extraordinarily great prior to the Velasco regime. At the turn of the century the mining society itself wrote the legal code under which that industry flourished for fifty years.[3] The society's larger members practically dictated the code's revision in 1950. In 1963-1964 the National Agrarian Society was, according to Carlos Astiz, the prime mover in adoption of the gutting compromises made in Belaúnde's agrarian reform legislation.[4] It is known that in 1967 Banchero's fisheries society successfully obtained a five-year lowering of export duties on fishmeal in an effort to revive the then-prostrate fishing industry. In the same year the National Society of Industries' rubber committee, under the leadership of Goodyear's Olbert, persuaded the government to suspend an elimination of all import duty exonerations, an act that would have injured all importers.[5]

With the 1968 coup, however, the influence of these associations seemed to decrease. The Revolution's agrarian reform went through on schedule despite the National Agrarian Society, and it included the coastal estates of Peru's sugar oligarchy. The comunidad idea and new controls over industry went ahead without major change, despite almost universal distaste for these innovations within the business and industry associations. When questioned on the influence of the groups under the Revolution, American businessmen were unanimous in perceiving a drastic shrinking of "clout." One executive in a position to know said the rubber committee had become "almost totally unhelpful." A high official at Cerro stated the mining society was "getting nowhere" in pushing for more proinvestor mining policies. A fishmeal producer remarked that the fisheries society had "almost no influence," with Banchero so discredited with the government that the generals would not be seen with him.

Yet it is my belief that a permanent and complete loss of influence on the part of the associations under the Revolution would be an oversimplification. It appears that for approximately two years the generals were anxious to disengage themselves from past patterns of influence, both as a symbol of independence from traditional economic interests and as a means of determining the basic course of the Revolution unhampered by negotiation over details. During 1969 and 1970 the tendency was for little communication between the associations (except CONOCO, perhaps) and their counterpart ministries. Industrialists complained that they were taken by surprise by radical new decrees that vitally affected their interests but about which they had had no specific forewarning.

By 1971 the business-government relationship was changing noticeably. General Ernesto Montagne Sánchez, the premier, was by now meeting monthly with a representative of each of the societies. Dialogue opened up on the ministerial and bureaucratic levels as well. Preliminary drafts of pending decrees were circulated to the associations for comment; this permitted the industrialists to know what was coming and also to request adjustments. Sometimes such communication was helpful to the businessmen, but it could also be frustrating. An American executive commented, "Whether they [the associations] really make a dent is unknowable—when the generals and the groups agree, cooperation seems to develop; but when they don't nothing is heard for six months until the final decree is published."

The new openness was not accompanied by a sudden collapse of the Revolution's ideals or a sharp departure from established courses of action. Yet significant adjustments in government policy which had been sought by the private sector were beginning to occur by 1971. For example, reduced taxes were promised for the troubled fishmeal industry in December.[6] Earlier in the year foreign exchange controls were liberalized so that foreigners employed in Peru could be paid in dollars and could take their savings with them when they left the country. This change had followed a concerted protest from the foreign business and diplomatic community against an earlier decree which had permitted only tourists or transients to take foreign currency out of Peru.

In June of 1971 an adjustment occurred in the taxation of mining which followed discussions with that industry. A 1970 decree, which had contained the basic outlines of the Revolution's mining policy, had excluded the comunidad concept and had set a reinvestment deduction allowance of 30 percent of pretax profits with a ceiling of 200 million soles. A 1971 decree that spelled out mining policies in greater detail (a customary procedure in Peruvian law) included the comunidad but raised the allowance to 40 percent with a ceiling of 300 million soles. My informants say this was a simple trade which had been agreed upon between the industry and the Ministry of Energy and Mines.

As for business associations speaking directly for U.S. interests in Peru, the American Chamber of Commerce continued a brave existence during the Velasco regime despite the distress most of its members felt about the Revolution. The usual charities and social functions were carried on although an older luncheon-club, booster-type of optimism began to fade. Never too influential within the internal politics of Peru because of its "gringo" image, about all the Chamber could do was transmit its views to other, possibly more influential, political actors. Closer ties were sought with other Lima business associations. The European chambers of commerce in particular were sought out as a means of access to the generals, who for a time seemed attracted to European and Japanese capital as an alternative to American resources. Contact also was continued on a regular basis with the U.S. Embassy; for some years the Chamber had been a focal point for the American ambassador's relationships to the U.S. business community. Occasionally the Chamber sent resolutions of protest to Washington as well. In 1971 it officially opposed the "Grace Amendment" before the U.S. House Agriculture Committee that would have set aside part of the Peruvian sugar quota for reimbursement to expropriated U.S. firms.[7] The belief was widespread in Peru at the time that the move by Grace would only harden Peruvian official attitudes and result in more drastic anti-investor moves from the military government.

Another U.S. business organization moved aggressively to establish a dialogue with the generals directly. This was the Council of the Americas, an association of more than 200 U.S. business corporations with investments throughout Latin America. Established in 1964 as the Council for Latin America, this organization promotes the interests of its membership in Washington and in Latin capitals. In addition it encourages behavior by the corporations themselves that works to their long-term rather than short-term interests. David Rockefeller is founder and chairman of the Council.[8]

In 1971, a year I am interpreting as critical in relations with the generals, the Council sought to assist the American business community's access by two distinct activities. First it brought to Lima, in January, a delegation of high-powered, parent-company executives to meet with Velasco ministers. The group included top officials of Westinghouse, Sears Roebuck, Celanese International, Bank of America, and Gulf Oil. Meetings were arranged with the ministers of Energy and Mines, Economy and Finance, Industry and Commerce, and Fisheries and the head of the Presidential Advisory Committee. The delegation's chairman, José de Cubas, president of Westinghouse Electric International, told the Peruvians that American business, too, was interested in development, change, and new ideas. But the fade-out doctrine of eventual minority ownership by foreign investors that had been adopted in Peru and by the Andean Pact "would cause very serious problems," de Cubas said. In answer the Peruvian officials defended stoutly the government's policies, insisted that the regime's image had been deliberately distorted in the United States, and refused to discuss the IPC case, which de Cubas described as "a very serious public relation problem" for Peru.[9]

The second action was undertaken by the Council's Lima office. (The fact that this office is physically located at the headquarters of the American Chamber indicates the closeness of the two organizations.) In mid-1971 it arranged several small dinner meetings with a key minister of the regime as guest of honor each time and with a group of local U.S. businessmen as guests. Recognizing the political delicacy of private meetings between the nationalistic generals and Yankee capitalists, these dinners were kept as closed and secret as possible. No other Peruvians were admitted, not even wives or servants, a condition laid down by the government's representatives. At these meetings informal conversation predominated although some businessmen prepared written questions in advance for presentation to the generals. The regime was clearly prepared to enter into dialogue but it was apparently fearful of seeming to be.

The fifth and last avenue of access is direct approaches by the corporations themselves. It is my contention that immediate and direct communication by corporate executives is definitely more beneficial to the enterprises than any of the indirect routes heretofore mentioned. This point should be stressed even though it tends to denigrate somewhat the importance of the business interest group, the most visible institution of business political pressure. Many executives have told me that the primary reason they belong to the business associations is that they are a good means by which to meet top officials; once personal acquaintanceships are made, further contact can be direct. (And we have just seen how the Council of the Americas utilizes its individual members as the principal point of contact.)

Evidence of the importance of direct access is both historical and contemporary. In the period 1914-1922 when IPC was struggling to avoid a tax schedule in accord with regular Peruvian law, Standard Oil did not rely on any external spokesman or group. It sent to Peru its own men, Walter C. Teagle, president of Jersey after 1918, and G. Harrison Smith, president of IPC. These officials made the top decisions on political strategy. Implementation of the strategy was in the hands of International's Canadian legal counsel, R.V. LeSueur. LeSueur took up residence in Lima for a number of years, ingratiated himself with sympathetic politicians and the upper class, and displayed prodigious lobbying skills. He developed personal relationships with Peruvian congressmen and newspaper editors, planted procompany articles in Lima dailies, furnished favorable material to U.S. publications, and caused a booklet to be published in Lima expressing the company viewpoint. LeSueur's lobbying in the Peruvian legislature was so effective that it delayed for years a tax increase affecting the company (he was not able to get all he wanted, however, including a general income tax he had proposed for Peru). Meanwhile, dealings with President José Pardo y Barreda were conducted personally by Teagle, who instructed the president on the advantages of foreign capital and informed him that the Peruvian government had "a moral obligation" to "come to some amicable arrangement with the Company."[10]

This type of direct approach, using high corporate executives, is still in effect today. The main difference is that with modern communications and air travel parent-company officials resident in the U.S. are more involved. It has already been mentioned how during the successive IPC crises of the late 1960's, for example, telephone calls between Lima and Coral Gables were made daily if not more frequently. Actual negotiations were conducted by Fernando Espinosa, IPC-Peru's general manager; at no time was an intermediary, outside lobbyist, or business group involved. Even the U.S. ambassador, very anxious to see an IPC settlement brought to fruition for the sake of improving U.S.-Peruvian relations, was essentially a passive participant. Although Ambassador John Wesley Jones was publicly charged in 1969 as being "Mister IPC,"[11] his main role was to facilitate negotiations rather than carry the company's torch. That was done by the company itself.

It is my belief that this is quite typical. Whenever a corporation is in political trouble, and especially when the "chips are down," so to speak, political dealings are conducted personally by the corporation's top executives. The extended negotiations over Lima telephone contracts and the talks leading up to the sale of ITT's telephone stock were conducted for the company by the local manager of Cía. Peruana de Teléfonos and the ITT Latin American Group executive from New York. Grace's negotiations over compensation for the sugar estates were in charge of a Grace vice-president, flown down especially from New York. Frank Archibald, the president of SPCC, personally conducted six months of negotiations prior to the signing of the Cuajone contract. Robert Koenig, for twenty years the president of Cerro Corporation, was a frequent visitor to Lima, and on occasion he called upon the president of the republic according to the protocol of what might be described as nongovernmental diplomacy. Koenig paid his first call on President Velasco only a month after the 1968 coup and just five days after Ambassador Jones had made his first visit to the presidential palace.[12]

The involvement of top executives is not just a matter of placing important responsibility at the top of the management hierarchy. Part of the corporations' adjustment to the Latin cultural environment is to avoid, in dealing with the Peruvians, the transmittal of company requests or bargaining positions via subordinates or impersonal written memoranda. In the New York business world agreements are often negotiated at lower levels and ratified at the top. In Latin America, however, the tendency is to regard a junior official as being without real authority and to stress informal, face-to-face encounters.[13] Use of external intermediaries would be considered an even greater blockage of top-level, personal communication than that of junior executives. One important exception exists to this statement, however: if an agreement is made that could be dangerous to reputations, such as delivery of a large bribe, a confidential intermediary is essential.

All corporate managers who know Peru are aware of this personalistic, direct style of government representation and they attempt to practice it well. They work hard to perfect their Spanish if it is inadequate. They methodically develop contacts in the right places by joining organizations of several kinds and by not restricting their social life to the American colony of Lima.

The opportunities for meeting high government officials and other important persons will, of course, vary. American telephone executives were assisted by the several elite Peruvians who had sat for years on the board of directors of Cía. Peruana de Teléfonos.* Goodyear's founder, Eduardo Dibos, is an extremely prominent Limeño and was still of political value to the company in 1971. A former GM general manager, Pedro Pessoa, of aristocratic (Brazilian) upbringing himself, was an expert horseman and thus able to mix with ease with the equestrian portion of Lima aristocracy. Robert Koenig's position as head of Peru's largest private enterprise and as a resident of the country in the Leguía days entitled him to membership in the exclusive Club Nacional. Cerro's conncections did not depend solely on Koenig, however, for the president of the Peruvian subsidiary for many years, Alberto Benavides, is a nephew of General Oscar R. Benavides, former president of Peru, and is related by marriage to Haya de la Torre.

Effective political behavior includes knowing how to adjust to changing conditions. The Velasco government, which saw itself as an enemy of the traditional oligarchs, was not approached at the racetrack or Club Nacional. A socially prominent Peruvian director or executive could be a hindrance as well as a help. Now contacts within the military services and the bureaucracy were far more important than within the economic and social elites. In some cases Peruvian executives of U.S. firms enjoyed personal friendships in the officer corps, for example, Dr. East of Marcona. Since many Peruvian military officers are from the middle class and are even of mestizo background (except in the navy), this kind of linkage was probably unusual.

Unlike the pre-Revolution period, when rapport between business and government elites was based on class, dialogue of the kind that was beginning to develop in 1971 seemed to have a predominantly functional basis. As the government engaged more and more in the task of directing economic life, it was perhaps inevitably pushed into closer contact with business managers and the technical problems with which they deal. This was evident in oil, rubber, and other industries by mid-1971. In those areas where government was assuming direct economic responsibility it sometimes brought private and even foreign influences closer in to policy-making councils. This happened when the Banco de la Nación purchased controlling interest in three private banks, two of them with strong American connections. Executives of the Banco Continental, previously controlled by Chase Manhattan, were able to liberalize the allocations of local credit available to foreign firms in Peru by persuading the authorities to construe consumer credit as not included within the limitations. This

*One of these, Miguel Mujica Callo, was Belaúnde's last premier. However, he was in office only 14 hours prior to the Velasco coup.

was quite beneficial to American business. It is paradoxical indeed if a government whose announced aims are to avoid foreign control and traditional capitalism is pushed into more intimate contact with foreign capitalists by the very nature of its policies.

Gifts, Payoffs, Favors

If American corporations in Peru do, in fact, lobby actively and at least on occasion with success, *how* do they bring pressure?

One of the most intriguing possibilities, raised explicitly by economic imperialism theorists, is the simple expenditure of cash. Venality in political leaders and bribery on the part of businessmen are known in all societies, but many believe them to be especially commonplace in Latin America. Those who are already suspicious of foreign investment are quite prepared to accept the assumption that foreign businessmen purchase favors and political influence on a grand scale. The companies are, after all, usually big—therefore they would seem to have almost unlimited funds with which to make payoffs. Do they bribe extensively?

Before presenting evidence the point might be made that blanket moral condemnation of payments or gifts could be considered presumptuous. It is easy to condemn a foreign capitalist for bribery, but it is not easy to condemn the poorly paid Peruvian official who accepts an informal remuneration for services rendered. Furthermore, various cash transactions must be judged within their particular cultural context. It seems "bad" for an American company in Peru to contribute to Peruvian political parties, but many might hesitate to find wrongdoing in contributions by Peruvian sugar growers to the re-election of U.S. congressmen chairing the committees that determine sugar quotas.

Let us deal first with gifts to political parties. In gauging the significance of political contributions in Peru, it is well to recall once more that the parties historically have had a secondary role in governing the country. Under Belaúnde they were important because of effective congressional opposition to the executive; but under Velasco the parties had no power whatever. The general alienation of American businessmen to the Peruvian party system should be noted again; in my interviews I perceived no sense of positive commitment to any party, including the most conservative. Any motivation to contribute would be, it seems, purely self-seeking.

The available evidence suggests that many corporations are asked to contribute money at election time to defray campaign expenses but not necessarily to provide continuous subsidization. When asked, representatives of some companies stated they had been approached for contributions in the 1962 and 1963 elections. One firm admitted acceding to the request, and I suspect that others did as well. The one candid enterprise was Cía. Peruana de Teléfonos; officials in both Lima and New York confirmed that all the parties approached them in 1962 and 1963 and that the company had provided some funds. One executive said APRA was given $2000; another stated that sums were given to all parties except the Christian Democrats.

I would speculate that this practice, although perhaps fairly widespread, is probably not universal among the American companies. Several observers expressed the belief that the dangers of party contributions outweighed their benefits. Revelation by an antagonistic newspaper or political figure of a gift could create very serious image problems for an *American* corporation. And a return on the investment would depend on the achievement of good will or a sense of political debt at a point in the decision-making structure that would be of specific value to the company. Usually in Peruvian politics a much safer bet would be to effect an exchange with individual ministers or bureaucrats rather than dealing with the haphazardly organized and continually changing party structure. When I asked former President Belaúnde whether Acción Popular had received contributions from U.S. companies, he replied he did not know what went on at the lower levels of the party.[14]

Cash contributions are made by business firms to journalists and newspaper editors from time to time. This practice is widespread in Latin American journalism and Peru is no exception. The benefit purchased is favorable newspaper publicity, usually in the form of slanted articles. Payments are sometimes made to the reporters personally but they may also be institutionalized to the point of periodic billings, just as for advertising. A purchased article is technically legal in Peru if the notation "Publi. Reportaje No.–" is included, indicating that it is registered publicity reporting; but a personal friendship or adequate cash award can lead to deletion of this line. On occasion reporters do not passively wait for payments but attempt to blackmail companies by threatening them with bad publicity if cash is not forthcoming.[15]

Although contributions to journalists are quasi-accepted in Peru, the Velasco government attempted to blacken further the name of IPC by releasing to the press, in early 1969, a list of thirteen journalists who were said to have received payments from IPC and the British oil company Lobitos. The list, obviously gleaned from seized IPC books, mentioned four daily newspapers, two radio networks, and one magazine. Annual payments per journalist ranged from 1,200 soles (less than $50 at the time) to 287,500 soles (slightly more than $11,000). Those journalists who answered the charges averred, however, that the payments were for articles written for company publications and not bribes.[16]

Of greatest interest in the realm of cash payments is, naturally, the bribery of government officials. It can categorically be stated that cash payments are definitely received by Peruvian government officials and that Amercian corporations definitely make them. But to understand these transactions an important distinction must be made. This is between the relatively small payment to a bureaucrat and the large-scale bribe to a high official. The difference is not simply one of degree; the bureaucratic payment is accepted as a normal and nearly universal feature of business life. The high-level bribe, however, is contrary to accepted public norms and can destroy reputations.

The smaller administrative payment is in reality a tip. It is known throughout the nonindustrialized world although by different names. Called "speed money" in India, "dash" in Africa, and "mordida" in Mexico,[17] it is referred to as "coima" in Peru. A relatively small amount of cash is paid to a minor government functionary as an informal tax or fee for facilitating a transaction with him. The payment may not be essential to the transaction, but it will speed up action and resolve any doubtful points in favor of the client. It may also permit the regulations to be stretched in his favor. The alternative is to wait endlessly for the wheels of government to turn and to expect no individualized or special attention. The phenomenon is not dissimilar to the tipping of waiters or barbers for the rendering of more than minimum service. In fact, Latin American buraucrats, like waiters and barbers, receive very low salaries and depend on customer remunerations to supplement their income.[18]

Some American businessmen in Peru initially balk at making such payments, but they soon learn to accept them as a routine cost of doing business. When a U.S. airline first established a sales office in Lima, the representative sent from New York was told by his superiors there to "play it above-board" in his dealings with the government, which meant the payment of no bribes whatever. Soon the American learned that it was virtually impossible to launch operations, let alone make them proceed efficiently, without making small payments to various officials. Headquarters personnel eventually accepted the practice, realizing there was little or no stigma attached to it.

In my conversations with company officials on this subject some were reluctant to admit they paid such tips, but others openly agreed that it was often necessary to "put a drop of oil"—as one respondent put it—on the bureaucratic machinery. The same interviewee conceded this was "hard to handle administratively," however, referring to the North American habit of justifying all business costs. At Christmastime the metaphor might better be "drop of liquor," for the practice at that time of year is to give a case of whiskey to individuals frequently dealt with, such as the mailman and customs official. Several executives explained that successful dealing with customs also required payments throughout the year; normally an extra charge is levied for each consignment of goods cleared, paid routinely through one's customs agent. Other officials regularly tipped are those who review tax records and issue import licenses.

If the bureaucratic tip has significance mainly for administrative efficiency, the high-level bribe has obvious implications for policy and politics.

Whether or not large-scale official graft is common in contemporary Peru, it is without question a part of the country's past history. Chapter Eight describes the engineering and organizational exploits of Henry Meiggs, a fugitive of California law who made a fortune in the 1860's and 1870's by building railroads in Chile and Peru. Meiggs's biographer, Watt Steward, writes: "That Henry Meiggs resorted to bribery to attain his ends cannot be doubted. By that means he managed the men who managed Peru." Meiggs's method of winning railroad contracts over all competing bidders consisted simply of outbribing them. He would find out the officials' "price," add that to his estimate for a construction job, and then pay off his benefactors from per-mile progress payments. William Clarke, a contemporary of Meiggs who supposedly heard the contractor's death-bed confessions, commented that such graft "may appear wrong, but it was one of the results of the evil form of Government which has made Peruvian bribery and corruption a by-word even in South America."[19]

During the Leguía administration official corruption also ran rampant in Peru, as noted earlier. American businessmen admitted making large payoffs to Leguía's son, Juan, and other Peruvians during U.S. Senate hearings conducted in the 1930's on stock exchange practices and the munitions industry. The Electric Boat Company, attempting to sell submarines to Peru, paid $15,000 in "commissions" to "political friends" in conjunction with orders placed in 1924 and 1926. In 1929 the company agreed to give Juan Leguía a $40,000 commission on the sale of two additional boats and it indicated a willingness to expend a total of $145,000 to settle the deal. In 1927-1928 two New York financial houses, J. and W. Seligman and Company and the National City Company, issued securities totaling $100 million for loans to the Peruvian government. According to historian James Carey, "promoters and grafters" of various kinds received no less than $567,000 in connection with these credits; Juan Leguía himself collected $416,000 of the amount merely for not stopping them.[20]

Is such corruption purely a thing of the past? According to reports from my informants the answer would be "no," but with several qualifications. First, large-scale bribery has occurred in the recent past but, most contend, not with great frequency. The big-time bribe is an unusual rather than commonplace phenomenon. In five years of interviewing I ran into very few rumors, let alone believable reports, of Leguía-type graft. The rate of occurrence certainly cannot be compared to that of administrative tipping. A certified public accountant who had been auditing corporation books in Lima for several years stated that although he had come across thousands of small payments by business firms to government functionaries in the

5,000-to-10,000 sol range (about $200-$400 at the time) he had not encountered larger payments.*

A second generalization that comes from informant reports is that British and American corporations are less inclined to engage in graft than Italian, German, and Japanese enterprises. This point was made time and time again by respondents of all types—from university intellectuals to Peruvian businessmen to Fernando Belaúnde, reputedly the only person to leave the Peruvian presidency a poor man. The reason attributed to the difference is not some superior Anglo-Saxon morality but, rather, a different style of business management plus a greater image problem. In American corporations particularly financial decisions are made collectively with many stages of review and in accord with rigorous rational analysis. A board of directors in New York, accustomed today to assessing capital items in cost-benefit terms, might well balk at making a $100,000 payoff to a Peruvian politician. The dangers in case of external discovery are also greater for the Americans; the political enemies of U.S. capitalism are legion in Latin America and they would gladly pounce on any allegation of wrongdoing.

In this connection it should be noted that the principal report of high-level bribery which I personally accept as verified from five years of inquiry concerns European and not American interests. In 1962 the Prado administration signed contracts with a consortium of British and German construction and banking interests to build a large hydroelectric project in the central Andes. The undertaking, on the Mantaro River in the Huancavelica Department was to cost in the neighborhood of $100 million. In mid-1965, a consortium of Italian interests—including both private and state enterprises—secretly approached the Peruvian government and proposed building the project (not yet begun) for some 15 percent lower cost. In late 1965 and early 1966, the Peruvian executive, supported by the supposedly opposition APRA-UNO coalition in Congress, renounced the Anglo-German contract in favor of the Italian proposal. At the time and subsequently, rumors flew that the aggressive Italian group, which had also been competing hard for construction projects in Turkey and Africa, paid a huge bribe to the Peruvian Minister of Development and Public Works and several other individuals (but not including President Belaúnde). Regardless of the truth of these allegations the British-German contracts were canceled in favor of the Italian consortium and the latter group proceeded with the project. It was scheduled for initial power generation in early 1973 and has cost not 15 percent less than $100 million but in the neighborhood of $237 million.[21]

Public works and other government contracts seem in general to be one of the more corrupt areas of government endeavor, which may be true all

*They could have been concealed or recorded in separate books, however.

over the world. According to Robert Koenig, who lived in Peru in the Leguía era, the contractor pays a standard percentage fee above the contract amount to an agent who secures the contract for him. The fee is reputedly 5 percent for military contracts and 5 to 10 percent for civilian public works contracts. Two percent is reserved to the agent for his commission, with the remainder going to a minister or other high official.[22] A Peruvian informant pointed out that in unusually large contracts several officials may be involved, including members of Congress when that body is sitting. When payoffs run to large sums they may be paid directly into one or more numbered Swiss bank accounts, with the Swiss bank countersigning the contract.

Still another generalization emerging from informant reports is that individual American companies differ significantly as to their political style as well as ethical scruples. The more recently established firms supposedly work hard to create a good image and are desirous of avoiding a single rash act that could damage their image permanently. Older companies, however, are in some cases more cynical.

Although categorizing companies this way is admittedly dangerous, it is my impression that Sears Roebuck and General Motors fell in the first group. For some years in the 1960's Sears was interested in building a third store in Callao, but it was unable to do so because it could not obtain the necessary municipal construction permits. A source claims this was a consequence of Sears's refusal to bribe municipal officials. Eventually the company gave up the idea and erected a store in Pueblo Libre, a section of Lima. GM also ran into attempted municipal bribery when it built its new assembly plant in 1965. In advance of construction local district officials told the general manager, Pedro Pessoa, that he had their informal approval to proceed. The formal permits could be obtained later, they said, and on the strength of these assurances construction went ahead. Later the officials reportedly demanded payoffs prior to issuance of the written permits. According to Pessoa, he told some of his journalist friends about the threat and then counterthreatened the authorities with front-page newspaper publicity if they persisted in demanding payment. This supposedly ended the problem.[23]

Two American companies among the top twelve were identified more often than the remaining ten as being involved in bribery at one time or another. These are the International Petroleum Company and Cía. Peruana de Teléfonos. IPC, some say, was bribe-prone prior to about 1962 but became "clean" after that. The telephone company, according to a few respondents, utilized graft to obtain its 1967 telephone expansion contract. Evaluating these allegations is most difficult. It is true that IPC had a reputation for tough and insensitive management prior to its mounting political difficulties of the 1960's. Yet when the company books were seized by the military government in February 1969, evidence of payments to journalists was revealed to the public but not of official corruption—a charge the generals could have made against the Belaúnde regime with some profit. As for the ITT allegation, we do know that the company made party contributions; it also pressed hard for diplomatic intervention in connection with a bill pending in the Peruvian Congress in 1967. Thus the company was capable of employing an interventionist and agressive mode of political behavior, but this does not necessarily include big-time bribery.*

A final point in connection with bribery is that payoff behavior varies over time. Obviously the companies are not going to give money to officials that do not accept it or give no indication they might accept it. In interviews of 1970 and 1971 the comparison was constantly made between the Belaúnde and Velasco regimes. Although President Belaúnde himself was universally characterized as honest, many of the approximately 100 ministers in office during his tenure were allegedly venal. The Velasco ministers, on the other hand, were widely acclaimed as being almost fanatically incorruptible. Schooled in the discipline of the armed forces rather than the maneuvering of civilian politics, they supposedly expected and received no bribes, at least from American business. (Public morality, in fact, formed part of the regime's ideology; the coup itself was rationalized in part on the basis of excising governmental corruption.) During the early years of the Revolution some rumors circulated regarding conflict of interest on the part of high persons (for instance, in government procurement), but none involving corporate bribery.

An understanding of political pressure in Peru must embrace exchanges other than the simple cash payment. Nonmonetary favors of a wide variety are granted. The value of these is material in some instances and in other instances not. The transaction involved is very different from the bureaucratic tip or bribe in that the intention is not necessarily an immediate quid pro quo; rather, it may be simply the cementing of close ties, the creation of lasting good will, or the establishment of eventual need for

*These words were written before ITT's behavior concerning the Allende regime in Chile was revealed, and in view of what has since come to light my conclusions regarding that company are not merely supported but made to appear grossly understated. As we now know, in 1971 ITT offered $1 million to the U.S. Central Intelligence Agency to prevent Allende's election. At a minimum, the corporation proposed fomenting economic chaos in Chile which would in turn lead the Chilean military to intervene. The contemplated methods were denial of credits and aid to the country, the closing of world markets to Chile, interruption of fuel supplies and arms shipments to the Chilean military, and a reduction of operations by other U.S. firms in the country. Some lower-company staff proposed subsidies to anti-Allende newspapers, but this was ruled out by senior executives. A few outsiders have speculated that part of the $1 million was intended for bribing Chilean legislators to vote against Allende. The ITT campaign was not waged, however, at least not in full, because of noncooperation from top U.S. officials. Also, other U.S. firms were apparently not interested, a point that is in accord with the broader conclusion of this book that companies differ greatly in political-behavior styles.

reciprocity. Another difference is that whereas bribery is normally between strangers favors are exchanged between friends. In fact friendship is one of the objects. This can be possible because, unlike large-scale bribery, the granting of favors is in no way considered unethical; to the contrary, it involves its own unwritten code of honor.[24]

Experienced American executives learn both to grant and seek favors in Peru, not only in their dealings with Lima officials but with local mayors, commercial suppliers, the press, and others. The practice is merely another facet of the personalistic, informal style of business negotiation found in Latin America.

U.S. corporations in Peru seem to grant two quite different types of favor in their dealings with government. These might be labeled "personal" and "institutional." The first are given to individual government officials for their own private benefit. Illustrations would be purchase of airline tickets for a government official who must travel to the United States for an operation or medical checkup; payment of his hospital bill; arrangement of the itinerary of an official traveling in the United States; and entertainment of government visitors when they are in New York, either at restaurants or at the homes of parent-company executives. None of these acts would be considered wrong or a crass bid for power, but they cement existing friendships and may lead to later deferences to the company by the officials involved.

A special type of personal favor that is somewhat unique in its consequences is the granting of a job to a friend or relative. This supposedly is done from time to time by American firms as they seek to make friends in important places. A salaried position in an American enterprise is highly valued by many Peruvians because of the relatively high pay and prestige attached. If one is given to the nephew of a minister this creates a political debt on the minister's part to the corporate employer. After the passage of time, the same employee may become a valuable route of contact back to the minister's department.[25]

Institutional favors, by contrast, constitute less personal gestures and they are granted to the government itself. Some consist of assistance to administrative programs and others of action perceived as generally supportive of the regime. A type of institutional favor employed by IPC on various occasions was the granting of credit or the facilitation of credit arrangements. In 1916 the Peruvian government, in dire financial straits, asked IPC if it and its affiliates could extend a loan of 30 million soles to Peru or join a group subscribing to such a loan. Standard Oil executives refused, but they did arrange for a Peruvian financial agent to meet with representatives of a group of New York banks headed by the National City Bank. The bankers were receptive to a loan but demanded as security the government's income from tobacco, copper, and petroleum taxes. Negotiations broke down, however, when it became clear that adequate petroleum taxes could not be pledged because of IPC's own unwillingness to accept a regular tax schedule for La Brea y Pariñas.[26]

On at least three occasions, however, International itself made loans to Peru. In 1936 a program of $6.4 million in credits was launched to finance highway construction. In 1946 the loans were repaid and a new credit of $5 million was granted.[27] Seven years later, with Odría now in power, the company extended a third road loan of $10 million, payable in fifteen years at 5 percent interest.[28] Although the company maintains that its "arm was twisted" in making these advances, they probably paid off quite well in not only expansion of the local gasoline market (new roads mean more auto use) but in political credits at the presidential palace.

Several illustrations can be given of favors granted to the Peruvian armed forces, recognized as politically important by the corporations long before the 1968 coup. IPC always enjoyed good relations with the Peruvian air force contingent stationed at Talara; part of the base housing was constructed from old company housing. (The army, however, hated the company because of several long-standing squabbles.) When Marcona constructed its modern facilities at San Nicolás the original facilities built at San Juan became obsolete. The old dock and two warehouses were given to the Peruvian navy with the idea that they could be used in the construction of a naval base at San Juan Bay. Goodyear, which sold truck tires to the army, made a point of making company tire crews available at military bases to assist in vehicle maintenance. General Motors, not to be outdone in making friends with the military, offered mechanic courses to personnel of all three services in its plant training rooms. This was of particular benefit to the army because of its many GM trucks.[29]

Two instances are known of where U.S. corporations offered to assist the government with investigative studies. In 1967 IBEC helped the Peruvian Agriculture Ministry and the U.S. Agency for International Development examine an idea for "minimarkets" in the barriadas. These were intended to increase the efficiency of food distribution to the poor. The idea was dropped, however, after IBEC found that the minimarket would be unable to compete with the traditional *bodega* or tiny family-run grocery store.[30]

After the sugar lands owned by Grace were expropriated in 1969, that company took a variety of steps to encourage a rapid settlement of the compensation issue along lines satisfactory to management. One such step was to propose to the government that Grace conduct a thoroughgoing technical study of integrated use of all the expropriated coastal estates. The basic idea was that the aggregated output of the several new sugar cooperatives could be harnessed to a unified industrial operation producing paper and chemicals. In short, the Paramonga concept of interrelated use of raw materials and multiple by-products would be expanded greatly in scope. The government initially expressed keen interest in the idea, inasmuch as the Andean Pact was materializing and this would mean a sizable market. Moreover newsprint could then be produced locally; control by the government of this imported commodity would have political advantages because of leverage the regime would then possess over the press. But despite initial indications that the government was favorably inclined it later rejected the idea for unknown reasons.[31]

During the economic crises of late 1967 a number of related incidents happened that illustrate perfectly the institutional favor, although on an unusually extensive scale. The currency devaluation of September 1 created an atmosphere of economic emergency that was to heighten as the weeks went by. The sol had dropped from 26.82 to the dollar to more than 38 and was rumored, by mid-October, to fall to 60. Pedro Pessoa, the effervescent GM manager, conceived the idea of organizing a campaign by Lima businessmen to stimulate confidence in the economy. His proposal was to arrange for a series of public statements by business leaders that expressed confidence in the future of Peru and which would be backed by announcements of new investment or expansion. The projects need not be newly planned or large, but, if announced together, he believed, they would create an impression of optimism.[32]

Pessoa approached several businessmen and was greeted by a mixed reaction. The mining companies were definitely not willing to cooperate and, after an initial acceptance of the idea, neither was Grace. Eventually, five entities agreed: Sears, First National City Bank, Lima Light & Power, Industrias Reunidas, S.A. (or INRESA, a Peruvian manufacturer of household appliances), and the Inter-American Development bank.

The campaign was launched November 2, 1967, with Pessoa announcing in a public statement that GM planned to spend 30 million soles in various additions to its plant "because General Motors has ample confidence in the soundness of the Peruvian economy and plentiful trust that the public authorities will solve this transitory crisis." Pessoa went on to tell reporters that "it is an hour that many of us join to conspire, but in favor of Peru, never against Peru."[33]

The next day John Gardner, the Sears president, issued a statement saying that his company was spending 33 million soles to build a warehouse and the new Pueblo Libre store. He specifically endorsed Pessoa's comments of the previous day and said: "This is the response to those who conspire against the stability of the Peruvian economy."[34] Three days later, November 6, Jack West, resident vice-president of First National City Bank, announced that the bank would open a new agency and, furthermore, had decided to purchase 40 million soles in Peruvian government bonds. West identified himself with what was by now being called the "conspiracy in favor of Peru" but he added that he did not like the pejorative connotations of the word "conspiracy."[35] On November 8 the Inter-American Development Bank representative came out with a similar statement of confidence and an announcement of plans for a $30 million loan to Peru.[36] On November 9 INRESA's manager—who happened also to be the current president of the National Society of Industries—told reporters that his confidence in the future of Peru was proven by his firm's plan to invest 25 million soles in plant expansion.[37] The campaign was completed on November 15 by a statement from Dr. Carlos Mariotti, general manager of Lima Light & Power, that his expansion program would continue and that, despite the devaluation, the World Bank had loaned the firm $17.5 million for new projects.[38]

It is impossible to know the economic effects of Pessoa's venture. Pessoa himself naturally feels it was a great success. Gardner doubted that it had had any economic impact whatever. Nevertheless the sol did not slide down further, at least for the time being. When questioned on the episode in 1970, former President Belaúnde expressed appreciation for it as a positive and helpful act.[39]

A particularly interesting aspect to the episode is that many observers felt the objectives of the campaign were not economic at all but political. A quite significant by-election was taking place on November 12, 1967. The most important contest was between Carlos Cueto of AP and Enrique Chirinos Soto of the APRA-UNO coalition over a vacant seat representing Lima in the Chamber of Deputies. All parties were watching the contest closely for signs of weakening government support. The Apristas and many others believed Pessoa was simply trying to improve the chances of Cueto. There was sentiment at IPC and elsewhere in the foreign investor community that the whole thing constituted an unhealthy "meddling" in politics. At any rate Chirinos Soto beat Cueto by the sizable margin of 90,000 votes, suggesting the outcome had not been affected. Pessoa himself insists the election had had nothing to do with his effort.

It is not known what General Motors itself got from the campaign, if anything, other than newspaper publicity and apparent goodwill with Belaúnde. But informant reports indicate at least two institutional corporate favors granted during the 1967-1968 economic crisis had a specific payoff. The decision by First National City Bank to purchase 40 million soles in bonds (approximately a million dollars worth) was made not just from kindness but in return for a government favor: the making available to the Bank of a quantity of dollar exchange for sale to its customers. Few Lima banks had sufficient U.S. dollars to supply customer demand, which was very heavy at this time because of the sol's weakness. First National City was delighted to get the dollars because it could satisfy its customers and earn the commission on exchange of currency.

Another quid pro quo associated with the economic crisis was a neat arrangement between the government and the Federation of Radio Broadcasters. This trade association agreed to have its member stations broadcast progovernment commercials in return for advancement in the

Peruvian Congress of certain legislation sought by the broadcast industry. Several spots were used; the text of one reads: "Many of the restrictive measures taken by the present cabinet are of temporary character for the crisis only. Overcoming this crisis rapidly depends on the conduct of each and every Peruvian. Peru asks your faith and confidence."[40]

When the coup struck on October 3, 1968, the companies that had been laboring hard to support the Belaúnde government suddenly found themselves with totally valueless political credits at the presidential palace or ministries. Very quickly, however, certain corporations that had been comparatively silent during the 1967-1968 economic crisis suddenly spoke out. These were Marcona and Belco Petroleum, two U.S. enterprises with long-standing expansion plans which chose to stress their plans publicly just a few days *after* the Revolution. Although officials of Belco deny this action had any political significance, Marcona executives frankly agree that the stimulation of favorable relations with the new regime was the objective. Marcona's statement, issued approximately one week after the overthrow, said in part: "Marcona Mining Company is interested in carrying out the expansion of its plant and installations . . . at the earliest opportunity. . . . An investment of approximately U.S. $25 million is required to carry out this expansion program."[41]

The chairman of Belco, Arthur Belfer, flew in from New York just ten days after the coup to confer with the new leadership. After his meetings a statement was issued, extracts of which are:

Belco Petroleum Corporation will increase its investments in Peru by $15 million annually and will start exploiting deposits on the continental shelf . . . within 90 days . . .

Belco thus proves its confidence in Peru and its decision to continue working and contributing to the development of the country and the solution of one of its most important problems: the deficit in the production of petroleum.[42]

Both of these corporations, it is worth noting, prospered under the Revolution and continued to expand their investments in Peru. Pessoa's GM plant, on the other hand, has been closed since 1970.

Mass Communications and PR

Use of the mass communications media to cultivate and mold Peruvian public opinion may be looked upon both as a potential avenue of access to decision-makers and as a possible means of influence. If decision-makers are at all responsive to public opinion, publicity may be an indirect route to governmental leadership. Then, too, the entire society may be the target of publicity. As we have seen, some writers envisage a kind of cultural subversion being perpetuated by the communication activities of U.S.

capitalism. In a state of mass psychological domination decision-makers could, conceivably, have little choice but to favor the corporations—or, more accurately, they may perceive no choice but to do so. This, supposedly, is a society in an advanced state of leprous penetration, to use Malpica's metaphor.

No attempt to operationalize the concept of cultural domination nor to measure it is made in this book. Limited materials which have relevance to this notion are presented when they emerge as a by-product of other lines of inquiry. But the very fact that there is a Peruvian "Revolution" whose aims and policies are associated with a reduction of foreign influences offers a prima facie case that if cultural "domination" exists it is not strong enough to keep the country's leaders from perceiving a need to increase independence and to intensify national pride. Nor is it enough to keep the Peruvian government from acting clearly against the interests of U.S. business.

Of direct interest here are the postulates concerning mass communications found in the first two hypotheses. Hypothesis I predicts that American corporations utilize "control of the mass media" as one means of influencing public policy. Hypothesis IA states the very different expectation that instead of seeking to control policies the companies will engage in one of two defensive communications strategies: minimizing public visibility or building a favorable public image.

We turn first to the matter of media control. As far as ownership is concerned, American investments in Peruvian broadcasting and publishing are minor. The Revolution's General Communications Law, decreed in November 1971, requires that television stations be at least 51 percent government-owned and radio stations 25 percent. Also their employees and private owners must be Peruvian-born and reside in Peru six months of each year. Even prior to these stipulations U.S. capital was little involved in the industry; to my knowledge none of the 19 television stations and only 2 of the 222 radio stations had significant American participation. The exceptions are SPCC's radio outlet in Toquepala and a Lima good-music station.

Revolutionary policy toward the press is grounded in the so-called "Freedom of the Press" law, decreed in January 1970. It stipulates that all proprietors, editors, and shareholders of newspapers and periodicals published in Peru must be Peruvian-born and reside in the country no less than six months each year. Aside from company house organs and cultural reviews, the only American-owned publication of prominence is the *Peruvian Times*, a weekly. The predecessors of this English-language newsmagazine can be traced back more than a century. Although widely read by the American and British colonies and some Peruvians, it is not a mass-readership publication. The *Peruvian Times* was able to continue publishing under the new law by rearrangement of its masthead; the

American publisher retired and a Peruvian long associated with the enterprise was named director.[43]

As for possible methods of control of the media outside of ownership, several forms of American involvement exist, but because of competition and other factors the degree of influence is in most instances problematical. In the magazine field *Selecciones del Reader's Digest* was for years among the top ten in sales and had a circulation of 40,000 in 1970.[44] Before its discontinuance the Latin American edition of *Life* also sold quite widely. But these publications have scores of Peruvian-owned and published competitors and are insignificant in the totality of the magazine market. A large share of international news is received by the Peruvian press via the wires of the Associated Press and United Press International. Agène France-Presse and Reuters are used, however, and since 1970 a Latin American agency has been operating (LATIN). Very possibly the most sensitive realm of mass communications with respect to cultural penetration is motion pictures. All the major U.S. film distributors are active in Peru; they must, however, obtain an import license and censorship approval for each film. Motion pictures of many other countries, including socialist, are exhibited.[45]

Commercial advertising is likely the single most sensitive area of mass-communications involvement by U.S. corporations in Peru. The two largest advertising agencies are American-owned, McCann-Erickson Corporation Publicidad and J. Walter Thompson Peruana. Together they handle approximately one-fourth of total agency billings. Of the top fourteen advertisers in Peru in 1969 (in billings) five were American companies: Sears, Proctor & Gamble, Colgate-Palmolive, Coca-Cola, and Braniff. Sears may be the biggest single advertiser in the country and certainly is in the newspaper field; in large part it introduced full-page, illustrated, announced-price advertising to the Lima press.[46]

One can only speculate as to the influence this advertising creates over editorial policy. Editorial pages of the Lima dailies are generally controlled directly by the prominent families that own the papers. The attitudes expressed vary greatly, however, including those toward American business. *El Comercio*, the leading full-size daily, was owned for decades by the Miro Quesada family and is usually critical of American investors and U.S. foreign policy. Its long-time vehement hostiility to IPC was a major factor in that company's expropriation. The second largest big daily, on the other hand, *La Prensa*, is generally favorable to American interests and was long owned by Pedro Beltrán, an economic conservative who served as premier in the second Prado administration.[47]

When Sears began its large-scale advertising campaigns in the mid-1950's, it sought to place its innovative ads in all major papers. *El Comercio* was unreceptive to the proposal and would not give Sears volume rates. *La Prensa*, on the other hand, immediately cooperated. As a result, Sears has been for many years an important source of revenue for that paper. And it is not a coincidence that Beltrán's morning daily carried frequent articles which gave favorable publicity to Sears; over a twelve-month period in the late 1960's at least twenty news articles appeared which extolled Sears's profit-sharing plan, local purchasing, year-end sales, and other activities. Sears did not pay for these articles; they were a return favor for the huge advertising purchases.

Increasingly in recent years television has replaced the newspapers as the principal medium of Peruvian advertising. Coca-Cola and American automobile and soap companies spend very heavily on this medium. Until its departure IPC did as well. For some time General Motors and Standard Oil of California (operator of "Conchan" refinery and service stations) had a notable advertising monopoly in television evening news programs. Only two extended evening commentaries were broadcast, one sponsored by GM and the other by Conchan. When Pedro Pessoa was asked whether he had ever had any control over the content of his program, the reply was "a few times"; the specific illustration given was when Belaúnde's picture was dropped from the show's format as popular confidence in the president waned toward the end of his administration. Pessoa says he insisted that the presidential image be restored—and it was.[48] By 1971 U.S. corporate sponsorship of television news had declined greatly; one of the major evening shows was sponsored by a government agency and the other by spots purchased by many advertisers.

In commercial advertising, then, we find perhaps the greatest point of vulnerability with respect to American influence in the Peruvian mass media. What about institutional advertising and other forms of public relations? To what extent do U.S. corporations engage in PR and to what extent does PR help them?

As Hypothesis IA states, we do find attempts by the companies to keep a low public silhouette, a kind of "non-PR." Of the top twelve firms of 1968, those who seemed to follow this strategy were Anderson Clayton and Grace. In all publicity these enterprises stressed the names of their separate affiliates and plants. These were given Spanish-language names and all company products carried Spanish names. Thus "Fábrica Monserrate" and "Ransa" were known in the popular mind as local producers and distributers of cottonseed oil rather than Anderson Clayton. "La Gaviota," "Arturo Field y La Estrella," and "Sociedad Paramonga" were given, to the extent possible, public identities separate from Grace. Even though collectively Grace was long one of the largest Peruvian firms, it never projected the image of giantism given by Cerro de Pasco or SPCC.

The opposite strategy is to carry on an active program of image-building. This was the policy of more than half of the top twelve companies. IPC, Goodyear, and the telephone company did this for many years. Relative newcomers to Peru such as Sears and General Motors were publicity-conscious from their arrival. For many decades Cerro de Pasco attempted to minimize its public visibility, but beginning in about 1965 a switch was made to a highly activist strategy. Southern Peru Copper Corporation went through a similar transition starting about 1967.

As for specific techniques, institutional advertising was stressed by the extractive industries. For some years Cerro placed newspaper and magazine ads which described the advantages to Peru of its medical centers, local purchases, and newly opened mines. In the latter 1960's the copy became increasingly sophisticated, emphasizing photographs rather than lengthy text and distinctly Peruvian themes rather than descriptions of new mines. SPCC frequently bought newspaper advertising space to proclaim the fact that it is the biggest income-tax payer in Peru and that more than half its profits go to the national treasury. Prior to its expropriation, IPC often published statements with headings such as "Communiqué from International Petroleum" in which it endeavored to answer charges of wrongdoing against it levied by *El Comercio* or other company enemies. (They were not run, however, in *El Comercio*.) IPC ran institutional ads on its television series from time to time; one of the devices used was favorable employee testimonials taken at Talara.[49]

Almost the whole gamut of other PR techniques was additionally employed. For years the words "Goodyear" and "Esso" blinked nightly in neon on Lima's skyline (they were replaced by "Toyota" and "Petroperú" with the Revolution). For generations the only roadsigns in more remote parts of the country were weatherbeaten Goodyear diamonds that also carried directions to the next town. Out of the hope that familiarity breeds more than contempt, the mining companies brought busloads of school children and other visitors to their company towns and mine-sites. IPC, which undoubtedly had the largest PR budget of any U.S. firm in Peru, produced expensive color documentaries for exhibition in motion picture theaters and brought to Peruvian television international films and a series ("Tempus") which portrayed Peruvian cultural history via art objects contained in Lima museums.[50]

Anxious to court the intellectuals as well as the masses, the IPC public relations department also sponsored journalism contests, held exhibitions for Peruvian painters, and published a quarterly cultural review, *Fanal*. This slick-paper, full-color magazine was devoted almost entirely to articles on Peruvian art, history, education, and other such topics and contained no political commentary or company propaganda. The review was distributed without charge and had hemisphere-wide circulation. The *Fanal* idea was later copied for a time by SPCC and Marcona. After IPC's expropriation Petroperú began publishing *Cope*, a very similar effort except that it contained considerable Revolutionary propaganda. Petroperú put out maps, calendars, a prestige volume on anthropology, and other items—obviously it was attempting to live up to the publishing standards of its predecessor.*

If Grace and Anderson Clayton kept their heads down, and IPC and the mining companies mounted professional PR campaigns, General Motors relied on the personal color and ingenuity of Pedro Pessoa. He once commissioned, amidst much publicity, the creation of a group of sculptured objects by a Peruvian artist to decorate the plant's central offices. He also insisted that a small symbol of Incan Peru—the *chasqui*—be placed on the rear window of all GM automobiles and hung from a give-away keychain. Even Pessoa's personal activities seemed designed to attract publicity; on one occasion he was prominently pictured in the newspapers leading, in a short-pants uniform, a street parade of Boy Scouts for whom he was leader. This behavior achieved much attention for the GM manager but it also generated considerable dismay among more dignified local businessmen.

The U.S. corporations, like their counterparts back home, customarily budget a certain amount of support for charitable good works. Grants to private individuals and groups are seen as a way of building good will and securing useful publicity. In Peru a particularly popular object of corporate giving is education; apparently its "goodness" is perceived as undeniable. Not infrequently gifts are made to finance the construction or improvement of school buildings or the purchase of furniture and books. Normally, although not always, the checks are handed over in a ceremony with press photographers present. The big companies generally have scholarship programs, with most of the stipends going to employees or employee children. In 1962 Dr. East of Marcona went beyond the usual limited company program and founded a permanent organization for cooperative scholarship-giving, the *Instituto Peruano de Fomento Educativo*. Over a decade this institution spent approximately one million dollars for loans, scholarships, and gifts of transportation, equipment, and tools. Its contributors have included not only Marcona but Sears, IBM, IPC, Grace, and the Council of the Americas.[51]

Usually the corporations try to give the impression of reacting generously to natural catastrophes. This is exemplified by conduct following the tremendous Peruvian earthquake of May 31, 1970. The worst disaster of its kind in hemisphere history, the quake wiped out several entire towns and killed 50,000 to 70,000 persons. Immediately Cerro, Grace, and Marcona each donated a million soles (about $22,000) in cash or goods and SPCC gave two million. IPC surprised the generals by sending $50,000

---

*Petroperú also inserted nationalistic themes into its commercial advertising. Its motor oil was promoted as "el lubricante con el aditivo decisivo ... PERUANIDAD ... es mejor ... y es nuestro!" ("The lubricant with the decisive additive ... PERUVIANNESS ... it is better ... and it is ours!")

down from Coral Gables. All told, $16.4 million was contributed from private U.S. sources compared to $10.3 million from the American government and $21.3 million from all other sources.[52]

More than just financial help was given, however. The mining companies were on the spot and had useful equipment. A Helio Courier plane owned by Cerro was the first to land in the Callejon de Huaylas area; this was not publicized by the company, however, out of fear of embarrassing the Peruvian air force. Considerable publicity was, however, given to a Cerro land convoy sent in the "back way" from Cerro de Pasco and Huánuco, that is, via the sierra instead of the coast. Cerro had originally built parts of the connecting road and had the necessary vehicles on hand to clear it. Later SPCC sent a truck convoy in from the sea to Cajatambo, a village that had not yet been reached. Because of its airport, nearness to the ocean, and communication and warehouse facilities, Paramonga became a logical staging area for many rescue operations. Peruvian military helicopters operated from the hacienda and U.S. helicopters flew from the aircraft carrier *Guam*, anchored offshore near Paramonga. Although most of these activites received ample publicity in the Peruvian press the PR payoff may have been slim; at this moment of great national emergency everyone was contributing who could, and help merely assured that adverse publicity would not result from a failure to assist.[53]

What of the effectiveness of corporate publicity activities in general? With their great financial resources and PR expertise, can the companies "purchase" sufficient favorable public opinion so as to bring indirect pressure upon governmental decision-makers?

The results of a number of public opinion polls conducted in Peru between 1958 and 1966 are available to help provide an answer. The most relevant data are reproduced in Tables 12, 13, and 14. Table 12 portrays the overall popularity of foreign business in Peru as of 1966. The picture is one of ambivalence strongly tinged with negativism. Although two-thirds of Peruvians believed that foreign capital contributes to "development" of the country and more than a fifth believed it contributes more than domestic capital, nearly 45 percent felt local firms contributed equally or more and over 70 percent believed they made less profits. When student opinion is examined it is found that a slim majority perceive American business as "harmful" and the vast majority believe that foreign business influence is "too much." Thus, almost all Peruvian students shared the fear of economic imperialism to some degree.

Table 13 presents data which permit comparisons over time. Polls were conducted in 1958, 1961, 1962, and 1966 in which identical questions were not asked but some kind of inquiry was made with respect to the desirability of getting rid of existing foreign assets in Peru. The outcome is a steady decline in the percentage that favored the enterprises. Whereas in 1958 only 36 percent of Lima residents wanted American investments limited, reduced, or eliminated and 59 percent wanted them increased, eight years later three-quarters wanted all or some foreign enterprises nationalized.

Table 14 concerns sentiment for nationalization as of 1966 in more detail. A plurality of Limeños favored nationalization of some enterprises but not all. When those "some" are identified one finds a wide range of feeling both by industry and company. Clearly, IPC stands in a class by itself; if the 31.2 percent favoring expropriation of all foreign enterprise is added to IPC's own 20.4 percent, the total is a majoritarian sentiment of 51.6 percent favoring nationalization. No other enterprise or group is nearly that high. The next worst in popularity are the communications and mining industries, which can only mean Cía. Peruana de Teléfonos and the gran minería. Yet when the ratings of Cerro, SPCC, and Marcona are

Table 12. Public Opinion in Lima on Contributions, Profits, and Influence of Foreign Business, 1966.

Question and response	General public (percentage of total)
Whether foreign enterprises contribute to development:	
Yes	66.0
No	30.8
Some or partial	2.3
Whether foreign enterprises contribute more or less than Peruvian enterprises to development:	
More	22.6
Equal	26.6
Less	18.2
Whether foreign enterprises make more or less profits than Peruvian enterprises:	
More	70.9
Equal	24.6
Less	3.2

	Students only (percentage of total)
North American business activities are:	
Helpful	42
Harmful	51
No opinion	7
Foreign business influence is:	
Too much	86
Right amount	8
Too little	1

Sources: Opinion of general public: survey conducted under auspices of Council of the Americas (unpublished). Student opinion: U.S. Information Agency, Research and Reference Service, "Political Attitudes of Latin American Students" (1966).

noted, it is found that their percentages are roughly in the 3 percent range, which is nothing compared to IPC and is even less than Lima Light & Power. By these standards Grace, Sears, and Goodyear scored even better.

What is the meaning of all this? First, the popularity of foreign capital sank very significantly in the latter 1950's and early and mid-1960's. It is difficult to interpret Peruvian society as psychologically dominated by foreign capital when three-quarters of the residents of the capital city want some or all of it expropriated. Second, a correlation does not appear between publicity effort and mass image. IPC, with by far the most ambitious PR program, had by far the worst image. The mining companies, Sears, and Goodyear all had activist PR strategies, but the gran minería did far worse than Sears and Goodyear. Grace, with its low silhouette, was intermediate. Obviously other variables are at work. Third, the Velasco regime was clearly riding the tide of popular opinion when it confiscated IPC. The telephone company also, apparently, was carrying

Table 13. Public Opinion in Lima on Limiting and Expropriating Foreign Business, 1958–1966.

Year	Inquiry	General public (percentage of total)
1958		
	U.S. business investments should be limited, reduced, or eliminated	36
	U.S. business investments should be increased	59
1961		
	Foreign property should be expropriated by the government	39
	Foreign property should not be expropriated by the government	39
1962		
	Large holdings and industries of foreigners should be expropriated	47
	Large holdings and industries of foreigners should not be expropriated	33
1966		
	All or some foreign enterprises should be nationalized by the state	75
	No foreign enterprises should be nationalized by the state	24

Sources: 1958 data: Survey conducted by International Research Associates, as reproduced in Leland L. Johnson, *U.S. Private Investment in Latin America: Some Questions of National Policy* (Santa Monica, Calif., Rand Corporation, 1964). 1961 data: U.S. Information Agency, Research and Reference Service, "The Climate of Opinion in Latin America for the Alliance for Progress" (1961). 1962 data: U.S. Information Agency, Research and Reference Service, "The *Alianza* After One Year" (1962). 1966 data: unpublished survey conducted under auspices of Council of the Americas.

more than its share of animosity prior to nationalization. But, obviously, the generals were not using this particular poll as a guide to policy, for they did not expropriate mining and they did take sugar.

Recapitulation

The corporations definitely "lobby" at the councils and bureaucracies of government. The use of professional lobbyists, legislative representatives, and political parties for this purpose is comparatively insignificant. However, business interest groups form an important avenue of access.

In some instances the corporations are in close association with conservative economic elites in this lobbying effort. Many companies cultivate contacts in upper-class circles via aristocratic Peruvians and organizations

Table 14. Public Opinion in Lima on Nationalization of Individual Industries and Companies, 1966.

Question and response	General public (percentage of total)
Extent to which foreign enterprises in Peru should be nationalized by the state:	
All enterprises	31.2
Some enterprises	43.8
No enterprises	24.3
Industries cited by those favoring nationalization of "some enterprises":	
Communications	7.1
Mining	7.0
Transportation	3.8
Banks	1.1
Public services	1.0
Textiles	0.7
Power	.5
Fishmeal	.2
Sugar	.1
Companies cited by those favoring nationalization of "some enterprises":	
IPC	20.4
Lima Light & Power	4.3
Cerro	3.2
SPCC	2.7
Marcona	2.6
Grace	1.1
Casa Grande	0.4
Sears	.2
Goodyear	.2

Source: Unpublished survey conducted under auspices of Council of the Americas.

such as the Club Nacional. The enterprises belong to traditionally elitist groups such as the National Agrarian Society when it is functionally logical to do so.

The corporations are not, however, bound to upper-class connections in their pressure activity. Some business groups are not associated with the old Peruvian oligarchy, a prime example being the American Chamber of Commerce. The fact that much lobbying is done directly by company executives permits the corporations to seek access to policy-makers not associated with the traditional elite, such as middle-class military officers of the Velasco regime.

It appears that the business groups, although extremely influential in policy formulation in the past, became much less so with the advent of the Revolution. They and individual corporations were unable to alter the basic course of reform. Although for a time the Velasco government held itself largely incommunicado from the business community, by 1971 it was circulating draft decrees and engaging in dialogue. By this time concessions became possible on the details of policy.

Informal cash gifts and favors are used to "buy" influence and services. The corporations make cash payments to political parties, bureaucrats, and journalists for reciprocal benefits. However, in doing so the companies follow local customs rather than introduce venality from the outside. Large-scale bribery, as distinguished from petty tips and contributions, occurred in the past but does not seem commonplace today. Apparently it is practiced less by American firms than by European and Japanese business interests. American companies are, however, often prepared to do favors for the regime or its programs in order to build good will or transact a specific quid pro quo. Typical favors are loans, operational assistance, and public statements of endorsement.

The corporations are self-conscious about their public image. Although they do not directly control Peruvian mass media to a meaningful extent, as major advertisers they are in a position to obtain favored treatment in some publicity organs. A few firms follow a PR strategy of low visibility; others are capable of mounting elaborate public relations campaigns and programs of charitable good works. But such efforts do not necessarily work. IPC, with its expensive and elaborate PR activity, could not avoid a uniquely adverse reputation on the part of the Peruvian public. Generally public sentiment toward foreign business declined radically in the period 1958-1966, giving no indication of cultural "domination" by the international capitalists.

Five   Behavior of the U.S. Government

It would be logical to expect the *American* government to aid *American* corporations abroad. Corporate requests for such aid would, perhaps, be similarly expected. Conceivably home-government support of foreign capital could become a major contributor to corporate influence vis-à-vis host governments. The most blatant form of assistance would be where the corporation, facing undesired host-government policies, seeks home-government pressure upon the host government to alter those policies.

The economic imperialism theorists contemplate precisely this type of collaboration and intervention. Hypothesis I predicts "intervention by the American government" on behalf of U.S. corporations in Peru. Hypothesis IA, on the other hand, incorporating the view that U.S. government and business seldom cooperate well, states that the companies "do not seek important intervention from U.S. authorities." This latter prediction assumes also that the firms do not get significant support, at least in response to requests.

Historical Cases of Intervention

At least as far as the historical past is concerned, the record is clearly not entirely in accord with the noninterventionist interpretation. Aggressive diplomatic interventions on behalf of U.S. commercial interests in Peru can be traced back to the beginning of that country's republican existence. Almost immediately upon U.S. recognition of the Peruvian state in 1826, American envoys in Lima were demanding payment by the young government of damage claims presented by American citizens. The early claims were largely minor matters, but this did not keep the United States from pressing the Peruvians incessantly, almost as if the objective were to teach them proper principles of international responsibility. Damages for which compensation was sought included the sequestering of American ships by the Peruvian military and the blowing up of American-owned mineshafts by revolutionaries. Eventually most claims were paid, but considerably below the amounts demanded.[1]

By the 1840's the Amazon basin had become an object of great romantic and commercial interest for certain North Americans. U.S. steamboat operators anticipated a bonanza and sought monopoly concessions on the Amazon and its tributaries. In 1848 one Audley H. Gazzam, a steamboat

entrepreneur from Baltimore, was vigorously represented before the
Peruvian government by John Randolph Clay, for many years the U.S.
chargé d'affaires to Lima. The Gazzam proposal was turned down, but
Clay continued to press by having bills introduced in the Peruvian
legislature that would admit Americans to this field of endeavor. Finally in
1867-1868 both Peru and Brazil opened their rivers to the vessels of all
nations, largely in response to intensive pressures from the U.S. government.[2]

The Peruvian guano boom of the mid-nineteenth century also stimulated
much international maneuvering by foreign governments in Peru. At that
time this natural fertilizer became of immense importance to British and
American agriculture. By means of unusually adroit pressure the British
were able to obtain control over the international marketing of this
commodity and in addition siphon off half of Peru's income from it to pay
defaulted London bondholders. It was in the interests of the English (and
the Peruvians, temporarily) to keep the world guano price pegged high.
The high price greatly perturbed tobacco growers of the American South,
however, and accordingly the tobacco lobby in Washington sought U.S.
government actions directed toward breaking the British monopoly.
Several congressional investigations were held on the subject. The U.S.
consul in Lima pleaded with the Peruvians to end the consignment
arrangements. President Millard Fillmore stated in his first annual message:
"Peruvian guano has become so desirable an article to the agricultural
interest of the United States that it is the duty of the Government to
employ *all the means properly in its power* for the purpose of causing that
article to be imported into the country at a reasonable price. Nothing will
be omitted on my part toward accomplishing this desirable end" [italics
added].[3]

No better illustration of this policy could be found than an incident that
occurred in 1852 concerning the Lobos Islands. This is a pair of guano
islands, one of which is only fifteen miles off the Peruvian coast. They
were clearly Peruvian territory, having been part of the Spanish viceroyalty
prior to independence. Even the British government recognized this;
London, in fact, had refused to support the claims of private British
citizens that the islands belonged to Britain.

But one A.G. Benson, A New Yorker, noted this British disclaimer and
persuaded a business partner, Captain James C. Jewett, to approach the
aging Secretary of State Daniel Webster on the possibility of claiming
American sovereignty over the Lobos. Webster responded by informing
Jewett, supposedly with President Fillmore's approval, that since an
American had visited the islands in 1823 they were therefore under
American control. Benson then chartered vessels with which to remove
Lobos guano. Webster helped by sending an American warship to the
islands to protect the operation. However, the dubious legal basis of the

scheme was soon made clear by the New York press, and after several months the embarrassed Fillmore administration was forced to reverse its position and recognize Peruvian sovereignty over the islands. Uncle Sam was no match for John Bull in the guano politics of the time.[4]

When Peru began to constitute a significant site of American investments around the turn of the century, the U.S. government actively promoted the establishment of American-owned enterprises in situations where capital of other nationalities was also seeking to secure a foothold. An early illustration of this is when the State Department assisted the Haggin Syndicate in establishing what was later to be known as the Cerro de Pasco Copper Corporation. To make the planned investment viable the syndicate needed to secure mining claims from a number of different owners. In purchasing these rights the group ran head-on with another mining enterprise, Empresa Socavonera del Cerro de Pasco, which was largely Peruvian-owned. A strenuous litigation arose between the two rival interests. The Haggin group, despairing of their chances in this fight, sought help from the American government. The U.S. minister in Lima reportedly devoted much of his time and energies to this matter between 1903 and 1906. Late in 1906 a syndicate representative, W.C. Gulliver, personally called on Secretary of State Elihu Root in Washington. By early 1908 the legation in Lima reported that the dispute had been successfully settled in the Haggin group's favor, with Root's "personal expression of interest in the matter" an important factor in determining the outcome.[5]

Once U.S. companies were established in Peru, American diplomats in Lima maintained close relationships with them. In the first decades of the twentieth century the American community in Lima was relatively small and New York headquarters were many days away. These factors encouraged a sense of intimacy and an identification of interest in foreign business-government relationships at the remote South American capital. The tone of contemporary diplomatic cable traffic between Lima and Washington is revealing in this respect. The following are excerpts from messages from the chargé d'affaires in Lima, Ferdinand L. Mayer, following the overthrow of Leguía by Sánchez Cerro in 1930. As is known, Leguía had been very good to American capital; local U.S. businessmen were jittery over what was to come and the uncertainty was amplified by a certain amount of rioting in Lima and suburbs. Mayer wired Secretary of State Stimson:

August 25 [1930], 4 p.m.: I do not like the look of things at all nor does Admiral [William S.] Pye [of the U.S. naval mission]. We believe immediate preparatory steps should be taken at Panama looking toward dispatch of naval force here for protection of American lives and interests . . .
August 26, 1 p.m.: . . . When I went downtown from the Embassy

yesterday afternoon to ask special protection for the National City Bank, the crowds were in a very nasty mood . . .
August 26, 11 p.m.: . . . Mr. Harold Kingsmill, local representative of Cerro de Pasco Corporation and for many years resident here, called upon me this morning and suggested the desirability of war vessels being sent here. He feels situation very unstable and that better wait and see what Sánchez Cerro will do in next day or two. Kingsmill somewhat apprehensive of conditions at mines as laborers using typical radical manifesto . . .
August 27, 1 p.m.: . . . If the Department agrees I should like to take this line of constitutional continuity with Sánchez Cerro [whereby he succeeds Leguía] in my first conversations with him which may be when introducing Mr. Kingsmill who wants to discuss Cerro de Pasco affairs with him at earliest moment practicable.

A few days later the absent American ambassador, Fred Morris Dearing, returned to Lima and recommended to Washington that the Sánchez regime be recognized. One of the reasons given was that the new president had immediately responded to the Embassy's request that Peruvian troops be sent to Cerro de Pasco to quell labor disorders. Another was that executives of several major U.S. firms, including Kingsmill of Cerro, had told the Embassy that they accepted and desired diplomatic recognition of the Sánchez government.[6]

Certainly one of the most aggressive diplomatic campaigns on behalf of foreign capital in Peru was the support given to the International Petroleum Company between 1915 and 1922. But London and Ottawa were the principal origins of the pressure rather than Washington, owing to Standard Oil's foresightedness in incorporating IPC in Canada. One of the reasons for this action had been that the British were known to be diplomatically active and adroit in protecting the capital of the Empire.

The lobbying by LeSueur and Teagle to keep IPC from being required to pay full taxes was accompanied by diplomatic pressure. In 1915, after the Peruvian government decreed that London & Pacific (controlled by Standard) would have to pay full taxes, Standard Oil wired the State Department in Washington that the Peruvians were "imposing and enforcing destructive and actual confiscatory tax" on the company. The telegram asked that Washington intercede to the extent of seeking delays so that London & Pacific could argue its case. Two days later the department instructed U.S. Ambassador Benton McMillin in a coded message that he should seek the desired delays. Later the ambassador replied from Lima that the tax was not new and was in fact owed by the company.[7]

London took a far tougher stance. The British ambassador in Lima delivered a note that demanded simply, "the Peruvian Government shall find a way to annul the Decree of March 15th."[8] When the Peruvians did not back down, IPC, in 1916, petitioned the British government to propose arbitration of the case or referral to the International Court of Justice at The Hague. To buttress its case the company told the Privy Council in London that if London & Pacific were required to pay full taxes this would constitute "confiscation." Such action in turn would make the property "available for German interests," who were reportedly willing to buy it. This barely disguised warning had high relevance to London in the midst of the Great War. But Whitehall was not moved by the national security argument and replied that all Peruvian remedies must first be exhausted.[9]

International arbitration of the case would in any event require approval by the Peruvian Congress, and Standard meanwhile acted to secure such approval. We shall explain in the next chapter how IPC threatened curtailment of company operations as a means of generating pressure. These local threats were overshadowed when, with great convenience to IPC, the Canadian government suddenly requisitioned for wartime purposes the two company tankers available for the Talara-Callao run. The result was an economic crisis; Lima had only a month's supply of oil. The Peruvian government appealed frantically for release of the tankers. Meanwhile IPC urged that the Peruvians agree to submit to arbitration. Finally Canada released one tanker, which went into Peruvian service in early November 1918. Within a month the Peruvian Congress had adopted a law authorizing submission of the La Brea y Pariñas dispute to international arbitration.

Still more Peruvian cooperation was needed to satisfy the oil company's needs. The arbitration statute authorized the president of Peru to reach an accord with the British on arbitration procedures. But the reluctant President Pardo did not move ahead. This problem was suddenly solved, however, when in July 1919 Leguía took over the presidential palace. The new president agreed to go ahead with arbitration providing IPC consented to pay one million dollars in cash to the Peruvian treasury. LeSueur recommended acceptance of the deal to Teagle and Smith, and they reluctantly agreed. Immediately the president went ahead with negotiations for arbitration and in 1921 an "Agreement for Arbitration" was signed between Britain and Peru.

Representatives of each of these governments plus the president of the Swiss Federal Court were to serve as the arbitration tribunal. Before the tribunal even met, however, a settlement had been reached. LeSueur had engineered a prior agreement which was signed in March 1922 in Lima by the Peruvian foreign minister and the British minister to Peru. This "Agreement for Settlement" provided for a pro-IPC compromise that taxed worked portions of the oil fields at the regular rate but unworked parts at a greatly reduced rate. The $1 million payment demanded by Leguía was provided for and was regarded as a final settlement of all claims pending. The tribunal then convened briefly in Paris the following April and merely declared this settlement as their decision. Supposedly it thus became binding as international law, although many Peruvians strongly reject any such notion. Some of the arguments against the "Award" or "Laudo," as it is called, are that the pro forma verdict of the tribunal was improper, that its Swiss member was not president of the Federal Court at time of signature, that the Peruvian Executive had exceeded his powers, and that the original arbitration documents do not exist. These allegations and several others are all strongly disputed by IPC.[10]

Contemporary Diplomatic Conduct

These examples of strenuous interventionist behavior and gunboat diplomacy occurred many decades ago and in some cases during the last century. Does such "imperalist" activity take place on behalf of U.S. business in present-day Peru?

In the process of answering that question it must be stressed that the bulk of diplomatic activity on behalf of American companies in Peru or any other country is quite mundane. Much of it consists of a mere interchange of information, such as between the corporate executives and embassy officers on the one hand and the embassy and the Peruvian government on the other. This intercourse almost always consists of informal conversation rather than the presentation of formal appeals or protests. Washington usually is not involved except for the receipt of reports.

John Wesley Jones, U.S. Ambassador to Peru from 1963 to 1969, inaugurated an institutionalized forum for the interchange of information between the U.S. corporations and himself. He established a monthly "businessmen's meeting" to be attended by twenty to thirty American executives and several from the embassy staff, with himself presiding. In doing this Jones was emulating a practice that had sprung up at several other U.S. diplomatic posts and was encouraged by the Department of State. The meetings were continued by Jones's successor, Ambassador Taylor G. Belcher. They were closed to all outsiders and a member of the embassy staff prepared a confidential summary of the discussion for the files. Ambassador Jones conducted the meetings quite informally, with himself typically briefing the executives on changes in American foreign policy and the businessmen in turn explaining whatever problems they were currently facing. General observations were exchanged on Peruvian political figures and events.[11]

These meetings were not the only method of communication between Jones and the executives. When a businessman had a particularly delicate matter to discuss he would see the ambassador by individual appointment. In fact, it seems plausible that the businessmen would not use these rather large forums with competitors present in some cases as the place to be totally candid about their dealings with the Peruvians.

The American Chamber of Commerce generally prepared the guest list for the meetings. Originally the Chamber (then known as CONOPROPE) invited only its own members. Jones terminated that practice because it meant that SPCC and Marcona were automatically omitted. The Chamber continued to make up the list of invitees, however. This was true even though the meetings were sponsored by the Embassy and not the Chamber and were held at the Embassy rather than Chamber offices.

U.S. diplomats are specifically assigned the function euphemistically referred to as "diplomatic protection." In relation to American business overseas this means acting on behalf of U.S. companies that are the object of actions that are interpreted as potentially discriminatory or illegal. In the words of the State Department's *Foreign Affairs Manual*, "Foreign Service posts are responsible for assisting legitimate American enterprises abroad when local authorities discriminate against them or violate rights granted by treaty or international comity. The nature and extent of post intervention depends in each case on the degree of prejudice to the American interests concerned." All such representations must be reported to Washington, the *Manual* goes on, and if they have potential political significance they must be cleared in advance.[12]

The bulk of protective actions involve Washington only passively; the ambassador and his subordinates handle many relatively routine requests on their own and do so in informal discussions with the Peruvian authorities. But, obviously, it is the nonroutine matters that interest us here, namely, those which might conceivably be construed as "intervention" in the sense that imperialism theorists would use that word.

The following pages present a variety of case studies of U.S. governmental action involving American business in Peru. First, three instances are examined in which the State Department alone acted; these might be looked upon as cases of "diplomatic protection" in the traditional sense. Second, three episodes are discussed in which other components of the U.S. government were also involved.

A "good offices" type of representation occurred in connection with Cerro de Pasco's livestock properties. As noted in Chapter Two, Cerro acquired much land in the sierra unassociated with its mining activities after smoke from the La Oroya smelter destroyed vegetation over a large area. In 1936 a taller smokestack was built and in 1941 Cottrell smoke precipitators were installed, making the lands usable for livestock grazing once again. On these lands, collectively amounting to 247,000 hectares, the company raised primarily sheep to furnish a mutton supply to company stores. Over time a prize-winning strain of sheep adapted to the sierra was developed, the "Junín."[13]

Under the agrarian reform law passed in 1964 the Belaúnde government moved to expropriate Cerro's lands. The action assumed unusual political importance because of the fact that Cerro was the landowner and also because of widespread popular feeling that the company had profited financially by its earlier desecration of the area. But Cerro was not prepared to cooperate with the expropriation. A decision was made to fight loss of the lands, even with compensation and even though agriculture was not an indispensable part of the mining operations. Cerro executives defended this position with the argument that the expropriation was technically illegal under the agrarian reform statute. Also, it was lamented, loss of the lands would mean destruction of the Junín breed and an end to plentiful meat for Cerro workers.[14]

In the ensuing controversy Cerro de Pasco acted largely alone without active embassy support. Negotiations took place directly between the corporation and government. However, arrangement of the negotiations was done by Ambassador Jones; he both encouraged and facilitated the holding of talks between Cerro de Pasco's Alberto Benavides and President Belaúnde. Jones did not himself enter the discussions or propose a solution or defend the company point of view.

Although a dialogue was achieved Cerro did not emerge from the episode totally victorious. Belaúnde at one point agreed to permit the company to keep half the lands but he later reneged. The matter then dragged on without settlement (but with Cerro continuing to possess the lands) until early in 1969, when the Velasco government decisively seized them. The corporation was paid 76 million soles cash for its animals (about $1.8 million) and 28 million soles in bonds (about $650,000) for the land itself.[15] These amounts were a fraction of what Cerro had demanded but, back in New York, Robert Koenig was not really dissatisfied.[16]

A case where Ambassador Jones intervened more actively was occasioned by the arrest, in June 1968, of the general manager of Xerox Peruana S.A., Leonard C. Ferry. An American citizen, Ferry was detained on the criminal charge of contraband. The arrest had followed a determination by Peruvian customs officials that Xerox photocopying equipment could not be imported under the duty classification of "printing material" as had been true in the past. Instead, Xerox copiers were classified "photo material," which carried a much higher tariff. The charges against Ferry had been predicated on the theory that conscious use of the previous classification constituted a customs violation. For its part, Xerox Peruana claimed that this classification had been previously accepted by the authorities themselves, in fact for some years.[17]

Ferry was taken into custody but not placed in jail. The American business community in Lima was shocked at what was considered a trumped-up charge. Ambassador Jones, without waiting for any formal request from the Xerox organization, immediately made urgent representations to the appropriate administrative authorities.[18] When this failed he called on President Belaúnde to present a formal protest. The president was personally skeptical about the validity of the charge because of

Xerox's international renown, but he did not interfere.[19] The case went through the normal Peruvian judicial processes and, four months later, Ferry was found innocent by a Peruvian court and released.

The third case of diplomatic conduct is very different, especially from the standpoint of who took the initiative. Cía. Peruana de Teléfonos was in serious political difficulties in the mid-1960's as Lima telephone service steadily deteriorated and the APRA-UNO coalition in Congress became increasingly hostile to an increase in telephone rates. In ITT's eyes a rate increase was essential to investments to expand and improve the telephone system. Yet public hostility over poor service made the rate increase a political football.

During this impasse, ITT was rudely taken aback when representatives of its main U.S. competitor, General Telephone & Electronics Corporation, suddenly appeared in Lima. Anxious to exploit ITT's weak political position and make inroads on its Lima market, in July 1965 GT&E sent two sales executives to Peru to lobby for an alternative solution to Peru's telephone problems. Their first idea, which many APRA-UNO congressmen and military officers found attractive, was to create a new national telecommunications company that would provide both local and long-distance service throughout the country. It would expand service rapidly, according to the promoters, with no cost to the Peruvian budget since its suppliers (GT&E, no doubt) would provide long-term credits.[20]

But when objections were raised to this project another tack was taken: promotion of international bidding for the financing and construction of telephone expansion in Lima. This idea caught hold in the Congress; in early 1967 a bill was passed which would require international bidding for telephone improvements. To become law all it needed was inaction by the president—a failure by him to recommit the measure to the Congress with his "observations." The time limit for this form of veto was February 3, 1967.

ITT executives in New York became so disturbed by this pending law that a telegram was sent to Secretary of State Dean Rusk over the name of Harold S. Geneen, ITT president. The cable, probably dated February 2, 1967, began as follows:[21]

This telegraph is to call your attention to a very urgent and serious situation that at this moment threatens important investments of International Telephone & Telegraph Corporation in Peru.

The Congress of Peru has passed a law which would, in effect, prepare the way for confiscation of our interests there.

The wire then outlined the nature of the legislation and defended a pending alternate settlement that had been worked out with the Belaúnde regime. Stressing the urgency of the situation, Geneen noted that the measure would become law on the following day if the president did not act. The telegram concluded:

> For these reasons, we request the intervention of your Department at the highest level possible. We have always received the fullest cooperation of J. Wesley Jones, your fine ambassador in Lima, as well as his staff in the embassy, but his efforts have been fruitless until now.
>
> We believe that this question concerns much more than the interests of ITT in Peru.
>
> The reputation of Peru as a friend of foreign investment and free enterprise is also at stake. The President of Peru cannot escape these aspects of the law which he has before him.
>
> We will continue to work with Ambassador Jones and with our local contacts, but we believe that an expression of your personal concern about this matter to the Peruvian Embassy in Washington would be very beneficial to resolving this situation. We would also appreciate it if Ambassador Jones would make similar representations to the highest authorities in Lima.
>
> ITT is prepared to discuss the details of this matter with members of your Department at any moment.
>
> Due to the February 3 time limit we are anxious that this law be held up in order to allow sufficient time for all those interested to discuss it sensibly and without pressure.

Specific information is not possessed with respect to State Department action on behalf of ITT. From the text of the telegram itself it would appear that Jones had provided "the fullest cooperation" to the company; yet it is known that generally diplomats dislike choosing sides when competing U.S. companies are fighting it out in an overseas situation. Another point is that there was little time for State Department intervention, for the very next day Belaúnde returned the bill to the Congress, thus killing it for the session. Washington would have had to respond almost immediately with instructions to Jones, followed by quick intervention by the ambassador. I suspect that by this time Belaúnde had already decided what to do anyway.

At this point it would appear that ITT had won the day. But in the midst of the acrimonious final day of the legislative session, February 15, Senator Carlos Carrillo Smith read to the upper chamber the full contents of the Geneen message. An uproar ensued, both in the Senate and subsequently in the press. Next day *El Comercio* and other papers carried the full text. Local managers of the telephone company, who had known nothing of the communication, were deeply embarrassed. In fact the general manager, Stephen H. Larrabee, was killed in a mysterious one-car automobile accident ten days after the incident. Larrabee's personal anguish over the outburst of bad publicity had been well known and is conjectured as a factor in his accident.

The explanation for the leak, as it turned out, was that the wire had been on the circuits of ITT's own cable company, All-American Cables. A less-than-loyal ITT employee in Lima had apparently seen the message, realized its political significance, and taken a copy to Carrillo Smith. In August 1967 a new telephone contract was finally approved, but it contained two ideas notably not present in earlier agreements: international bidding for part of the system's future expansion and arrangements for eventual "Peruvianization." ITT's victory had been temporary.

Recent Economic Sanctions

We turn now to cases which involve more than requests for or acts of diplomatic protection. Three instances are described in which components of the American government other than the Department of State acted and, more importantly, in which economic sanctions were either brought or threatened against Peru. The cases involve the International Petroleum Company, American tuna-fishing interests, and W.R. Grace. They are the most prominent U.S. actions related to the welfare of U.S. corporations in the 1963-1971 period and have been selected to test whether blatant interventions such as occurred in the nineteenth and early twentieth centuries are still possible.*

The lengthy and complex dispute with IPC over the La Brea y Pariñas oil fields provides us with more than one situation to consider with respect to U.S. intervention. In fact, during the Jones ambassadorship three separate episodes can be identified that shed light on Standard Oil-U.S. government interrelationships. One occurred at the beginning of the Belaúnde administration, a second at the conclusion of it, and a third at the start of the Velasco regime.[22]

July 1963-December 1964. Upon taking office on July 28, 1963, Belaúnde promised that a solution to the La Brea problem would be prepared within ninety days. For the next three months intense negotiations took place between his government and IPC. The talks broke off without success, however, in late October. In November the Peruvian Congress renounced the 1922 arbitral award that established the oil field's tax schedule. In early 1964 negotiations resumed, and they almost achieved fruition in terms of a settlement that would have involved IPC's

---

*Although several other important instances of external economic pressure occured during the period they did not directly involve business interests. According to Teresa Hayter, the Agency for International Development, World Bank, and International Monetary Fund urged the Belaúnde administration to undertake a number of financial reforms in 1967 with the possibility of credits as leverage. Also in the Belaúnde period the World Bank intervened in the location of irrigation projects and the State Department pressed the Peruvians to purchase U.S. military planes. See Hayter, *Aid as Imperialism* (Harmondsworth, Eng., Penguin Books, 1971), pp. 146-149.

operation of the fields under contract. But in late December 1964 Belaúnde retreated from this formula.

During this time Fernando Espinosa, the Peruvian general manager of IPC, was in frequent contact with Ambassador Jones. The ambassador offered his "good offices" and encouraged and arranged negotiating sessions with the Peruvian authorities. According to my sources (which are varied and corroborated) the company—at this time—did not ask Jones to bring explicit pressure on the Peruvians on its behalf.

Yet by a combination of accident and intent, the State Department did in fact do this. Shortly after taking office Belaúnde had asked Teodoro Moscoso, Coordinator of the Alliance for Progress, to prepare a U.S. aid program to Peru that would be implemented upon resolution of the IPC problem. Accordingly AID officials prepared an economic assistance package totaling $64 million. But, as we have seen, no IPC settlement emerged. Thus the package was not delivered.

According to press reports (neither denied nor confirmed by the State Department) Assistant Secretary of State Thomas C. Mann determined in early 1964 that not only would this special package of assistance not be given to Peru in the absence of no IPC settlement, but that existing flows of aid would be slowed.[23] This was done over the next two years. Although technical assistance grants, Food for Peace assistance, and certain other forms of aid continued unabated, new commitments for development loans were drastically curtailed. The commitment level of $30 million for fiscal 1964 was cut to $2 million in fiscal 1965.[24] In February 1966 Mann's slow-down order was withdrawn and loan commitments began to rise again. Shortly thereafter Mann left the Department.

June 1967-August 1968. The IPC issue rose to another peak of prominence when, on June 22, 1967, the APRA-UNO coalition introduced in the Peruvian Congress a bill that involved a government take-over of the La Brea deposits. The measure was passed in modified form and, among other things, voided IPC's title to the fields and placed the oil deposits in the national reserve. Furthermore, the president was authorized to expropriate any and all surface equipment and property.

As it turned out this legislation was to have little practical significance in the eventual outcome of the dispute, but at the time it appeared to be a dramatic blow against IPC. By sheer coincidence the author was conducting interviews at the offices of Esso Inter America in Coral Gables on June 23, 1967, the day after the coalition bill was introduced. The information had been telephoned from Lima the night before. Throughout that day I talked with and observed several of the highest Esso executives. They seemed plainly worried and appeared to perceive the situation as a crisis. It was equally plain that they had been through similar crises many times before. As for steps to be taken, the dominant theme of their conversations on the topic was to wait for further information and, upon receiving that, file the appropriate appeals in the Peruvian courts. I asked the then president of Esso Inter America, Howard Kauffmann, if he would likely enlist State Department help in an instance such as this. He instantly and vigorously denied the possibility, remarking that he did not even know State's telephone number.[25]

My acceptance of this denial was shaken a few years later during a conversation with a State Department officer who had been directly involved with the IPC dispute in this period. He stated that Kauffmann had in fact telephoned the department very frequently during 1967-1968, raising the question of whether, in light of Peruvian actions regarding IPC, the American government should approve additional loans to Peru. The official even added that Kauffmann "not only knew our number, he must have known it by heart!"

Meanwhile, back in Lima, IPC and the Peruvian government engaged in inconclusive litigation and fruitless negotiation. IPC was, however, temporarily permitted to continue operating La Brea. On July 25, 1968, a minor bombshell broke when top company officials suddenly informed the Peruvian minister of development that they were willing to give outright the company's mineral rights and production facilities (not the refinery) to the nation in return for a quitclaim on any debts and agreeable refining, marketing and exploration concessions. This represented a sharp change of policy for Standard Oil, for previously it had been demanding that an operating contract (for the fields) be in hand before any rights or property could be given up. The proposal was essentially accepted by the Belaúnde government, becoming the basis of the short-lived "Act of Talara" agreement, signed August 13, 1968. Three weeks later the government had fallen, however, and the Talara properties were expropriated.

Mr. Belaúnde has speculated to this author that if the July 25 proposal had been made five years earlier, the chances would have been excellent that IPC would still be operating in Peru today.[26] That is, of course, merely conjecture. It raises the question, however, as to why the company did not make these concessions at an earlier time.

My reconstruction of the situation, based on a number of sources of information, is that the Standard Oil management was internally divided on what to do. A "dove" faction (known by that name) advocated greater concessions in order to avoid a later total confiscation. An opposing "hawk" faction argued that such concessions would be observed by the more than 100 governments round the world with which Jersey Standard dealt. According to this view, "backing down" in Peru would be construed as a sign of weakness and would signal an onslaught of new demands in numerous countries. The hawks won.

Ambassador Jones, meanwhile, did not try to tell IPC what to do. He simply urged a continuation of earnest negotiations so that *some* settlement could be worked out. He supported the negotiations leading to the Act of Talara but was not present during them. Jones has been criticized by some for not taking a more active role in urging concessions on the part of the company, which is perhaps a valid point.[27] But he did not aggressively press for concessions by the Peruvians either. The ambassador did, however, feel obliged to remind them of the potential threat to Peru inherent in the Hickenlooper Amendment. Unfairly, in my view, the Peruvian magazine *Oiga* pictured him on its cover with the captions "Mister IPC" and "Jones—Embajador de UEA o de la Standard Oil?"[28]

October 1968-August 1969. The famous Hickenlooper provision in the Foreign Assistance Act was passed in 1962, over the objections of the Department of State. It requires suspension of foreign aid to any government which expropriates U.S. property and then does not, within six months, "take appropriate steps" to make "equitable and speedy compensation."[29] In 1965 a similar provision was added to the Sugar Act which requires suspension of the U.S. sugar quota for any country in which American property is taken without compensation.[30] (Peru's quota was worth, in 1969, about $45 million in added national income.) No escape clauses exist in these laws, it should be noted, although the meaning of "appropriate steps" would be open to interpretation in a given circumstance.

When the revolutionary government seized IPC'S Talara properties on October 9, 1968, the Hickenlooper provisions were brought into play. The six-month time period began immediately, thus setting April 9, 1969, as the deadline for suspension of foreign aid and the sugar quota.

The Talara installations were worth, according to the company, $120 million. The Peruvian government gave no sign of being willing to pay IPC this amount. In fact, for years the Peruvians had maintained that IPC owed Peru large sums because of its "illegal" status. The military government put this debt at $690 million, the value of all oil and gas extracted by IPC since 1924. The obvious implication was that no compensation to Standard Oil would be forthcoming.

The American government tried anyway. During the remainder of 1968 its approach was quite low-key. The new Lima regime was recognized, and generally polite notes were exchanged on such points as whether IPC were Canadian and hence not subject to U.S. protection. (The issue arose from the company's registration in Canada.) The Hickenlooper provisions were noted by State Department press officers but not overly stressed.[31]

Soon after the Nixon administration took office in January 1969, however, a tougher line emerged. Washington press dispatches of January 29 reported that a State Department spokesman had declared, in reply to a reporter's inquiry, that Peru would be subject to sanctions if IPC went uncompensated. In a public speech on February 6, 1969, President

Velasco accused the United States of making unjustified and unjustifiable threats against Peru and insisted that Peru would not be intimidated. This defiant official attitude was supported throughout Peru by countless resolutions, public declarations, and newspaper editorials. Washington continued to press, however; in a March 4 news conference President Nixon said that if compensation was not forthcoming "we will have to take appropriate action with regard to the sugar quota, and also with regard to aid programs."[32]

Soon Washington's posture seemed to change again. A few days after his news conference Nixon sent a special emissary to Lima, John N. Irwin, who discussed matters quietly with the Velasco regime. He returned to Washington on April 3. April 7, two days prior to the Hickenlooper deadline, Secretary of State William Rogers announced that invocation of the Amendment was being "deferred" inasmuch as IPC had available to it a Peruvian administrative appeal process that constituted "appropriate steps" toward compensation.[33] This was, it would seem, merely a way of saving face and formalistically obeying U.S. law. The administrative appeal, predictably, was adverse to IPC in August. The Hickenlooper Amendment was not then formally invoked. Instead, economic assistance to Peru was informally curtailed to minimum levels without public announcement.

In the context of our purposes here, a question of importance is whether Standard Oil was requesting use of the Hickenlooper Amendment as a threat and subsequently a sanction against Peru. Publicly the company did not; no official statements were made either way. When queried about the matter, IPC executives said they did not advise the State Department on what should be done, but merely answered all of the many requests for information that the department submitted to them.

The underlying realities, according to reliable sources, were otherwise. Internally the company's management was once again divided along hawk-dove lines. The president of IPC during this period, James Dean, informally but not publicly let it be known to business associates and friends that he felt the Amendment should be imposed. This viewpoint of Dean's was known at the Department of State. The company did not, apparently, specifically lobby at the Department or White House in favor of threats or sanctions.[34]

To sum up, Standard Oil seemed progressively to move from "go it alone" bargaining with the Peruvians to a policy of seeking help from Washington. In the early 1960's it was keeping the U.S. ambassador informed; in the mid-1960's it was suggesting to the State Department that no new loans be approved; and in the late 1960's it was informally urging the imposition of Hickenlooper by the president.

Interestingly, Washington's behavior was more than once out of step with that of Standard Oil. In early 1964, when IPC was launching a new negotiating session with the Peruvians and was not, according to my information, pressing for sanctions from Washington, Assistant Secretary of State Mann ordered the development loan curtailment. Then in 1969, when the company was informally campaigning for application of sanctions, Washington took the softer approach and deferred invocation of the Hickenlooper Amendment. In short, although the U.S. Government frequently attempted to assist Standard Oil in its Peruvian difficulties, Esso and Washington were not in a kind of subserviant or conspiratorial relationship that would yield perfect coordination.

In any event U.S. actions helped the company little. A settlement was temporarily effected (the Act of Talara), but this grew out of major company concessions rather than U.S. pressure. IPC was eventually evicted from Peru with no likelihood of compensation. Major pressures in the form of both economic sanctions and the threat of same had failed.

Another instance in which U.S. economic sanctions against Peru played a part was not on behalf of U.S. business "in Peru" in the sense normally used in this book—direct investment on Peruvian soil. Yet it concerns American business operations that are "in Peru" according to the Peruvians' own standards, namely, U.S. commercial tuna fishing within 200 miles of the Peruvian coast.

When American fishing vessels operate within 200 nautical miles of the Peruvian coast they are, according to Peruvian law, under Peruvian governmental jurisdiction. This "200-mile limit" has been claimed by Peru since 1947. Most other Latin American nations also claim it. The United States, on the other hand, insists that international law recognizes only a 3-mile territorial limit and a 12-mile fishing jurisdiction. It is not necessary to go into the numerous legal and technical arguments involved here, although it might be said that a substantial case can be made for the Peruvian position on the basis that its offshore fishing grounds are an integral part of the country's ecological system.[35]

For many years Peru has regulated commercial fishing in the 200-mile zone by means of a licensing arrangement. Foreigners are free to fish within the zone provided they pay registration and license fees, whose proceeds go to marine conservation. Many foreign fishing crews pay the fees and operate unhampered. Others, particularly American tuna fishermen operating from San Diego, refuse to make the payments on grounds that "freedom of the seas" begins 12 miles out. The Peruvian navy possesses rapid cutters with which they can easily intercept unlicensed vessels, and more than thirty-five interceptions of U.S. boats were made between 1953 and 1970. The offenders are escorted to the nearest Peruvian port where they are required to pay fines and penalties amounting to as much as $15,000 per boat.[36]

The southern California tuna industry did not accept these seizures gracefully, to put it mildly. A strenuous campaign for protection and retaliation was waged by the American Tunaboat Association, representing the boat owners, the International Longshoremen and Warehousemen's Union and other unions, representing the crews, and the tuna canners and southern California press. With help from friends in Congress, such as Representative Thomas Pelly of Washington, a number of laws were passed to these ends. The Fishermen's Protective Acts of 1954 and 1968 call for reimbursements by the U.S. government of fined fishermen and subsequent reduction of any reimbursements from foreign assistance to the country that levies the fines.[37] The Kuchel Amendment to the Foreign Assistance Act encourages discontinuance of aid to a boat-seizing government,[38] and the Pelly Amendment to the Foreign Military Sales Act makes an offending government ineligible to purchase U.S. arms.[39] Still another law terminates authority to loan warships to countries that take possession of an American fishing vessel.[40]

In addition to lobbying Congress the American tuna industry has made specific requests for Executive Branch action, including use of armed force. One of the more notable incidents provoking such requests occurred on February 14, 1969, and is known as the "Saint Valentine's Day" incident. The tuna boat *Mariner* was taken at sea while an accompanying tuna clipper, the *San Juan*, refused to submit to boarding. It was consequently machine-gunned, resulting in considerable damage but no injuries. Back in the United States, industry leaders and friends expressed outrage and demanded immediate action. On February 17 a union official wired President Nixon, "We urge you to take strong action to protect American fishing interests on the high seas. . . . Such protection should include the use of naval vessels if necessary." Congressman Pelly appealed to the president, "The United States has tried reason and sought unsuccessfully to settle these disputes by mediation and in the International Court of Justice. Therefore, I urge you to provide naval protection to our fishing fleet on the high seas." Representative Edward Garmatz, chairman of the House Merchant Marine and Fisheries Committee, demanded that the State Department "retaliate and get tough" with seizing nations.[41]

Although gunboats were not dispatched, the State Department acted and acted vigorously. On Saint Valentine's Day itself military sales to Peru were suspended, in accord with the Pelly Amendment (the language of this provision is such that the cutoff is supposed to be automatic, although a presidential waiver is permitted). No announcement of the suspension was made, not even to the Peruvians; not until April 3 was the Peruvian government itself informed through its embassy in Washington. The step did not become publicly known until late May, when U.S. congressmen, disgruntled over additional tuna seizures, leaked the story to reporters.[42]

The reaction in Lima was extremely hostile. The Velasco government claimed it had been insulted by the fact that it had never been informed, finding out about the move months later via the press. General Velasco ordered the forty-one U.S. military mission personnel then in Peru to depart immediately. At the same time he made it clear that Governor Nelson Rockefeller was not welcome to stop in Peru on a scheduled Latin American tour for President Nixon.

Meanwhile, before the sales cutoff became known, the State Department had taken other measures. Immediately after the February 14 incident Secretary of State Rogers summoned Peruvian Ambassador Fernando Berckemeyer in Washington and expressed "serious concern" over the attack. On February 19 Ambassador Jones presented a formal protest in Lima. Six days later additional pressure was applied in Washington when a State Department press spokesman strongly hinted that an overage U.S. destroyer on loan to Peru would be withdrawn if the Peruvians did not pay compensation for the $50,000 of damage inflicted upon the *San Juan*. "Our actions will be determined in accordance with the relevant statutes," the spokesman said.[4 3]

Despite the threats of sanction and, when it later became known, the implemented sanction of suspending military sales, the Peruvians did not back down. Nor did they later retreat. After considerable negotiations between Jones and the Velasco government a four-power fishing conference was held, in July and August of 1969. The United States hoped to convince Peru, Ecuador, and Chile to join in the formation of an international fishing conservation and control organization. Fishing fees could then be paid to the organization, thus side-stepping the issue of national jurisdiction at sea. But the conference achieved nothing. The Peruvians paid no compensation for damages to the *San Juan* and continued to seize unlicensed vessels.* For its part, the United States continued diplomatic efforts aimed at a negotiated international solution but tried no more economic threats.[4 4]

The final case involving U.S. economic sanctions concerned the W.R. Grace & Co., although it also was supposedly intended to benefit other U.S. firms in Latin America and elsewhere. Grace's two sugar haciendas, Paramonga and Cartavio, were expropriated by the Peruvian government in 1970 under Velasco's agrarian reform program. The estates were appraised at $10.1 million by the Peruvians, and according to the law most of this amount would be paid to Grace in 20-25-year bonds at an interest rate of 5-6 percent, plus a small amount of cash. To Grace both the method and amount of payment were unacceptable. The company claimed the properties had a replacement value of $46.7 million and a current value of $26 million. Moreover the bonds were considered largely worthless because of the low interest rates and their nonredeemable nature unless invested in

---

*After very few seizures in 1970-1972, during which time schools of tuna failed to appear off Peru, at-sea captures became common once again in 1973.

approved industrial projects. Grace executives were, moreover, irritated over long delays in negotiations over compensation; by April 1971, 17 months after the take-over, Grace had not even been permitted to appeal the officially appraised value.[45]

A decision to apply pressure on the Peruvian government was thus taken high in the New York hierarchy of Grace. It was proposed to the House Agriculture Committee of the U.S. Congress that the Sugar Act, going through one of its periodic renewals in 1971, be amended so that proceeds from the sugar quota of any country that expropriated U.S.-owned sugar-producing properties would be held back in the amount of $15 per ton. This action would follow a determination by the Foreign Claims Settlement Commission that the expropriation had not been accompanied by a "just and adequate compensation." The funds withheld would then be paid to the owners of the taken properties. James P. Freeborn, the Grace vice-president who testified on behalf of the proposal before the committee, calculated that the $15 penalty would absorb approximately one-third of the sugar quota's value to Peru and would pay off Grace's $26 million in slightly over four years.[46]

Obviously primed for the charge that the company was not playing fair with the country of its birth, Grace officials insisted that the corporation supported continuation of Peru's sugar quota of approximately 435,000 tons. It was true that existing—but moribund—sugar legislation directed the president to suspend the sugar quota of a country whose expropriation of U.S. property went uncompensated for six months. Perhaps more important than this dead-letter amendment, a move was at the time underway in the House Agriculture Committee to reduce Peru's quota anyway, along with the quotas of four other big producing countries, so as to make room for allocations to additional African and Caribbean nations. James Freeborn argued to me that the "Grace Amendment" could actually be looked upon as a means of heading off more severe action against Peru, including a complete termination of Peru's quota. This argument was used also by the corporation with Peruvian Ambassador Berckemeyer, to whom Freeborn's House testimony was shown in advance.[47]

That certain U.S. congressmen were in a mood to apply more severe pressure on Peru than Grace proposed was shown by subsequent events. The House Agriculture Committee, under the prodding of Congressman Pelly, enlarged the coverage of the expropriation amendment to cover *any* business—including, obviously, seized tuna clippers. Restrictions or discriminations other than outright expropriation were introduced into the reach of the provision. The amendment was changed so that the president rather than the Foreign Claims Settlement Commission would make the determinations and the withholding amount was upped to $20. Finally, the president was given the option of suspending all or part of the offending country's quota. Peru's new quota was set at slightly under 419,000 tons.[48]

The U.S. Senate went even further. Castigating Peru for its IPC expropriation, Finance Committee Chairman Senator Russell Long secured the further reduction of Peru's quota to under 392,000 tons. More importantly, the expropriation language was tightened by the Senate Committee so that an offending country's quota would be automatically terminated following Tariff Commission proceedings. A fee equal to one-half the U.S. premium price on that quota would then go to corporations suffering losses.[49]

In conference committee, where the White House threatened a veto if Senate expropriation language was retained, the House version of the amendment was essentially retained. Peru's quota, however, was cut to the level set by the Senate. The final outcome, then, was introduction into the Sugar Act of a new sanction against a country that expropriates U.S. business, but to be invoked at the pleasure of the president.[50] To this writing the provision has not been implemented.

Of particular interest is the reaction of various interested parties to the Grace action and to the idea of sugar-quota sanctions. Perhaps somewhat surprisingly, much of the American business community in Lima was incensed. Although Koenig of Cerro supported Grace,[51] the managements of most other U.S. companies were of the opinion that Grace had made a profound mistake. The president of SPCC was worried that the U.S. Congress would now start levying penalties on other Peruvian exports, including copper.[52] The head of Goodyear got in touch with the parent company in Akron and asked that the company's Washington lobbyist oppose the restrictions.[53] Most members of the American Chamber of Commerce were strongly opposed to the action, and in a meeting of its board of directors Grace's Anthony Navarro was subjected to a vigorous and concerted denunciation of his company's move. The Chamber president at the time, Howard G. Crawford, wrote identical letters to the chairmen of the House Agriculture and Senate Finance Committees in which Peru's present quota was strongly supported. The letter said in part:

While Peru is currently implementing political and economic changes, some of which may be detrimental to some U.S. businesses, it still remains a fact that the majority of U.S. enterprises continue to operate success-fully. A radical reduction in the U.S. sugar quota allocation to Peru at this time could produce a disturbing reaction prejudicial to those U.S. interests.

The principles of the agrarian reform program initiated in 1969 had been recommended by several international U.S. sponsored Agreements. It is the considered opinion of this Chamber that under the adopted program, the Government of Peru has taken and is taking measures to compensate former owners of sugar estates. While we recognize that a more rapid settlement with a more flexible form of compensation would be desirable, the program, if properly administered, should eventually resolve the issue.[54]

The *Peruvian Times* commented:

The situation is moderately complicated, but Grace's new move has surprised many people in Lima as being heavy-handed at best and even more probably quite dangerous. Quiet pressure up in Washington is one thing, according to one diplomatic authority, but Hickenlooper-like-amendments, it is felt, were thoroughly and finally discredited at the time of the International Petroleum Company; damaging to Peru, maybe, but with a proven 100% fracaso* rate.[55]

My own inquiries at the American embassy and elsewhere verify strong State Department opposition to the entire idea. Embassy officers argued that the strategy failed to recognize the Peruvian regime's own political need to satisfy Leftist factions supporting it. Furthermore, it was said, a commodity penalty would be a bad precedent in terms of spreading to other exports and in restricting further the administration of foreign economic policy.[56] In Washington the State Department itself vigorously opposed the Sugar Act restrictions, probably for similar reasons. Deputy Assistant Secretary of State Julius L. Katz infuriated Grace officials, in fact, by discussing with them their Peruvian problems just a day or so prior to stating the Department's position before the House Agriculture Committee and saying nothing of this opposition to Grace. To the businessmen of Hanover Square the American government had turned its back on American enterprise.

The position of the Peruvian government is also worth noting. Although the Lima press raised a great protest, the regime itself took the matter cooly. President Velasco made it appear that he did not care what happened. His government took no official position on the Grace Amendment but it did instruct Peru's sugar lobbyist in Washington, Edwin H. Seeger, to testify before the two relevant congressional committees on behalf of continuing Peru's quota at its current level. Ironically, one of the arguments used in behalf of the quota turned the compensation issue on its head; Seeger said that Peru needed sugar earnings to pay off its large external debt—owed in part to U.S. banks and government agencies.[57]

Despite the strong misgivings over Grace's strategy within the Lima business and diplomatic community, was it truly a tactical error? One might be hard-pressed to agree that it was, although at this writing all evidence is not in. Just ten days after the Freeborn testimony before the House committee in Washington, negotiations between the company and Peruvian authorities in Lima, suspended for months, were resumed. By November 1971, a major agreement had been arrived at whereby the

*Failure or "flap."

company's industrial properties were to be sold to the government over a ten-year period with Grace maintaining managerial control for at least seven years. The basic outlines of a method of compensating for the sugar estates were also worked out. In both cases the amounts of compensation were still to be agreed upon, however.[58]

Recapitulation and Analysis

In the historical past the U.S. government intervened on behalf of U.S. business interests in Peru on a number of occasions. American envoys in Lima pressed with great vigor on behalf of American commercial interests. Diplomats and businessmen in Lima could be very close, even to the point of polling the executives prior to United States recognition of a new Peruvian government. Governmental actions against Peru included sending a warship to Peruvian waters and withdrawing oil tankers vital to the Peruvian economy.

Contemporary relationships between the U.S. business and diplomatic communities in Lima involve systematic, institutionalized communication. The American ambassador, in cooperation with the American Chamber of Commerce, holds monthly, confidential meetings at which views and problems are shared.

The U.S. Embassy in Lima performs the function of "diplomatic protection" of American business in Peru in a variety of ways. The ambassador may offer his "good offices" whereby he encourages and arranges negotiations without taking an active part in them or announcing his preferences as to outcome. He also may file a formal protest when a businessman has been deemed the object of illegal or discriminatory treatment. Informal inquiries and representations are more common.

With respect to U.S. intervention in Peruvian affairs beyond the realm of diplomatic protection, we find that on at least three recent occasions economic sanctions were threatened or used on behalf of U.S. business interests. In 1964-1966 new development loan commitments were curtailed, in 1968-1969 invocation of the Hickenlooper Amendment was threatened, and in 1969 military sales to Peru were suspended.

A wide variety of behavior is seen on the part of both the corporations and the U.S. government. Cerro fought the sheepland issue largely alone with essentially passive diplomatic assistance. In the Ferry incarceration Jones protested on his own before Xerox requested help. ITT frantically pressed the State Department to intervene on its behalf but it is uncertain as to whether U.S. authorities acted at all. For many years IPC tended not to encourage U.S. assistance but once the situation became critically threatening the company reversed its strategy. In the IPC case Washington also appeared to reverse its approach at least a couple of times, from conciliatory to hard-line to conciliatory again. California fishing spokesmen assiduously sought both legislative and executive action against Peru, whereas Grace concentrated on congressional action. The style of these overt, public moves on behalf of tuna and sugar interests were almost at the opposite extreme of private pressures brought by ITT and IPC.

Intimate collaboration between American businessmen and officials no longer obtains. Assistant Secretary of State Mann acted on behalf of IPC interests presumably without consulting Standard Oil; Deputy Assistant Secretary of State Katz opposed the Grace Amendment without informing the Grace organization. Spokesmen for the tuna interests and Grace officials heatedly characterize the State Department as unreliable and even disloyal. American business executives in Lima generally look upon the U.S. Embassy as an unreliable and largely impotent ally, even though most of them go to the monthly meetings.

Clearly the corporations do not form a monolithic bloc with respect to demanding assistance, nor does the American government with respect to giving it. True, Lima executives universally condemned the Ferry detention because, perhaps, they all saw themselves as possibly facing the same predicament some day. But, as was pointed out in Chapter Three, many businessmen were not overly disturbed by IPC's expropriation. Inside Standard Oil itself a wide gulf of opinion existed with respect to political tactics in Peru. In the negative reaction to the Grace Amendment on the part of the American Chamber of Commerce, a dramatic instance of internal division within the American business community may be seen. As for divisions within government, the Lima Embassy was deeply disturbed over Mann's sanctions, as was the Department of State in general over restrictive amendments attached by Congress to foreign aid and sugar legislation over the years. In short, a true American "conspiracy" in relation to intervention against Peru is difficult to substantiate at almost any level of analysis.

The effects of the described diplomatic protections and economic interventions were in all instances outcomes that were more positive from the American viewpoint than might be imagined. Cerro was compensated, in part and after long delay; Ferry was released, after several months; ITT's monopoly was preserved, at least for a couple more years. As for the IPC, tuna, and Grace cases, one notable achievement in each was the opening of negotiations. In the Grace dispute the talks resulted in a tentative settlement for the Americans, but in the other two matters the Peruvians were absolutely unyielding. U.S. intervention in behalf of the corporations occurs, but it does not always fully work.

Six   Bargaining over Investments

Quite apart from lobbying, PR, and appeals to the U.S. government, the corporations could conceivably gain considerable influence over Peruvian public policy by investment bargaining. They could, for example, offer to make new investments in Peru but with the proviso that the Peruvian government give them in return certain rights or guarantees associated with the investments. In this situation the companies would be seeking to influence a narrow range of public policies. Such an effort may very well work if (1) Peru wants the investment badly enough and does not have alternate sources of capital, and (2) the investors can afford to risk being scorned. Bargaining leverage can also conceivably arise from existing investments; one possibility is that the corporation could threaten to curtail operations in Peru or go home entirely unless policy concessions are made. Also, perhaps, the company could actually slow down or terminate operations and make their resumption contingent upon cooperation from the Peruvians. Still another possibility would be to hold out to the government the prospect of improving its payoff from existing operations, for example, by indicating a willingness to pay higher taxes. Delivery of such "bait" would depend on making prescribed concessions of policy.

Hypothesis IA predicts that the corporations "are able to bargain effectively over investment terms" because of "a degree of economic dependence on U.S. capital." That is, it is hypothesized that Peru *does* want and need American investments badly enough to yield to the corporations' considerable bargaining leverage. The hypothesis differentiates, however, between leverage attainable from new capital as over against existing investments; the former is predicted as more able to induce "clout" than the latter because once capital is committed the corporation finds it difficult to withdraw from its end of the bargain. The Peruvians, on the other hand, can always change their minds with regard to concessions previously made. They also then have the U.S. assets within their legal jurisdiction and subject to local laws.

In Chapter Three we did not find a generalized, pervasive economic dependence by Peru on U.S. capital, but certain specific points of vulnerability were noted. Two industries of critical importance that were dominated by U.S. capital prior to 1968-1969 were petroleum and telecommunications. A critical sector which continued to be American-dominated after the Revolution was mining. Let us examine these three industries in turn for evidence that verifies or discounts the hypothesis with respect to investment bargaining.

Bargaining over Petroleum

As might be expected, the richest source of information with respect to bargaining over oil investments is the lengthy La Brea y Pariñas dispute. In 1916 Standard Oil already controlled and managed the La Brea fields, but the Peruvian government was threatening to undo the extremely light tax regime that had applied to the property for more than a quarter-century. To counter this threat the corporation applied an interesting array of bargaining tactics.

In November 1916, Walter Teagle, the rising Standard executive who headed Peruvian operations at the time, approached President José Pardo y Barreda. Teagle warned him that unless a satisfactory tax settlement was reached "future operations here could not be continued on a profitable basis." The oil official added, however, that IPC needed and wanted to make further investments at the La Brea fields, but that going ahead with them could not be recommended to the stockholders under prevailing uncertain conditions. At the same time Teagle provided material on the company point of view to several U.S. newspapers, apparently attempting to bring indirect pressure upon the Peruvians.[1]

Late in 1917 the Peruvian Senate finally passed a La Brea tax measure but included in its stipulations that IPC be subject to jurisdiction of Peruvian courts and that the company renounce all rights of foreign diplomatic intervention. As a result further pressures were applied by Standard Oil. In April 1918 Pardo was again informed that if favorable legislation was not passed the company's Peruvian operations would be curtailed. In June the Congress adjourned without the lower house acting, in effect calling IPC's bluff. Behind the scenes, the Standard management was uncertain as to what to do; Teagle proposed a partial reduction of wages and G. Harrison Smith, by this time IPC president, wanted a complete shutdown at Negritos, a partial closing at Talara, and dismissal of all workers with a small severance payment. But the master lobbyist, R.V. LeSueur, urged noncurtailment for the time being and his viewpoint won out. The company interpreted a promise by Pardo of immediate reconsideration of the legislation at the next session of Congress as a pretext for continuing operations.

But, to the oilmen's discomfiture, the next Congress acted even more strongly against company desires and interests. A bill considered by the Chamber of Deputies in October 1918 was perceived by International as meaning it would eventually lose its investment. Now even LeSueur was unwilling to stand still.

In a newspaper interview LeSueur suddenly stated that a shutdown was impending at both Talara and Negritos. An outburst of popular indignation followed. Lima newspapers said this action constituted an economic attack on Peru and proposals for nationalization of the property were made. Unswayed, IPC moved to increase the pressure by seeking diplomatic intervention; as related in the last chapter, this came in its most crucial form as a requisition of company tankers by the Canadian government. As a result, oil shipments from Talara to Callao were in fact temporarily cut off, creating a fuel crisis in Lima. The curtailment threat had become implemented, although in the form of an interruption of transportation rather than production.

As has been seen, the Peruvian Congress capitulated in December 1918 by authorizing international arbitration. Within four years an arbitration award had been handed down that embodied a settlement hammered out by LeSueur and President Leguía. Its terms were decidedly procompany by today's standards, reflecting perhaps the combined effect of the era, IPC's tactics, and Leguía's pro-U.S. scale of values.

For approximately the next two decades things went well for IPC. Its investments at La Brea were greatly augmented. During the five years following the award the company's production of crude oil and its number of workers doubled. With a near-monopoly on production, refining, and distribution within Peru, the company enjoyed a high degree of both horizontal and vertical integration. Exports as well as internal sales were profitable. Moreover the political scene remained comparatively quiet on the petroleum question, with the exception of a strenuous effort after Leguía's ouster in 1930 to gain nullification of the 1922 Award by the World Court. This failed, however.

IPC's pleasant and prosperous Peruvian career began to wane after World War II. A politically unsettling issue appeared: the domestic price of gasoline. In 1939 the prices of petroleum products had been frozen along with those of other consumer commodities. In 1949 the Odría government unfroze all prices except those of bread and gasoline. IPC, experiencing rising production costs and an increasing percentage of its sales in the domestic market (rising from 30 percent in 1939 to 75 percent in 1957), lobbied hard for a price rise. Nothing substantial happened until 1952, when a new General Petroleum Law was enacted. This law, in addition to offering generous terms to new concessionaries, provided for a flexible pricing policy that would have affected IPC. Prices were to cover all costs and provide a "reasonable" profit agreed upon by the company and government. For the moment things looked better for IPC.[2]

Even though many other American-owned petroleum companies benefited from the Petroleum Law, Standard Oil did not. In 1953 a small rise was permitted in gasoline prices but not enough to counterbalance IPC's declining profits. The company continued to press, and in 1954 a decree raised the price slightly more and provided also for semiannual reviews of petroleum prices. The new price was still inadequate to make Peruvian sales profitable. In addition, in mid-1955 the government, under pressure from the powerful chauffeur union, postponed the first semiannual review. Soon IPC was losing substantially on its Peruvian operations. At this time Peru's price of gasoline was one of the lowest in the world.

IPC hoped for more responsiveness to its pleas from the second Prado administration, which took office in 1956. The president and each of his cabinet ministers were visited by the current IPC general manager, Jack Ashworth. The new government seemed sympathetic in these talks but did nothing to satisfy the company. In March 1957 a price increase was recommended by the government's Petroleum Bureau but was overruled at a higher level.

In August 1957 International reoriented its strategy on the price issue. Investment bargaining pressure, rather than mere lobbying, was brought to bear. The first move, undertaken in August 1957, was an outright offer to exchange the privileged status of La Brea y Pariñas for ordinary concession status under the Petroleum Law. Presumably IPC hoped that this exchange would appeal to the government politically and also open the way to a price increase under terms set forth in the Petroleum Law. The offer was rejected, however, and so in early 1958 curtailment of part of La Brea's drilling operations was suddenly ordered. Over 1000 company workers were declared surplus, although they temporarily remained on the payroll pending completion of severance pay negotiations.

A vehement public outcry followed. To counter it IPC purchased newspaper advertising space in which it defended its action as necessary in view of the nonprofit status of Peruvian operations. This effort seemed only to exacerbate the situation; reacting angrily, the premier warned that further pursuance of curtailment tactics would be regarded as an "unfriendly act." At the same time, however, the initiation of negotiations was promised.

By September 1958 the talks were underway and at them IPC reintroduced the proposal of conversion to concession status. The idea was again rejected, on grounds that it would allow too great a price increase. In October the discussions were suspended by the Peruvians; in November IPC responded to the newest balking by suspending its remaining drilling operations and declaring more workers surplus.

The stage was now set for an explosive revival of the La Brea y Pariñas controversy. Peru was at this time facing a general economic crisis. A new premier was appointed, Pedro Beltrán of the procapitalist *La Prensa*. In July 1959, shortly after Beltrán's appointment, a substantial increase in the price of gasoline was decreed. This brought a storm of protest in Congress and in *El Comercio, La Prensa*'s rival daily. Deputy Alfonso Benavides Correa, a Lima independent, launched a vitriolic campaign against IPC and the 1922 Award.[3] His line of attack was not directed specifically against the company's curtailment tactics but constituted a generalized broadside against the company. The act of arbitration was declared illegal and its nullification demanded; the company was charged with all manner of crimes, including treason in Peru's recent border conflicts and complicity in two murders. Huge sums of money were declared as owed to Peru by IPC because of allegedly illicit profits or unpaid taxes. All charges, no matter how wild, were given instant publicity in *El Comercio*. An almost incessant drumbeat of attack continued for some two years, making life not only uncomfortable but dangerous for IPC officials resident in Lima. The company had paid a high premium for its price increase.

During the Belaúnde administration (1963-1968), the political temperature of the La Brea y Pariñas dispute went up and down several times. As mentioned in the last chapter, Belaúnde came to power promising a "solution" to the problem within ninety days. Company-government negotiations began in August 1963 and continued into October. In these talks IPC proposed exchanging its rights for a thirty-five-year concession, during which half of company profits would go to the government. IPC also offered a cash payment—the amount to be negotiated—payable over twenty years. The government responded with the demand that current La Brea rights be disavowed prior to a contract, that two-thirds of profits be paid to the government, and that the special payment of $50 million be paid over five years. IPC then brought in a counteroffer of accepting the two-thirds tax level and the $50 million payment, but with the latter strung out over twenty years instead of five and an exchange of rights rather than unilateral disavowal. The negotiations then stalled at this point on the eighty-ninth day. Belaúnde proposed to Congress that IPC be told it must accept the government's terms or be expropriated. But the coalition-dominated legislature instead merely declared the award as null and void, thus tossing the problem of a settlement back in the president's lap.[4]

In April 1964 discussions resumed. By July negotiators for the two sides had agreed on a new formula, among whose provisions were exchange of rights for a twenty-five-year operating contract, the ceding of surface and subsoil ownership rights in exchange for a quitclaim on all debts, and 65 percent government participation in profits. The company now thought the dispute was over and all that was needed was congressional ratification. However, in December the Peruvian minister of finance, overruling the negotiated position, denied in effect that any agreement had been arrived at on the contract and quitclaim. A proposal was now made that management of the oil fields be vested in a five-man commission to which the government would name three members. Loss of managerial control was an anathema to IPC and its spokesmen made this very clear.

During 1965 discussions dragged on but without progress. Bills were introduced in Congress to expropriate IPC. Unwilling to make further significant concessions at this point, the company tried a new tactic: instead of promising exchanges related to current investments it offered the possibility of new investments. In 1966 IPC announced that it was considering expanding the Talara refinery at a cost of $8 million. The enlarged facility would not be owned by IPC but by a new Standard Oil subsidiary, "Esso Peruana." The company characterized this reorganization as a means of isolating the La Brea problem and proceeding normally in other areas. Company opponents called the proposal a plot to dilute IPC'S assets, which by now they considered as security on Standard's "debt" to the nation. Soon it was apparent that the expansion plan was a failure and it was never carried out.

On June 22, 1967, the APRA-UNO coalition seized the initiative by introducing a bill that challenged the continued operation of the fields by IPC. In its enacted form the measure revoked the company's oil field ownership title and authorized the Executive to expropriate IPC and establish a new entity to manage the properties. As it turned out, IPC was not to be expropriated until more than a year later, but in the interim various government actions built up a gradually increasing political head of steam. These included registering the La Brea deposits in the national reserve, tendering bids from other companies to operate the fields, making formal findings that IPC owed more than $144 million in debts, and attachment of International's bank accounts.

On July 25, 1968, Standard played its last card in a desperate attempt to bargain its way out of the increasingly threatening situation. Whereas in 1963 the company had offered to give up its rights for a concession, and in 1964 for an operating contract, now the price named was simply a quitclaim on all debts and certain substitute concessions. This meant that for the first time IPC was offering to relinquish not only ownership rights but operating rights at La Brea. The fields, all production facilities, and the town of Talara would be owned and operated by the state oil company, Empresa Petrolera Fiscal (EPF). Standard would continue, however, to own and operate the Talara refinery and its service-station network. Also, according to the proposal, IPC would purchase EPF crude oil on contract, supply oil field services to EPF, and would receive new exploration concessions elsewhere in Peru.

The Belaúnde government, sinking in prestige by this time for several reasons, accepted the proposal almost in its entirety. Modifications were essentially matters of detail, except that new concessions were delayed for later negotiation. At the moment it appeared that a clever bargaining move had saved the company in the nick of time. But, as we know, political opponents of Belaúnde and IPC, led by the disgruntled head of EPF, Loret de Mola, opened a campaign several days after the Act of Talara to discredit it as a gigantic fraud and dishonor to Peru. In an atmosphere of increasing political chaos General Velasco led a successful coup d'etat. In a matter of days the Talara properties were expropriated, and in early 1969 the remaining IPC assets were seized. Standard Oil was now out of Peru for the indefinite future, and with no compensation in sight.

Thus a long history of investment bargaining, incorporating a wide variety of lures and threats—coupled with proffered exchanges and actual curtailments—had come to a rather ignominious end. Resourceful and multiple bargaining tactics had worked (in combination with political pressures) brilliantly a half-century previously but at great cost a decade before. The eventual price was loss by the company of all Peruvian assets, including its Peruvian reputation.

Bargaining over Telephones

When International Telephone and Telegraph purchased controlling interest in Cía. Peruana de Teléfonos in 1930 the system was antiquated, tiny (10,000 telephones), and regulated on an ad hoc basis. During the 1930's ITT invested considerably in its new property, more than doubling the number of phones by 1938. Automatic exchanges were installed throughout. The government awarded a tariff increase in 1935.[5]

During the 1940's no significant improvements were made, despite a second tariff boost in 1947. In 1950 the Odría administration awarded still another increase, and following that the company embarked on its first postwar expansion program. By 1956 the system contained 47,500 telephones. Also in that year—Odría's last—the first telephone regulatory law was passed. Among its provisions were a guaranteed level of earnings for the company of 10 to 12 percent on the average total of invested capital, and also a right to apply for revaluation of assets whenever the company felt its rate base was undervalued. In addition an immediate rate increase was granted. For its part, the company was obligated to add 38,200 new telephones over a seven-year period, 6,800 of which were to be installed during the first three years.

ITT was thus blessed with both important guaranties and a modest expansion obligation—the number of phones was to be increased at a rate less than 12 percent annually. The company applied new capital to the extent that improvements to the system were pushed along far ahead of schedule, and by 1958 nearly 23,000 additional telephones were in service.

During 1958 Cía. Peruana de Teléfonos's position began to deteriorate, however, as it saw its earnings drop from around 10 percent to the 6 percent level, or about half the guaranteed amount. A tariff increase was applied for in October. The response from the government—with Prado now in power—was coldly negative. On top of this, in December the Odría-negotiated telephone law was abrogated in its entirety. The telephone expansion program was then immediately terminated, substantially short of its seven-year target.

An eighteen-month impasse followed, involving informal lobbying, a law suit, and extended negotiations. Finally in July 1960 the Prado administration issued a new telephone decree that was only slightly inferior to Odría's. The principal change was to guarantee a 12 percent rate of earnings, but calculated on the average total of ITT's equity in the company only, a substantially inferior base than provided for in the previous law. But a provision was added which stated that such guarantee could not be changed to the detriment of the company as long as it was in debt for expansion purposes. This was hoped by ITT officials to provide a means of avoiding recurrence of the 1958 abrogation.[6]

By September 1961, however, the company was again facing unfavorable conditions. Despite the earnings guarantee, profits were down to nearly 3 percent.[7] A tariff increase was requested and this was granted in February 1962. It is undoubtedly not coincidental that during that same month a new expansion program was announced. It was estimated to cost $45 million, with $20 million to come from a hoped-for World Bank loan and the remainder from New York banks and internal ITT sources. The program was scheduled over six years with a target of 90,100 new phones, equivalent to an expansion rate of 18.4 percent.

The program went ahead, raising hopes among the 85,000 anxious new-phone applicants that by now existed. But in July 1962 a military coup was staged against Prado; the generals that came to power established a new regulatory agency, the Junta Permanente Nacional de Telecomunicaciones. In January 1963 the company applied to this Junta for revaluation of its assets, as was its right under the 1960 decree. The regulatory body refused, however, to process the application because of differences with the company over procedures. Angered, the ITT management halted the current expansion program, which by now had resulted in only 6,600 new telephones.

On March 26, 1963, company executives delivered a statement to General Nicholas Lindley, then Peru's president, stating the conditions under which expansion would be resumed. After Lindley failed to respond to the company's satisfaction its position was restated in the most explicit terms. A letter was sent to Lindley in which it was stated that without revaluation "investors within and without Peru will be unwilling to risk their capital in telephone operations." The reference to non-ITT sources of capital was an attempt to place part of the onus for the company's recalcitrance on the World Bank and private U.S. banks. The letter went on to spell out the specific requirements for resumption of the expansion program:

Perutelco [Peruvian Telephone Company] is anxious to proceed with the expansion program which is now suspended, and if the Government does wish to have more telephones now, it should take the actions necessary to accomplish the following, in order to permit financing to be obtained and to enable the program to start moving.

1) That Executive Decree 488 be given force of law to strengthen the assurances offered investors that Decree 488 and a recent Decree Law 14198 be compatible. This has been pending since September 25, 1962.

2) That the Finance Minister issue promptly a written statement, incorporating the terms discussed, backing Perutelco's application to the World Bank. This has been pending since March 1, 1963.

3) That a guarantee of the Government be granted when the loan is offered. This cannot be accomplished until after the World Bank acts.

4) That the Government proceed promptly with the revaluation provided for by the terms of Decree 488. This has been pending since January 25, 1963.[8]

Even this ultimatum failed to produce results and the regime to which it was addressed passed from power in July 1963. Although it was eventually apparent that the new Belaúnde regime was more conciliatory to ITT, it could not at the moment appear protelephone company for political reasons. Moreover the APRA-UNO coalition in Congress was strongly anti-ITT despite its otherwise conservative orientation. This was first made manifest in November 1963 when the Congress raised the stamp tax affecting telephone operations. For the two smaller provincial telephone systems owned by Peruvian, Swiss, and Swedish interests, the tax was raised from 0.45 to 1 percent. For the ITT, however, it was increased to 4.45 percent and later 5 percent. Meanwhile the ministry of labor decreed higher wage rates for telephone workers each year.

By the mid-1960's the deepest telephone crisis yet was brewing. With higher taxes and labor costs and the same tariffs as granted in 1962, the telephone company's profits were down to around 4 percent. Meanwhile unfilled telephone applications increased by the thousands, as Lima experienced its population explosion of the 1960's. Telephone service deteriorated to an abysmally low point; five minutes or more were required to get a dial tone, and even then completing a call was highly problematical.[9]

By mid-1965 the Peruvian Executive was ready to come to terms with ITT to meet the growing crisis. In July a nonbinding "Memorandum Agreement" was signed with the utility whereby it would be granted a new twenty-year concession, a 12 percent guaranteed earnings rate, and a tariff increase as of September 1. In return ITT would undertake a $74 million expansion program which would add 143,000 (later 145,000) new phones over five years, an expansion rate of 31.3 percent.[10]

By August the company had fulfilled its end of this bargain to the extent of placing an order for sufficient equipment to expand by 25,000 phones. At the same time new tariffs were applied for. Belaúnde completed his part of the arrangement by signing—secretly—a decree that would increase tariffs. Soon this act became public knowledge. The resultant outcry on the part of the APRA-UNO coalition in Congress was so vehement that Belaúnde was forced to rescind the increase. ITT then countered with a measure that is possibly rare in contemporary foreign investment politics, a sending of individual warning letters to each member of the Peruvian Congress. Dated November 30, 1965, the letter asked that objection to a tariff increase be withdrawn. A key paragraph reads:

The failure to implement tariff increases will not only destroy all possibilities of obtaining the financing of more than Two Thousand Million Soles [$74.6 million] that is required to complete the expansion program of more than 145,000 telephones, but will also place the Company in the grave situation of not being able to comply with the commitments it has assumed to initiate the massive expansion of the telephone service in Lima, Callao and suburbs by installation of the first 30,000 telephones between May 1966 and December 1967. The material impossibility of obtaining financing to effect these payments with the existing tariffs and within the limitations to which our company has been subject, is an indisputable fact which can easily be confirmed by any impartial study. The repercussions of this new situation in which the company is being placed and the immense damages caused do not require further comment.[11]

Congressional opposition continued unabated. But nevertheless the regulatory Junta finally agreed to open negotiations on a new settlement. In September 1966, after months of talks, the draft of a new telephone contract was approved. It contained substantially the same terms as the 1965 agreement, with two exceptions: two government members were added to the company's board of directors, and purchase of ITT's telephone company shares was opened to the government or new telephone users. The contract was approved (but not signed) by the Executive in November. The first rate increase in four years went into effect in December.

Meanwhile Congress expressed its distaste for these moves by passing a resolution against both the contract and the rate increase. Opposition legislators discussed the possibility of opening future telephone expansions to competitive international bidding, an idea that had been favored by anticompany forces for some time. APRA senators bitterly questioned Belaúnde ministers in parliamentary interpellation regarding details of the pending contract and conjectured that pressures had been coming from the U.S. government. The company responded with newspaper advertisements and public statements defending the rate increase and contract. Referring again to potential actions of external creditors, a statement of January 10, 1967, said in part, "The financing of the expansion program depends substantially on capital and credits which may be obtained by the Company. It is not possible to obtain this capital and credits without a stable economic organization supported by adequate tariff rates."[12]

The next month Congress passed a bill requiring international bidding, as described in Chapter Five. We know that Belaúnde did not approve it. When the Geneen letter to Rusk requesting U.S. intervention came to light a few days later, the congressional opposition was presented with one more brickbat to hurl at the Belaúnde contract, which still had not been made final and binding.

Finally, on August 12, 1967, Belaúnde signed the contract in substantially modified form, obviously making concessions to his critics. The principal changes were incorporation of the concepts of international bidding and eventual Peruvianization of the company. ITT would go ahead with installation of 67,000 new lines over the next three years. Meanwhile the government would tender bids for an expansion program of 150,000 additional lines. If no satisfactory bidder was found, ITT could then add 43,000 more lines. (Two bids were submitted; neither was accepted.) In any event the company was to be Peruvian-owned by the end of 1971; this was to be accomplished by nationalization, purchase by a private bidder, or creation of a subscriber sinking fund. The last-named method, implemented temporarily, imposed a surcharge on new telephone installations and monthly bills, the receipts of which were to be used to buy out ITT.[13]

The corporation found this contract acceptable under the circumstances despite these innovative concepts, and it went ahead with expansion. During 1967 some 13,000 lines were installed and considerable new central-office equipment was purchased. When the devaluation of the sol occurred in September, however, wage and material costs began to climb. The company continued with expansion but applied for yet another tariff increase. To obtain public acceptance of it public statements were used; a March 1968 advertisement was headlined, "Prospects for Telephone Expansion Good—If Rate Hike Approved."[14]

The Junta de Telecomunicaciones approved the tariff increase in May and the company continued with its latest expansion program well into 1969, despite the disruption of the 1968 revolution and the aftermath of uncertainty. Once again, however, the program was jeopardized by ITT perceptions of trouble. In May 1969 the Revolution's minister of transport and communications, General Aníbal Meza Cuadra, announced that he was seeking ways to finance immediate purchase of ITT's shares in the telephone company. He stated that Peru was one of the few countries whose basic communications network was not entirely in government hands. Within the Peruvian military the sentiment was strong that nationalized telecommunications were essential to national security.[15]

In the meantime, the company had asked for yet another rise in tariffs.

In July 1969 it was flatly turned down. Immediately the current expansion program was slowed. In the same month the government charged that during 1967 and 1968 Cía. Peruano de Teléfonos had spent approximately $2 million for unnecessary expenses, among which were padded expense accounts and superfluous public relations advertising (note the advertisement quoted above). In August 1969 General Meza Cuadra declared the 1967 contract "an impossible juridical act" and void.[16]

At the same time these moves were taking place publicly, privately the ministry of transport and communications and ITT were negotiating a mutually acceptable settlement of the corporation's overall status in Peru. The outcome was an agreement whereby ITT would sell its 69.11 percent of the telephone company's equity to the government. ITT was willing, and the only issue was price. Initially the enterprise wanted $19.4 million in cash. But these terms soon went by the board. When the government's negotiators made it clear they were going to demand that at least half the proceeds of the sale remain in Peru, ITT proposed that its Sheraton hotel subsidiary use part of them to construct a luxury hotel in Lima. After some deliberation Meza Cuadra accepted the idea, with the proviso that it be designed by a Peruvian architect of the government's selection. This was agreed to; it was determined that $12 million of the sale's proceeds should go to the hotel and an excellent parcel of downtown land was sold to ITT for the site. (The 20-story building was completed in 1973.)[17]

Realizing that the hotel project would consume only part of the value of the telephone stock, negotiators for the government then proposed that ITT construct a telephone equipment manufacturing plant in Peru. The corporation accepted the idea after some consideration. It was agreed to form the Fábrica de Equipos de Telefonía S.A., which would be a joint venture with ITT holding 60 percent and the government 40 percent of the capital. After eight years the government could increase its share to 50 percent. (The plant began operating in 1971.)

Other aspects of the settlement included contracts whereby ITT would supply equipment for expansion of the Lima telephone system; ITT technicians would temporarily advise the ministry's telephone management; and ITT would receive $4.2 million in cash. The plan's basic features were announced in October 1969 and its details worked out by March 1970. ITT executives privately say they got "quite a good deal" from the settlement in that they had received the equivalent of $17.3 million in cash and guaranteed new investments, almost 90 percent of their initial price. In addition, the manufacturing contract was extremely liberal from the company's standpoint in terms of protective guarantees. Finally ITT's general position in Peru was undoubtedly strengthened in that its investments were now in politically less sensitive form.

There is evidence that the government, too, was not displeased by the outcome. In fact the agreement was used to attempt to mollify the hostility and uncertainty about Peru in international financial circles that had arisen from the IPC affair and other actions of the Velasco regime. When the basic elements of the settlement were announced in October 1969 the two parties issued a joint statement that declared that ITT "will receive what it considers to be a fair and just value for its equity." The statement added, "The Agreement demonstrates the willingness and sincere interest of the Revolutionary Government of Peru to work constructively with foreign private companies and investors."[18] In November 1969 and January 1970 the amicableness of the nationalization was described in paid advertisements placed by the government in the *New York Times.*[19]

In sum, ITT—unlike IPC—emerged from several decades of activist investment bargaining with its original properties gone but with its vital interests protected. The principal strategy had been holding the Lima telephone system hostage to accomplishment of desired government policy. On several occasions expansion of the system was held out as a lure and suspension of ongoing expansion imposed as a sanction. This was done specifically, deliberately, and at times arrogantly. Quite effective at first, the strategy nevertheless brought, with the passage of time, increasingly delayed and unfavorable governmental responses. But, before it was too late, the company was able to strike an entirely new bargain that was not only inherently attractive to ITT but which created a reestablished investor-host relationship that was far safer for both sides.

Bargaining over Minerals

It might be anticipated that pressures generated from investment bargaining by the mining companies would be particularly strong. It is in mining that Peruvian dependence on American capital is most acute; it is also in this sector that U.S. capital is most heavily involved in Peru, making the stakes for the investors as well very high. Evidence has been gathered on bargaining over minerals for three periods: 1947-1954, 1965-1968, and 1969-1971.

1947-1954. During this first period, it must be remembered, Cerro de Pasco was the one and only giant mining company in Peru. Marcona and the Southern Peru Copper Corporation came on the scene shortly afterwards.

As World War II ended, the management of Cerro was uncomfortable with developments in Peru. Labor costs were rising in the postwar inflation. Export taxes, which are unrelated to income or profits, were being progressively increased. The company's net profits as a percent of sales fell from the 11-14 range in the early 1940's to the 5-7 percent range in the latter part of the decade. Moreover the Bustamante administration,

elected in 1945, had imposed foreign exchange controls, a policy traditionally despised by exporting firms.[20]

Pressures were applied by Cerro to improve the situation. A source of
bargaining leverage was conveniently at hand: the corporation wanted
eventually to construct a major zinc-lead refinery at Cerro de Pasco as a
part of its metals diversification program away from copper. To supply
power for the refinery a large hydroelectric plant was also needed.
Together these projects would cost in the neighborhood of $50 million, a
large sum for those days—its investment would about double U.S. mining
assets in the country.

In 1947 the Cerro management specifically sought tax relief. In November of that year a government commission was appointed to reassess the
tax situation but by year's end no action had been taken. Cerro's 1947
annual report, published in early 1948 (a place where the company often
transmits pointed messages to the Peruvian government—texts of the
report are widely reprinted in Lima newspapers), continued to hold out
the prospect of the major investment but warned that "conditions" must
be appropriate: "Under conditions recently prevailing in Peru, it has been
necessary to defer a decision to make these investments in a zinc refinery
and hydroelectric plant, but . . . the decision must not be too long
delayed."

A series of events favorable to Cerro's interests then occurred. In March
of 1948 a reduction of mining taxes was decreed. The following September exchange controls were liberalized. In October the best thing of all
happened—the overthrow of Bustamante by General Odría.

Unprepared to take the new situation for granted, the corporation
pressed for still further modifications of mining policy. By 1949 the
zinc-lead project was still hanging fire and hence available for a quid pro
quo. The 1948 annual report, issued in early 1949, stated with respect to
the project, "There has been no change in conditions which would have
justified a commitment by the Corporation for such a large investment."
With the project still not begun in early 1950, the 1949 report reiterated
the warning, only this time adding that a needed loan from the Export-
Import Bank would depend on acceptable policies: "A condition precedent to borrowing funds will be appropriate assurances of the Peruvian
Government with respect to such matters as exchange control, export and
import restrictions and taxes."

But by this time the Odría government was already moving in the desired
direction. In August of 1949 a study commission had been formed to
propose changes in the mining code, the basic law of the industry. The
code had not been comprehensively revised for half a century despite
several attempts by Cerro and the other mining companies to this end. By
January of 1950 a draft was ready; this was approved in May and
promulgated in July.

The content of the Mining Code of 1950 was greatly influenced, if not dictated, by the wishes of Cerro de Pasco Corporation and other members of the Sociedad de Minería y Petróleos. Robert Koenig, who had become president of Cerro in 1950, described the code to me as just what the industry had wanted.[21] The new law simplified and reduced mining taxes, provided low canon payments on concessions, and permitted concessionaires to retain exploitation rights for an indefinite period even if the concessions were unworked. Two features of the code were of particular importance to Cerro: A depletion allowance of 15 percent modeled in concept on U.S. tax law and authorization for special investment contracts in which the regular tax arrangements would be substituted by a negotiated profit-sharing deal. The latter was provided for in Article 56 of the code.[22]

Investment "conditions" in Peru were now such that Cerro felt it could go ahead with expansion. Contracts for the zinc program were signed in December 1950 and January 1951. Over the next five years the company placed new capital in the country at an annual rate of $9 million compared to a $2.4-million rate during the previous five years. Cerro made good use of Article 56's flexibility; in fact, as long as Odría was still in power the corporation could quite literally write its own ticket on special contracts. Koenig recalls how once he approached the president to propose a new investment project under Article 56. Odría told Koenig, whom he had known well for many years, not to press him with the details but simply to inform the finance minister what was wanted. This Koenig did; after telling the minister what the president had said a telephone call was placed to the palace to check whether blanket approval had in fact been given. A contract exactly along the lines desired by Cerro was then written.*[23]

Article 56 was also the legal basis for the largest single private investment in Peru's history, the huge Toquepala open-pit copper mine. Although no details are known of the bargaining that preceded this investment, the basic contract was signed in November 1954 while Odría was still in power. It provided for a sharing of 30 percent of net income with the Peruvian government in lieu of other taxes. In 1954 Peruvian corporate tax levels were such that this percentage constituted a moderate but not enormous tax reduction. But the arrangement was to be in effect not for a specified number of years but for the length of time it took SPCC to recoup in profits its initial investment in the mine complex. It was the corporation's interpretation that depreciation and depletion allowances were *not* to be considered "profits" for the purpose of computing when investment recovery had been made. As has been mentioned, Cerro owned 22 percent of SPCC (the enterprise created for the venture), with the American Smelting & Refining Company (ASARCO) holding 51 percent. An investment of $215 million was at first contemplated, of which the

*Koenig completes the anecdote with the remark that today this is no longer possible.

Export-Import Bank provided $100 million in initial long-term credits; eventually the project required almost $250 million.[24]

1965-1968. Toquepala went fully "on stream" in late 1959 after four years of construction and preparation. The enterprise was greatly successful, especially in view of the precipitous climb of world copper prices in the 1960's. This meant that recovery of investment proceeded faster than expected. As Mikesell and other foreign investment economists would anticipate, the profitability of Toquepala began to draw complaints within Peru that the corporation had been given too favorable a deal. Opposition to the Toquepala contract intensified following Belaúnde's election and soon serious moves against it were developing in the Peruvian Congress.

In response to prodding by a group of Aprista deputies, an investigating commission was formed in 1965 to study the matter. The commission's report, issued in February 1967, was exceedingly critical not just of the contract but of SPCC itself. The corporation was accused of refusing to provide the commission with the financial information needed to assess its tax liability and also of misrepresenting the true dimensions of its investment and profits by use of double or even triple sets of books. But even without the desired data, the commission concluded that recovery had already been achieved if depreciation and depletion allowances *were* included in net income. This interpretation of the contract's meaning became the basic rationale for a demand that it had, in fact, expired. Although a minority of the commission members wanted to have the contract unilaterally declared void, the majority recommended that SPCC be required immediately to begin paying regular taxes (now around 48 percent). In November 1967 legislation was passed which authorized the Executive to renegotiate the Toquepala contract; as with La Brea y Pariñas, the ball had been tossed in Belaúnde's lap.[25]

Meanwhile the SPCC management stuck to its guns by insisting that depreciation and depletion were not to be counted toward investment recovery and that as of mid-1967 only $120 of the $215 million had been earned. To recover the remaining $95 million five to six more years of the existing profit-sharing rate were required, it was said, and thus the corporation was entitled to them.[26]

To SPCC the stakes were, however, higher than a few million dollars of extra income from Toquepala. Significantly, the stakes were greater for Peru as well. Adjacent to Toquepala were two other huge deposits of copper as yet untouched, Cuajone and Quellaveco. Cuajone, twelve air miles away, was known to be the biggest of the three ore bodies and could be exploited in substantial degree by means of the same railroad, port, and smelter already servicing Toquepala. SPCC had rights to mine these deposits as a result of ASARCO's possession of the appropriate concessions from several years back. In short, the possibility was open to Peru that tremendous new sources of revenue and foreign exchange were within a few years' reach. To SPCC opportunities lay ahead of doubling or tripling its Peruvian output. The situation was ripe for nonzero-sum bargaining.

To investors an obvious bargaining goal at this stage was to make the terms of Article 56 more ironclad so that prior interpretations of taxation privileges would not become "unstuck" after the investment was in place. In February 1967 the presidents of Cerro, ASARCO, and the Anaconda Company (concessionaire to the undeveloped Cerro Verde copper deposit) requested a joint audience with President Belaúnde. According to Koenig, from whom I learned of this meeting, the three mining heads specifically informed Belaúnde that they each had certain capital investments in mind for the near future. But, they said, it was impossible that the projects go ahead without revision of Article 56 along certain lines. Koenig did not tell me what lines, but from later developments it can be inferred that tax stability was one of them. According to Koenig the proffered projects were "minor," although it is difficult to believe that the possibility of developing Cuajone or Quellaveco was far from the minds of those present.[27]

To complicate matters, soon another issue emerged to accompany Article 56 as a topic of investment bargaining. In September 1967 the Belaúnde government devalued the sol, and Peru's economic crisis deepened. In November the regime, in a desperate attempt to raise added revenues, placed a 10 percent surcharge on the gross value of practically all exports, including minerals. Technically the charge was a prepayment of future income taxes, and tax credit certificates were issued on it. But to the mining companies this was just one more drain on current income. In Cerro's annual report for 1967 the charge was described as "inhibiting"; it would, the report complained, "adversely affect Cerro's near-term operating results." In oral comments at a stockholder's meeting Koenig was more candid, calling the tax credit certificates "worthless paper." At the same time it was made clear that if the Peruvians did away with these harassments great things were possible. With regard to Cuajone, Cerro's 1967 report said, "Further progress toward bringing this property into production depends on legislative developments in Peru which bear on the ability to obtain financing for the project and on other factors."[28]

Whether or not pressures generated by these new-investment offers were responsible, in 1968 the Belaúnde administration accommodated the mineral interests in varying degree on both of these questions. In February 1968 a revised Article 56 was approved; the new version was not precisely what the foreign investors had wanted but was acceptable. It explicitly provided that all contractual rights would remain in force for the period of recovery of investment. Depreciation and depletion funds were to be counted as net income to be applied against recovery, but in exchange for this progovernment feature a postrecovery period of six years was guaranteed during which only taxes in effect at the time of contract signing would be owed. Clearly the corporations had made a net gain.[29]

In May settlement of the export surcharge issue was achieved. Here again a compromise was struck, but probably more in the interests of the government than the companies. Its terms were proposed by none other than the Marcona Corporation, the one member of the gran minería not directly involved in the February 1967 offer to Belaúnde.[30] (Marcona has frequently been able to avoid identification with the Cerro-SPCC group, to its own advantage.) The proposed solution was to convert the tax credit certificates to bonds. It was accepted by the government and beginning in July the export charge was terminated, but the large mining companies (not other exporters) were required to purchase government securities in the amount of 10 percent of exports.[31]

It hardly seems a coincidence that shortly after these concessions by the government in the first half of 1968 the investors would then make their moves. June 18, 1968, Minister of Finance Manuel Ulloa announced that a new Toquepala contract had been signed with SPCC whereby the corporation would pay 51.4 percent of its net revenues to the government. This was, in the company's eyes, a loss of the 30 percent rate three years prematurely. *Just one week later* Frank W. Archibald, then SPCC president, announced that the company was now planning to move ahead with Cuajone, assuming satisfactory completion of current negotiations. He stated that he expected such negotiations to be satisfactorily concluded "shortly." In his announcement Archibald included an explicit endorsement of the Peruvian regime, no doubt aimed at the New York financial community but obviously not displeasing to the Lima government: "The full cooperation of the Peruvian Government to complete the arrangements necessary for the development of this mine has created a favorable climate for new mining investments in Peru."[32]

1969-1971. If Archibald did indeed perceive the investment climate as "favorable" at that time it was soon to become more forbidding. The coup of 1968 resulted in sweeping changes in the structure of the Peruvian mining industry. In September 1969 the corporations were told to submit detailed, rapid schedules of development of unworked mining concessions or risk losing them. Some 900 schedules were filed, but most of these were declared inadequate and most unexploited concessions were subsequently withdrawn without compensation. Anaconda lost Cerro Verde, Cerro had to give up four properties, and ASARCO was relieved of Michiquillay, a huge copper deposit in the Cajamarca Department. SPCC lost Quellaveco but retained Cuajone.[33]

In April 1970 the 1950 mining code was displaced by an entirely new basic mining law.[34] It applied new incentive concepts to the industry and enlarged the state's role in it. A government instrumentality, the Empresa Minera del Perú (Mineroperú), was given a monopoly in foreign mineral trading and in the refining of metals, except that Cerro's zinc-lead refinery was not disturbed. The industry was not otherwise nationalized although tax differentials encouraged state participation in mining enterprises. The old depletion allowance was wiped out, substituted by a reinvestment deduction allowance; this was initially set at 30 percent of pretax profits to an upper limit of 200 million soles and was later changed to 40 percent and 300 million soles. This liberalization was in return, I am told, for a decision, publicly revealed in June 1971, to apply the comunidad concept to mining.

Thus the "rules of the game" had been modified. Although the mining companies had been permitted to comment on early drafts of the new decrees their desires were largely ignored. Koenig and other veteran mining executives were angered and even bitter about the new situation; they proclaimed having no further interest in investing in Peru.[35] Nevertheless, it should be pointed out, the foreign mining corporations had not been taken over or forced out. In fact, with the exception of unworked concessions, existing contracts and arrangements were permitted to stand. Taxation and control of foreign exchange were revised and the comunidad concept was added, but otherwise existing operations could continue.

Even SPCC's right to develop Cuajone under the old Article 56 was unabrogated. The gradual coming to fruition of this vast new mining complex provides a fascinating example of how mutual self-benefit can drive two parties with divergent interests to eventual agreement. Both sides had enormous stakes involved, most tangibly revenues and export earnings for the government and profits for the corporation. Also, I am told, the government was anxious to prove to the international financial community that it could work with foreign capitalists and SPCC was anxious to protect the flank of Toquepala, in which almost a quarter of a billion dollars had already been invested.

Unfortunately "inside" details of the Cuajone negotiations are not known. But from outward appearances SPCC's strategy was to avoid threats and instead to underscore its ability to live with the Revolution. In December 1968, just two months after the coup, the corporation reported that a formal application for a Cuajone contract had been completed. In early 1969, when U.S.-Peruvian relations were highly strained and it was unknown whether President Nixon would apply the Hickenlooper Amendment, the SPCC management assured the minister of energy and mines, General Jorge Fernández Maldonado, that Cuajone would go ahead "con Enmienda o sin Enmienda" (with the Amendment or without the Amendment).[36]

In the final months of 1969 bargaining over the contract intensified and in December an agreement was announced. The terms included a tax of

47.5 percent during the recovery period and a maximum rate of 54.5 percent during the six-year post-recovery period. The press treated the signing of the contract as a highly significant event inasmuch as an investment of at least $355 million and possibly $550 million was involved. The Velasco government hailed the project in a paid *New York Times* ad as "one of the greatest investments ever made in the world by a single corporation." The ad copy also said, "To invest money in Peru does not mean taking a risk. The Cuajone contract . . . is great proof that between the foreign capital and the nationalist way of the Peruvian revolution, an understanding is possible."[37]

It still remained, however, to obtain financing for the enormous project. Toquepala had been in part financed by Washington but, because of the U.S. government's coolness toward the Velasco regime, for Cuajone this was out of the question. SPCC approached a European consortium for financing in 1970 and a group of Japanese smelting firms in 1971, but in both instances investment risks were apparently deemed too great for expected payoffs. Finally it became clear that SPCC would have to go ahead alone and finance initial stages of the project itself or risk losing the entire concession.[38] In fact the Velasco government set October 1971 as the critical deadline—by that time SPCC had to commit at least $25 million in preliminary development costs or lose everything. SPCC determined that its own interests lay in continuation of the Project, and by June of 1971 $90 million had been committed. This capital was not, however, newly imported to Peru but consisted of reinvested profits from Toquepala.*

The mining companies, then, had engaged in investment bargaining with the lure of new capital as the principal tactic. This powerful attraction drew successive Peruvian regimes into procompany revisions of the mining code and tax law. In the 1940's and 1950's it permitted Cerro de Pasco virtually to dictate public policy of immediate interest to the company. Yet in the 1960's and 1970's the corporations found that compromises, concessions, and even substantial progovernment alterations in the basic rules of the game were necessary. But, with great dependence by Peru on the gran minería for export earnings and government revenues, enormous pressures were exerted to come to terms with the foreign capitalists. The Revolution, despite its otherwise radical nature, was made compatible to huge and even growing American mining investments. The added expansion—particularly at Cuajone—cemented even further the tight interdependence of investor and regime.

---

*Two years later, after an intensive search in world money markets for the remainder of Cuajone's financing, sufficient capital was secured to assure completion of the project. The funds include $175 million from a 30-bank consortium led by Chase Manhattan (with most of the banks American) and $215 million from supplier credits and advance copper sales.

Tacit Bargaining?

Thomas Schelling defines tacit bargaining as "bargaining in which communication is incomplete or impossible." It differs from "explicit bargaining," in which each parties' offers, intentions and agreements are relatively well articulated and communicated. Tacit bargaining may occur, he says, when the parties will not or cannot negotiate or where mistrust blocks explicit agreement; an example is the nonuse of poison gas in World War II.[39]

Tacit bargaining is exceedingly hard to perceive and impossible to verify, for its central characteristic is lack of communication and hence visibility. Thus its description and analysis must rest largely on conjecture in most instances. Yet evidences of it may surface here and there in the form of vague "signals" to the other side; alterations in the behavior of both sides that coincide and which are logically linked and mutually beneficial may be identified as possible tacit agreements.

One is strongly tempted to speculate that certain events occurring during the Velasco regime are related to forms of tacit bargaining. American capital and the Peruvian Revolution were, for at least a time, communicating meagerly and in a state of mutual distrust. Yet each side's self-interest lay in revealing what was acceptable and what was unacceptable. Furthermore each side could conceivably benefit from a détente provided it was not openly recognized.

Consider, for example, certain actions of the Belco Petroleum Corporation, whose Peruvian subsidiary had been engaged in offshore drilling operations in northern Peru since 1960. As has been mentioned, a few days following the 1968 coup the company issued a statement that expressed its "confidence in Peru." The firm was able to negotiate directly and effectively with Petroperú the following year over the price of crude oil delivered to Talara; in fact the company suspended deliveries for a time to gain bargaining leverage. In March 1970 Alfredo Rosenzweig, then Belco's local general manager, was quoted in the *Peruvian Times* in a manner that contained no explicit threats to cease deliveries again or to depart from Peru, but nevertheless the impression was left that such was possible if the government went too far: "As long as the government considers that Peruvian oil should have preferential treatment here, and that the set-up should include the necessary incentives to make production here economically possible, we'll continue to do our very best to look for ways and means to exploit the area. So far we have received these incentives, and there is no indication that this attitude will change."[40]

A parallel statement was made by Charles Robinson, president of the Marcona Corporation, at almost exactly the same time. Marcona had also, in effect, endorsed the new government when it came into power and had negotiated successfully with the Santa Corporation over a new contract.

And, like Belco, Marcona apparently wanted to tell the Peruvians that the enterprise could and would leave the country if the policies of the Revolution became intolerable. Yet any departure warning had to be nonexplicit to avoid requiring the generals to retaliate in order to save face. In March 1970 an interview with Robinson was published in *Forbes* and subsequently in the *Peruvian Times*; it said in part, "I am really quite discouraged with Peru. . . . They don't know what they want and may have to go pretty far to learn the economic facts of life." Stress was given in the *Forbes* article to Robinson's new concept of Marcona as an international "resources transportation company" rather than mining firm. "If we had to," he said, "we could rapidly deploy our fleet elsewhere in the ore market and not show a substantial drop in revenues." *Forbes* editorialized that what Robinson was saying in less diplomatic language was "Without Marcona, where would the Peruvians sell the ore and how would they ship it?"[41]

Let us carry the speculation one step further and argue that changes occurred in investment actions and government policies in 1971 which are indicative of formulation of a tacit agreement. As was shown in Chapter Three, the book value of U.S. investments in Peru had dropped precipitiously after 1969. The flow of new private capital into the country came to an almost total standstill when the radical contours of the Revolution became evident. The only infusions of foreign investment worth mentioning in 1969-1970 were associated with the small Madrigal copper mine opened by the Homestake Mining Company of San Francisco and the Bayer acrylic fiber plant built by the Germans in Lima (and the latter had been committed prior to the coup).[42] The new Sheraton Hotel, the ITT telephone equipment plant, and Cuajone's development all involved reinvestment of capital already in Peru. U.S. businessmen during this period frequently referred to a "hold-out" on new investments in the country and spoke in such terms as "nothing—absolutely nothing—is happening down there now."

In about mid-1971 the picture seemed to change, with respect to both investor behavior and to governmental posture. In June Petroperú signed an oil exploration contract with the Occidental Petroleum Corporation, a U.S. firm. In a rather unusual arrangement proposed by Petroperú, the state remained concessionaire while Occidental explored for oil under contract. Instead of splitting income or profits as is normally done, any crude oil brought to the surface was to be divided 50-50 between the two parties. Petroperú then purchased Occidental's half and the company was excused from all but minor taxes. At this same time several other international petroleum companies expressed interest in such contracts and within a few months several additional, similar deals were concluded. Investor interest in Peruvian oil heightened further when, in November 1971, Petroperú itself spudded a first successful well in the Marañon-

Pastaza Basin of the selva. By year's end talk was being heard in industry circles of investments up to one billion dollars in selva oil during the 1970's.[43]

In other sectors signs of reawakened investor interest were also visible. In August 1971 bids were opened for construction of a diesel engine plant; seven offers were made, including a very comprehensive one from the Continental Motors Corporation of Detroit. Meanwhile British and Belgian consortia began competing for rights to exploit the Cerro Verde copper deposit, formerly owned by Anaconda. The Britons won, signing a contract in October that envisioned an initial investment of $70 million.* About this time another British group signed a contract to build and finance, along with the Inter-American Development Bank, the $110 million Majes irrigation project. Together these projects represented the biggest British financial commitment on the West Coast of South America in over half a century.[44] In December Goodyear del Perú announced that it was considering diversification into other products than tires and tubes with the prospect of augmenting nontraditional exports from Peru.[45] In January 1972 the Inter-American Development Bank announced a $12 million loan for the agrarian reform cooperatives and ENTURPERÚ, the state tourist company, signed letters of intent with Holiday Inns, Marriott Corporation, and Braniff Airways to construct six hotels worth $15 million in Peru.[46] Clearly foreign-investor psychology had changed, at least in certain areas.**

Meanwhile 1971, unlike the previous year, was turning out to be very bad from the standpoint of the Peruvian economy. In contrast to the excellent export earnings of 1970, a serious balance of payments deficit was being experienced, mainly as a result of low earnings from copper and fishmeal. Fishmeal was suffering from a chronic liquidity problem and mining was being plagued by declining world prices and a rash of strikes called by the left-wing CGTP union.[47] Reduction of copper income was hurting the government's budget as well; during the first half of 1971, SPCC was making a fifth of its usual profits and Cerro and Marcona were actually losing money. The resultant tax loss was at least $30 million for the first six months of the year.

As 1971 progressed a number of actions on the part of the Revolutionary government were noted with great interest by the foreign investment community. In April Rear Admiral Jorge Dellepiane, minister of industry and commerce, was replaced by Rear Admiral Alberto Jiménez de Lucio; Dellepiane had been responsible for the Industrial Law and was strongly

*The following year the arrangement was revised, with Eurocurrency loans providing much of the capital.

**It is worth noting that Table 10 (Chapter Three) shows a significant drop in the book value of U.S. direct investments (in current dollars) between 1969 and 1970, but none between 1970 and 1971.

disliked by business leaders, whereas the youthful Jiménez de Lucio was considered "moderate" and "rational." Following this switch, communication between the ministry of industry and commerce and business leaders became more cordial as was happening elsewhere. Revolutionary decrees were now being circulated systematically in draft form for business comment and deadlines imposed on the corporations were occasionally extended when requested. For a few months the possibility even seemed to open up that foreign firms would not have to "fade out" after all, although this was eliminated by later clarification.[48] Negotiations with Grace over compensation for its sugar properties and sale of its industrial properties resumed in May and culminated in an agreement in December. Throughout the latter part of the year talks were proceeding with the fishmeal industry as to what tax and credit adjustments could strengthen that sector. Finally, and perhaps most importantly, toward the end of the year the government made it clear that it was no longer going to tolerate lengthy CGTP-inspired strikes in the mines; in November the army moved against strikers at the immobilized Cobriza mine with the consequence that five miners were killed and several injured. Several other strikes were forcibly ended without serious violence.[49]

My interpretation of the significance of this congery of events is admittedly tentative and conjectural. Yet the deterioration of the economy, relaxation of policy, and resumption of investment could be plausibly linked. The generals' interpretation of the Peruvian public interest could have been affected by the payments and budget deficits; an increase in industrial output was essential in the short run. In the long run continuing population growth and migration to Lima mean it is necessary to create 130,000 new jobs annually just to keep even; hence a reversal of the investment "holdout" may have been perceived as eventually necessary anyway. President Velasco could not, of course, admit making concessions to the foreign capitalists, and in May and then in November of 1971 he found it necessary to deny explicitly that structural transformation of the society was being sacrificed to economic growth and that business was becoming a new privileged class.[50]

Yet, the businessmen—at least some of them—were starting to feel better about the Revolution. Part of this was, no doubt, a consequence of simply getting used to the new order. Another part was likely a realization that for the time being the armed forces were electing to remain in power; at least political conditions would remain reasonably stable so that the "rules of the game" were knowable. And the "rules" did not look so bad by comparison to what was by now going on in the Marxist regime of Chile.

Business executives with whom I spoke in mid-1971 were plainly keeping their ears open for encouraging signals from the Peruvian government. They furthermore conceived of the payments and budget deficits as the kind of problem the hard-headed generals simply could not ignore.

Even if the Revolutionary leadership was *not* worried the businessmen *thought* they were, and thus business was ready to view any government concessions as understandable and relatively sincere.

In short, the events of 1971 make some sense as a "tacit agreement" whereby the generals and the capitalists agreed without saying so that a rapprochement was mutually desirable provided each side's vital interests were left undamaged. The Revolution could not sacrifice its basic principles and the foreign investors could not do without profits. And neither side could afford to be very open. Yet the right kind of nonzero-sum exchange could potentially improve both parties' position. True, not all corporations or government entities relaxed; Cerro de Pasco and the ministry of energy and mines remained cool and unbending. Also it should be remembered that coincidental, nonpolitical factors such as the selva oil find were at work. But *something* had happened, and only the perspective of time will help to clarify what it was.

In any event it is fascinating to consider how American corporations in Peru may possess a subtle, undirected "influence" whereby the most radical government in the country's history eventually begins to make its peace with them.

Recapitulation and Analysis

The corporations definitely engaged in investment bargaining, that is, exchange of prospective economic benefits associated with corporate investments and operations in return for specified public policies.

IPC employed several investment bargaining tactics in its campaign to avoid full taxation prior to 1922, secure a gasoline price increase in the 1950's, and counteract the political movement against it in the 1960's. In 1916, 1918, and 1958 the company threatened to curtail Talara operations or actually did so. In 1916 and 1965 hints of new investment were made. In 1957-1958, 1963-1964, and 1968 the privileged status of La Brea y Pariñas was offered in return for different arrangements.

ITT's investment bargaining revolved around expansion of the Lima telephone system. It appears that offers of expansion were used to press for tariff increases in 1950, 1956, 1962, and 1965. A 1963 ultimatum to General Lindley and a 1965 letter to members of Congress flatly conditioned expansion on tariff rises. In 1967 and 1968 the company publicly linked expansion and tariffs in newspaper advertisements. In 1958, 1963, and 1969 expansion programs currently underway were halted or curtailed in retaliation for refusals to increase tariffs or revalue assets.

The mining companies utilized primarily lures of new investment to gain bargaining leverage. In 1947-1950 Cerro offered the zinc development project as bait to secure liberalizations in taxation, exchange controls, and the mining law. In the following few years all three of the gran minería negotiated favorable investment contracts under Article 56 of the 1950 Mining Code. In 1967 the prospect of Cuajone and lesser mining projects was used to seek modification of Article 56 and probably termination of the export surcharge.

It is speculated that "tacit" bargaining occurred between several companies and the Velasco regime. In 1970 Belco and Marcona appeared to send "signals" to the effect that departure or curtailment of operations would follow imposition of unacceptable policies. In 1971 an apparent "holdout" of new American capital was eased at the same time that the government was sending what might be interpreted as "signals" of desired conciliation. A subsequent "tacit agreement" to cooperate more fully is conjectural, however.

With respect to the outcome of bargaining, it would appear that in general the corporations did better in the past than in recent years. In 1918-1922 IPC got precisely what it wanted in terms of making secure La Brea y Pariñas. The company's efforts to obtain a gasoline price increase in the 1950's were eventually successful but at enormous cost. Its attempts to secure a new footing for La Brea in the 1960's succeeded temporarily in 1968, but the cost this time was removal from Peru without compensation. In somewhat parallel fashion, ITT quite easily obtained tariff increases and new telephone rights up to and including the Odría period. But the Prado government balked for months before giving in and the Belaúnde regime resisted for years, in large part because of congressional opposition. As with IPC, just when the telephone situation seemed to be finally settling down in the late 1960's, the Velasco coup interrupted with a demand for nationalization. The mining companies, Cerro in particular, were able almost to dictate mining law and contracts during the Odría years. Under Belaúnde they no longer controlled the situation outright but nevertheless were able to bargain quite effectively by dangling new mining projects. After Velasco's rise to power mining policy turned sharply against investor interests but yet all major investments survived and Cuajone proceeded.

If one considers what strategies seemed most effective, the lure of new capital rather than offers or threats surrounding existing capital seems to have generated the greater leverage, with important exceptions. ITT and the mining companies made virtually all their gains with the new-investment strategy. The tacit agreement of 1971 (if it existed) was based on an inflow of investments. At the same time, however, it must be recognized that IPC's most effective bargaining was based on curtailment tactics; moreover, Belco and Marcona did well following their tacit threats. Offers to exchange existing investment terms generally failed when employed by IPC; SPCC's revised Toquepala contract of 1968 and ITT's hotel deal of 1969 were reluctantly accepted exchanges rather than bargaining ploys.

Part III   **Implications for Community
and Society**

Seven   Politics in the Company Town

A potential political consequence of American business in Peru outside of affecting *national* independence is the impact on *subnational* politics. As was mentioned in Chapter Two, eight Peruvian towns between 4,000 and 35,000 in population were economically dominated by U.S. companies in mid-1968. Since that time three of the towns have been affected by nationalization and another set of American company towns is being built at Cuajone. The U.S. company town continues to be of significance in Peruvian society even though a relatively small proportion of the total population lives in them. The towns are all important regional centers and their economic and social impact is widespread.

Essentially Hypothesis II postulates that *economic* domination of these communities by U.S. firms translates into *political* domination. To summarize, the specter is raised of a "state within a state." If true, any departures from U.S. economic imperialism on the national level in contemporary Peru may be compensated for at specific points on the subnational level. The hypothesis anticipates that political domination will stem from economic dependence itself, opportunities to control mass communications, and an ability to "buy" influence through bribes, favors, and worker benefits. Paternalistic patterns of support are predicted as declining but not necessarily leading to a reduction of company influence.

Capacities to Control

Let us examine selected factors which could underlie management's political domination of the towns. In Chapter Three we noted the extent of American control of the corporations, finding it effective if not complete. The same is true with respect to corporate managements located in the towns: local assets are wholly owned and local operations are closely controlled from the Lima or U.S. headquarters. Managerial personnel located in the eight towns were, in 1968, aggregatively 26 percent American, 15 percent other foreign, and 59 percent Peruvian. (This compares to the 30-14-56 proportions at Peruvian headquarters discussed in Chapter Three.) In all towns but two, however, the top-ranking corporate executive was American, making these percentages secondarily important. The exceptions were the two Grace plantations, where Peruvian nationals were almost completely in charge. In 1968 not a single American resided in Cartavio except for occasional visiting consultants. By contrast, SPCC operations were almost entirely directed by Americans; at Toquepala only a single Peruvian had department-head status in 1968.[1]

We turn next to the extent of corporate economic domination of the towns. Table 15 presents data on two measures of relative economic importance of the companies in their respective towns, namely, jobs (and income from them) and property ownership.

Being the principal source of employment places the firms in the position of being the principal source of material security and economic status in their respective communities. If alternate opportunities for employment are slim or absent the jobholder will think twice about alienating management by opposing the company or engaging in political activity. Peruvian labor law protects workers from arbitrary dismissal, but the desire to avoid prejudicial action or to maintain favorable assignments or to obtain promotions could nevertheless be inhibiting. An estimated 42 to 100 percent of the town populations were dependent directly on company employment in 1968, as the table shows.

In addition to wage payments, the companies support many residents indirectly. Relatives of workers or others in the community earn livings in small retail or service enterprises whose markets are created from the primary economic base. It is estimated that no less than 63 percent of the population of any town was dependent on the companies for income either directly or indirectly. In Cartavio, Paramonga, La Oroya, Pueblo Nuevo, and Toquepala income dependence was total.

The degree to which the towns are company-owned in the literal sense is important because everyone needs (or would like) a house in which to live. Further, independent retailers need stores if they sell elsewhere than in the street or public market. Hence opportunities for managerial leverage are created in the allotment of houses and commercial space. As the table indicates, in all towns most residential property was company-owned and in five of them this was true with respect to commercial buildings.

Some fairly substantial differences can be seen between the towns. If one calculates a rough index of economic domination by summing the percentages of population dependence ("by all means") and residential property ownership, he finds the rankings of least-to-most domination to be: Talara, Cerro de Pasco, La Oroya, San Juan, and—equally—the towns of Grace and SPCC.

The explanation for Talara's low ranking is that in the years prior to its expropriation IPC was implementing a deliberate "community integration" plan in which land and a stadium were ceded to the municipality, the company's cinemas were sold, and in-town tracts of land were set aside for private residential developments. At the exact moment of expropriation in 1968 ways were being sought to sell the company hospital and potentially all worker housing. For some years IPC had encouraged the

Table 15. Measures of Economic Dominance in Company Towns, 1968.

Company town	Company	Percentage of population dependent on company		Percentage of property owned by company[c]	
		By employment[a]	By all means[b]	Residential	Commercial
Talara	IPC	42	63	75	85
Cartavio	Grace	52	100	100	100
Paramonga	Grace	60	100	100	95
La Oroya	Cerro	80	100	60	10
Cerro de Pasco	Cerro	49	70	80	5
San Juan	Marcona	73	90	95	10
Pueblo Nuevo	SPCC	100	100	100	100
Toquepala	SPCC	66	100	100	100

[a]Calculated by multiplying company employment by 4 (roughly the average size of the Peruvian nuclear family) and dividing this product by town population.

[b]Management's estimate of the proportion of town population whose income derives directly from company payrolls or is obtained indirectly via the extended family or economic services to persons benefiting from the payroll.

[c]Management's estimates.

establishment of other industries in Talara, with Belco the most prominent to come.[2]

Cerro de Pasco and La Oroya are just short of being complete company towns because of the existence of several independent mines at the former and the Central Railroad at the latter. In addition, independent retail businesses are numerous. The fact that Cerro de Pasco is an ancient settlement and hence was not created de novo by the company has led to much independently owned property. At La Oroya an entire sector of town not owned by the company exists across the Mantaro River from the mining facilities.

San Juan was built almost completely by the Marcona Mining Company beginning in 1953; prior to that time it consisted of a few fishermen's huts along the beach. Fishing still supports some residents, and the company has permitted local businessmen to own their own buildings in a prescribed zone.[3]

The virtual 100 percent company towns are the two former Grace plantations and the two SPCC mining camps. Income dependency is total in all four places and every building, with the exception of a handful of houses at Paramonga, is company-owned. These communities were originally built to support corporate farming and mining and no substantial independent sections of town were allowed to grow. Until recent years Grace ran all commercial institutions such as stores and cinemas. At its mining centers SPCC still owns and operates all commercial outlets and places of entertainment except for stalls at the public market, which are leased and regulated by the firm. Toquepala's isolation in the sierra means that company monopolization there is complete; Pueblo Nuevo (formerly Ciudad Nueva) is adjacent to the fairly important port city of Ilo, hence the significance of its economic domination is diminished.

A third factor that could underlie political domination is corporate control of mass communications. We found earlier that U.S. capital is involved in the Peruvian mass media on a national scale mainly through commercial advertising and film and publication imports. In the towns, however, an opportunity for direct media control could conceivably exist because of the isolated nature of some of the communities.

With respect to television, none of the firms operates its own station even though a usable TV signal is received in five towns and sets are in abundance at them. At Cartavio and Paramonga outside commercial channels are received directly; at Talara, San Juan, and Toquepala the company constructed relay towers by which to import a commercial signal. In all cases the programs are similar to those shown throughout Peru, and the extent of the company's control of content would depend on influence at the originating station only.

The medium of radio broadcasting lends itself more fully to company control. Transistor radios are ubiquitous and all classes of people can be reached via audio broadcasting. Radio stations are relatively cheap to build and operate compared to television stations. Perhaps surprisingly, in only two towns are the companies directly involved in radio broadcasting. At San Juan a station operates that is ostensibly independent of management but in fact is not. Although the station is not officially owned and operated by Marcona, the individual who manages it is a company employee. Moreover it is physically housed in a company-owned building. My informants in San Juan say that the station is definitely procompany in its news programs, especially during tense periods such as strikes.

SPCC operates a radio station at Toquepala whose signal is also received in Pueblo Nuevo, Ilo, and one nearby village. This is "Radio Cultura Toquepala," call letters OAX-6S. The license, transmitters, and quarters are all directly owned by the company and the staff is employed by SPCC. Daily programming includes, without commercials, a series of brief music, educational, sports, and news programs. Although the station's head (a Peruvian) perceives himself as having autonomy in determining programs, occasionally the company gives him "special announcements" to be read over the station. The station's audience is very large, owing in part to the inferior programming of a competing commercial station.

The companies own and operate motion picture theaters in five of the towns: La Oroya, Cerro de Pasco, San Juan, Pueblo Nuevo, and Toquepala. But only in the SPCC towns do the company theaters have a monopoly on motion-picture exhibition. Presumably management selects films with a conscious consideration of subject matter, and conceivably this could have a long-range effect on community values. It would be interesting to study corporate film-selection systematically to determine what, if any, biases exist; a quick spot check at Toquepala indicated a higher percentage of American films than is shown in Lima. As a tool of local political control the films could hardly have other than passive effect, however, since their content deals with the world beyond the town.

But if outright company propaganda is not prevalent in broadcasting and films, it is not uncommon in local printed media. The managements in all eight towns publish "house organ"-type newspapers or magazines. These appear weekly, biweekly, or monthly, are prepared by the industrial relations or public relations departments, and are distributed gratis. An analysis of fifty-six copies of nine different publications put out in 1967 and 1968 shows that 29 percent of column-space is devoted to articles on the community, 20 percent to reports on individual workers and their families, and 19 percent to company operations. Articles in the first two categories usually have an impartial or nonpolitical flavor, giving much attention to industrial safety, public health, sports, and various contests. But write-ups on the company are aimed at sheer indoctrination. News and comment concerning the national and world scene are rare.

Very likely Toquepala comes closest to a mass communications monopoly. Not only does the company have control over all films seen and most of the radio programs heard, it also determines for many persons what news they hear other than by word of mouth. Daily the company distributes a news summary covering local, national, and international events for affixing to camp bulletin boards. The only alternative printed source of daily news is the Tacna edition of *El Correo*, one of a national chain of newspapers, of which 600 copies are imported for sale each day.

In summary, a number of conditions exist in the towns that make them susceptible to political domination by corporate managements. In all but two towns top management consists of Americans. In five of the towns all residents are directly or indirectly dependent on the corporation for income, and among the remaining three, 63 percent is the lowest proportion. In four towns all residential property is company-owned and among the other four the lowest percentage is 60. The companies do not own many broadcasting stations but they operate cinemas in more than half the towns and publish a great variety of house organs. At Toquepala these conditions for foreign political domination are particularly complete; and I am told by SPCC management that at the new Cuajone towns being built the situation will be very similar.

Relations with Town Government

Management's relations with the officially constituted local authorities are obviously vital to this subject. For if the companies are politically dominant in their towns local government officials must in some way be made subservient or removed from vital decision-making. Otherwise the companies are merely pressure groups trying to influence local government, which is not the same as political domination.

The institutions of Peruvian local government have something of a French flavor. The country is divided into 24 departments which are in turn divided into nearly 150 provinces; these provinces are then subdivided into more than 1500 districts. Each unit at each level has a capital at which are located three types of authority: (1) courts or justices of the peace, (2) prefectoral officers representing the central government (prefect at the department level, subprefect at the province level, governor at the district level, and lieutenant governor at other places), and (3) local councils consisting of a mayor and five councilmen in the case of districts and nine and fifteen council members at the province and department levels, respectively. All of these positions are appointive; although mayors and council members were elected in 1963 and 1966, that practice is not traditional and was abandoned by the Velasco regime.[4]

Relating this system to our eight company towns, Cerro de Pasco is a department capital, La Oroya and Talara are provincial capitals, and San Juan and Pueblo Nuevo are district seats of government. Cartavio,

Paramonga, and Toquepala theoretically report to the district capitals of Santiago de Cao, Pativilca, and Ilabaya, respectively.

One dimension of the political importance of this local officialdom is its functions. They are not impressively vital in communities below the department capital level. The central government retains all important powers in law enforcement, economic matters, education, and communications, and meaningful decisions in these areas are taken by the prefects or at the ministries in Lima. The police throughout Peru is the national *Guardia Civil*, for example. Left for local authorities are such activities as provision of water and electricity, construction of local public works, operation of sports fields, cleaning of streets and collection of garbage, fire protection, maintenance of vital statistics, and settlement of local disputes. Local public charity societies run hospitals and cemeteries.

In the company towns the responsibilities of local government become even less, however, because of their frequent performance by management. This is actually required by Peruvian law in many instances. The haciendas and mining camps are obliged to provide free medical service to employees, for example, and hence they build and staff local clinics and hospitals. Also the companies must construct elementary school buildings and pay for their operation; but the Ministry of Education hires the teachers and runs the schools. In all eight towns except La Oroya and Cerro de Pasco management provided the public water supply, generated and distributed electricity, and maintained the streets. At all communities except Talara and the Cerro towns the company also collected garbage and provided sports fields or stadia. In each community company fire-fighting equipment constituted the town's fire department (except for older parts of Cerro de Pasco). Although the Guardia Civil is nominally the only police force, in most towns the company employs industrial security guards who are sometimes armed and usually patrol executive-staff living areas at night. At San Juan company guards also round up beggars and at Toquepala they very strictly control entry and exit to the entire community via continuously manned gates. SPCC licenses peddlers, inspects markets, operates its own post office, and registers all firearms. This displacement of local responsibility lightens the administrative burden of town officials, but it also dilutes their importance as decision-makers. Moreover company performance of functions such as control of citizen movement and regulation of firearms may add positively to management's raw political power.

Another potential source of corporate influence is associated with the resources of local government. Local bodies receive small financial grants from the ministries in Lima and are also entitled to a share of locally collected property taxes. Town councils often levy minor taxes and impose small fines, thus generating additional income. But, like local governments everywhere, there is never enough money. In the company towns management customarily steps in with additional help even though the corporation itself is already performing several public functions.

The assistance is in several forms. Office space is often provided free of charge to officials in company-owned buildings; furniture and public utilities are sometimes thrown in as well. Part of the financial cost of a program may be borne by the company; IPC paid for half the cost of contracted garbage collection in Talara, for example. The municipal agent at Toquepala—in charge of collecting vital statistics on behalf of the Ilabaya district—was employed as librarian in the SPCC-sponsored workers' club. The providing of equipment and materials, such as trucks and gravel for street projects, is quite common. This kind of aid is either free or at cost; some managements ask for no payment while others consider it good policy to require small rental fees and reimbursement of expenses. Cerro is unique in a practice of adding to the revenues available to the La Oroya and Cerro de Pasco councils by generating electricity and then selling it at wholesale cost to them, who in turn retail it at an approximately 100 percent markup. The company has a similar arrangement with respect to the public water supply. Finally, on occasion the companies make loans to town governments; for example, Grace provided a short-term loan to the Santiago de Cao council for the purposes of constructing a road between it and Cartavio.

This assistance to local government is obviously of financial benefit, but it also can—and no doubt does—contribute to management's leverage with town authorities. The same bargaining strategies discussed in the last chapter could be used to wring concessions from local authorities. The possibility of losing vital assistance could be generally inhibiting to local officials in their behavior toward the company. With respect to equipment and materials at least, the requests for help are always greater and more numerous than management feels it can provide, with the consequence that company officials are put in the position of deciding which community projects will go ahead and which will not. The company administrator or superintendent becomes, in effect, something of a one-man appropriations committee to local government.

If individual town officials can be reliably influenced, control of town government is of course established. Decades ago this could be a relatively simple matter—at Talara, for example, IPC had its general manager appointed as mayor. Today the companies no longer control appointments, for these are a jealously guarded prerogative of the central regime. The corporations can, however, seek influence with those named. According to informants U.S. managements frequently dispense payoffs and favors in an effort to make friends and secure good will among local authorities. It would appear that these tributes are usually not in the form of simple cash but are rather such gifts as free liquor, repair of private vehicles in the company garage, payment of bills run up at local stores, and bestowal of guest privileges at the staff club. When the officials are also employees of the company—possible for the mayor and councilmen, whose governing responsibilities are part-time—management is in a position to offer such favors with respect to dwelling and work assignments. In mid-1968 company employees sat on all town councils except that of Ilabaya (Toquepala's district). At Cartavio, La Oroya, San Juan, and Pueblo Nuevo (the Ilo council at that time) half or more of the councilmen were on the company payroll. At Cartavio and San Juan even the mayors were company employees.*

Paternalism and Antipaternalism

We move now from possible mechanisms of political control over town government to those embracing the population generally. Community residents and groups too can conceivably be coopted or bought off by company beneficence. Generous company paternalism could create ties of perceived obligation or, more likely, lay the basis for intimidation via threats to withdraw benefits. More deeply, the provision of "free" goods and services and the assumption of normally personal responsibilities can, possibly, create a state of psychological dependence in which company authority is never questioned. Note the following view of Casa Grande, Peru's largest sugar hacienda, as it appeared to an American visitor around the turn of the century:

There is, indeed, something patriarchal in the relations between the manager of Casa Grande and the families living on the vast estate under his direction. Or probably it would be truer to say that this relationship is something like that which, in times long past, obtained between the Inca and his subjects. Be that as it may, all those who are connected with the company, especially the peons and their families, are well cared for, as one soon learns who visits the people in their homes. All seem contented and happy. There are no strikes and none of those clashes between capital and labor that are so frequent in the United States and Europe. The rule governing the workmen, while engaged in the large factory at Casa Grande, may be summed up in the words over the main portal—*Tace, ora et labora*— observe silence, pray and work.[5]

And yet, as discussed in Chapter One, ambiguous forces may be generated by paternalism. Literature on the modern company town suggests that the outcome is not just tranquil gratitude but rather incessant carping against management for being unconcerned, unfair, and slow to correct wrongs. Part of this may be due to management becoming the

*At this time the council posts were elective. Inquiries were made as to whether the companies attempted to influence the outcome of local elections, such as by contributing to campaigns. No evidence of such involvement was uncovered.

target of inevitable community conflicts and frustrations; perhaps another ingredient is discontent created by feelings of obligation to and dependence on an impersonal corporate entity. Unlike the Casa Grande of seventy-five years ago, the running of these towns is comparatively depersonalized and bureaucratic. Moreover, unlike decades past, workers are protected by labor laws and unions and cannot be fired outright; protests can be made with relative impunity and through established grievance channels.

Being responsible for all aspects of the workers' lives is thus not only expensive to management but a giant headache. As a result the trend has been toward the so-called "clean wage," payment in cash only rather than noncash benefits such as free housing and food. Experiments have been conducted in "self-help" and community-development type projects designed to create a positive substitute for paternalism. As stated in Hypothesis II, these attempts to reduce or replace paternalism can conceivably work both ways with respect to management's political power; they could lessen dependence and hence company influence or they could establish a new form of employee docility that results from company-imposed need-satisfactions. Let us examine our eight company towns for evidence.

Fifty years ago Cerro paid Indian laborers in chits that were convertible to company scrip rather than Peruvian currency. The scrip was valid for only one week and could be spent only at the company mercantile.[6] This kind of monopolistic economic grip does not exist today—all workers are paid in cash. Excluding free housing and other generalized benefits, supplementary noncash remuneration is unusual; the only cases which I encountered in 1968 were at La Oroya and the Grace haciendas. At the former, workers living in housing (hovels is the better word) without gas stoves received free firewood. At Cartavio management provided workers with a weekly ration of meat, rice, and salt from a company distribution outlet. Cartavio workers were given as part of their pay an allotment of coupons which entitled them to purchase food at low cost from another distribution center operated by management. At Paramonga food rations were given out as recently as 1959[7] but had been eliminated a decade later. However a practice of furnishing field workers with two hot meals per day—delivered in the fields— was still extant, although in 1968 it was in the process of elimination, too.

In all towns workers are freely provided housing, medical care, primary education, and certain "social service" activities. In practice the schools and clinics are sometimes made available without charge to nonemployed town residents as well. In some instances the company supplements what is required by law and provides, say, a trade or high school as well as an elementary school. At all towns except the Cerro communities public utilities are provided free with no metering.

Peruvian law requires that a "social service" program be conducted at each company town. This is a combination of individual and family counseling, extension-type teaching of basic home economics, and sponsorship of recreational activities. The recreational programs are carried out by means of social clubs, sports clubs and leagues, women's organizations, and other groups. Although the degree of independence of the groups varies, in all cases some kind of company support is provided. This usually includes a building, set of rooms, soccer field, or other facility. Equipment, uniforms, transportation, and staff assistance are usually provided.

At Talara, Cerro de Pasco, San Juan, and the two Grace haciendas, company policy in 1968 was largely to permit these organizations to function independently. Officers were freely elected by members. Boards of directors or their equivalent determined and ran their own programs with a minimum of interference. This was particularly true with respect to sports programs, but each town's "obrero club," "empleado club," and "staff club" (or their equivalents) were also largely run without intervention. Elected officers collected membership dues and controlled the expenditure of club income.

Such independence was not, however, allowed at Toquepala and Pueblo Nuevo. Except for the sports teams, all social organizations were managed directly by SPCC's Department of Welfare, a division of Industrial Relations. This body appointed organization officers and planned, scheduled, and executed activities. No funds were permitted to be held independently by the clubs; at one time the *Club de Empleados* of Toquepala controlled its own money, but when this was "misspent"—in management's opinion—the privilege was withdrawn. Even the credit cooperative at Toquepala, theoretically owned by its depositors, was company controlled. It is notable in this connection that for many years the SPCC welfare department was headed by former Peruvian army officers. When I visited the camp in 1967 and 1968 the department head was an efficient excaptain; his predecessor was a former major who had incurred local ill-will by killing two workers during a strike.

Other companies had the diametrically opposite policy of SPCC in the late 1960's and were actively seeking to reduce worker paternalism. Ironically, the two firms most aggressive in these efforts have since had their towns expropriated, namely, Grace and IPC.

The former Grace plantations were perhaps among the most logical candidates for depaternalization in that they inherited decades (and centuries in the case of Cartavio) of patrón tradition. In fact, in former years the Grace management itself was not above a personalistic, patrón style of stewardship. At one time the company's president, R. Peter Grace, a staunch Roman Catholic, periodically received figures as to attendance at mass in hacienda churches. When, some years ago, Mr. Grace was urged by others in the company to sell Cartavio because of its lack of promise for long-run earnings, he reluctantly decided not to do so because of a feeling of moral obligation for the welfare of the plantation's residents.

During the 1960's, however, the company was trying hard to shed some of the day-to-day problems connected with running the towns. In the 1966-1968 period the general stores at both haciendas were sold to consumer cooperatives, although ownership of the buildings remained in company hands. At Paramonga union leaders were sent to Lima at company expense for training in cooperative techniques and upon their return they organized the co-ops with management's blessing. One company-managed retail outlet remained at each estate, however: the food-coupon sales outlet at Cartavio and a pharmacy at Paramonga. In mid-1968 an effort was being made to sell the pharmacy.[8]

Other antipaternalism efforts at Paramonga included a program to persuade the field hands who received two hot meals per day to accept an increase in cash wages instead. By mid-1968 about 30 percent had done so. Another undertaking was encouragement of worker bicycling so as to avoid a need for company-provided bus service around the plantation. Bicycles were made available at a mere 200 soles each (about $8 at the time) and soon adult cycling was common, a very unusual spectacle for Latin America.

Grace also attempted to facilitate worker ownership of residential housing at both haciendas. One element of this effort was associated with the aftermath of the earthquake of 1966, which as a seismic event was nothing compared to the quake of 1970 but nevertheless damaged many north coastal towns. The Grace management saw the incident as an opportunity to rid itself of company housing. In Lima the companies lobbied for a law that would permit sale of damaged but repaired homes, with government earthquake damage loans providing part of the capital. Pressure from the unions and Peruvian land owners delayed the measure for a year. However it passed in 1967 and provided for half of the home financing by earthquake benefits and the other half by the buyer. Undamaged homes could also be bought, with management guaranteeing nongovernmental credits.[9]

Coincidental to this effort was a "self-help" housing program sponsored by Grace. The idea was to sell hacienda land to housing cooperatives, which in turn would finance the purchase of individual plots by workers. Groups of five families each were encouraged to invest their cooperative labor in the construction of each family's house, with Grace providing house plans and technical advice. The houses would then be connected to hacienda utility lines at an appropriate monthly charge. The company strongly promoted the endeavor; at Paramonga, for example, management formed a *Comité Pro Vivienda* to serve as a forum for persuasion and negotiation of the housing program.[10]

But the effort essentially failed. At Paramonga a private residential development, "Las Mercedes," was established at the edge of the hacienda. Despite the fact that the cost of the houses was originally about $1000 and twenty-year mortgages at 5 percent interest were made available, worker interest was minimal. Only about fifteen homes were built by retirees. The company had all but abandoned the program prior to expropriation of the towns in 1969.

Talara has also been the scene of attempts to lessen the degree of paternalism inherent in management-worker relationships. In the years immediately prior to IPC's expropriation in 1968-1969 the company's Peruvian management was debating whether to adopt a program of trying to convert Talara entirely to a normal, open city with private ownership of property and municipal responsibility for public utilities and services. Dr. Guillermo Gorbitz, IPC's medical director, was championing the idea but others in the company opposed it on grounds of cost. An unpleasant experience for IPC at the nearby town of Negritos may have contributed to the hesitation. This former company camp was sold when all oil field operations were centralized at Talara, with the result that residents remaining at the town were suddenly deprived of free water and power. When the company tried to present claims for payment of bills on delivered utilities much bitterness resulted.[11]

The more progressive elements of IPC's management were, however, able to execute some depaternalization plans. One was establishment of a children's club whose intended mission was not babysitting, as is true with most company-sponsored *Clubes Juveniles*, but rather the fostering of values of group participation and initiative. Called *El Club de Niños*, the organization was formed in 1960 and housed in a small wooden building behind the Talara obrero club, whose directors had originally proposed the experiment. The IPC social service director provided staff to design and run a program. Talara boys and girls nine to twelve years of age from IPC worker families were invited to join. The children elected officers, including president, vice-president, a "secretary of culture" (a girl) and a "secretary of sports" (a boy). With adult guidance the club leaders planned craft projects, parlor games, soccer matches, poetry readings, and excursions. To finance incidental expenses, and eventually to acquire a small "library," the children taxed themselves one sol per meeting and determined themselves how the proceeds would be spent. Meetings were held twice per week, with the sexes segregated at some meetings and mixed at others. A club song was written, a motto composed ("Love the club— mutual help—cooperation"), and a club emblem designed, on which was incribed "CN" and—interestingly—"Esso."[12]

In addition to worker benefits company paternalism takes the form of donations to various groups in and around the towns. We have already noted that management gives the town governing authorities assistance of various kinds. Help is rendered to various charities, schools, churches,

hospitals, and governmental units in the surrounding region. Most companies maintain a regular "donations" account in their budget to cover this
activity; Cerro, for example, regularly spends $35,000 a year in this way.
Sometimes the gift is in the form of cash, to be spent for such things as
scholarships, school books, a new schoolbuilding roof, and disaster relief.
Contributions of services or materials are made; examples are sheep-
husbandry advice (Cerro), the digging of drainage ditches (Grace), and
provision of barbed wire for an Army infiltration course (SPCC). Management receives hundreds of requests for aid each year and, as in the case of
donations to town government, it selects which ones it will honor.

The corporations have the option of whether to furnish the aid freely or
to require some kind of payment. To ask for compensation is a less
paternalistic approach and this course is followed by some corporations
for social rather than financial reasons. Cerro de Pasco is one firm which
changed its policy in this regard in recent years. At one time it neither
asked for nor expected compensation of any kind. This policy was
reevaluated when, some years ago, the company was requested by the
Indian village of Alis (near the Yauricocha mine) to install a water pipe to
the community. Although management initially intended to provide only
the pipe and require the villagers themselves to lay it, this plan was met
with inordinate delay and considerable bickering. Finally Cerro went
ahead and did the entire job itself. The residents of Alis, an executive says,
"have hated us ever since."

At a later time Cerro was asked by the Indians of another village, Laraos,
to construct an access road that would open up the community to the rest
of Peru. Unlike the Alis case, management deliberately took no responsibility for the project and merely made available a rock drill and air
compressor.The villagers were charged a rental fee for the equipment plus
wage costs for the operator. Dynamite and other materials were sold at
cost. The road was built and it is claimed that company relations with the
village have since been excellent.

At Toquepala the unilateral donation was still practiced as of 1967. An
SPCC executive expressed great distaste for the task of deciding which
requests would be honored and, when asked whether he thought the
contributions "paid off" in good will, said that they only lead to more
demands. The net result may even have been greater hostility, he felt,
because of the growing number of unsatisfied requests.

A different policy from that at SPCC headquarters in Toquepala was
followed at Pueblo Nuevo, near Ilo. The top-ranking company man at the
town, the smelter superintendent, was conscious of the supposed superi-
ority of a self-help approach and not only asked for compensation in many
cases but himself promoted community development projects. When it was
determined that a squatter settlement was dangerously situated under an
SPCC high-voltage power line, for example, the superintendent did not

simply remove the squatters, as he was legally entitled, but sought out prefect government officials, local parish priests, and Peace Corps volunteers of the area to discuss the problem. Together they approached the squatters and offered assistance in constructing permanent housing at an alternative site. The offer was accepted and a new settlement was subsequently built by the people themselves with help from SPCC and other organizations in the form of building materials and heavy equipment. Concrete dwellings, a medical post, and a school were eventually put up, known collectively as *Barriada John F. Kennedy.*[13]

The outstanding case of community development involving American companies in Peru to occur in recent years was the rebuilding, under IPC auspices, of Cabo Blanco, a fishing village twenty miles north of Talara. Once famous for its deep-sea fishing, this little town along the water's edge was the temporary residence of Ernest Hemingway in the early 1950's. At that time Cabo Blanco was what North Americans would call a slum: the houses were wooden shacks, pigs and cattle wandered freely in the village, and no power, water, or sewage facilities existed. The smell of fresh dung and dead fish permeated the area. The villagers were not "poor" in the sense of having an inadequate base of income, for the offshore waters were so good for fishing that the men went out only two or three days per week.

International Petroleum executives had long known about these conditions because they fished in the area for recreation, IPC oil wells were nearby, and a company desalinization plant was located on an adjacent beach. Belco Petroleum also had a tank farm nearby. No interest was shown in the village, however, until one day when the fishermen asked Dr. Gorbitz whether IPC would provide the materials to construct a new church. His reply was that they might better think about rebuilding the entire town. This idea was received favorably and, at Dr. Gorbitz's suggestion, a community group was formed to consider what could be done. Soon the *Junta de Progreso de Cabo Blanco* was formed, and it elected as its leader the town's most illustrious citizen, the owner of the small hotel-bar where Hemingway had been a guest. The Junta then proceeded with small-scale urban redevelopment: pens were built down the beach so as to isolate the animals and, one by one, the shacks were replaced with row houses. These were made from cinder block manufactured by the villagers on the beach. At first IPC contributed materials and equipment but later asked for remuneration; agreeing to this, the fishermen levied a tax on themselves and fished an extra day each week to raise funds. Later the company sold water to the Junta from its desalinization plant, which in turn retailed it at a markup in order to increase revenues. By mid-1967 almost all housing had been rebuilt and a school was half-finished. The undertaking was so successful that it could have been taken out of a community development manual.[14]

Competition and Controversy

So far in this chapter we have left almost unmentioned economic or social entities other than the corporation itself that may have interests at stake in town politics. Is this because there are none—at least of significance—leaving management without competitors for power? Or have possible political counterforces been overlooked?

In surveying these eight communities only two potential counterweights emerge. These are the labor unions and their occasional political party alliances on the one hand, and the local Roman Catholic clergy on the other.

Labor unions are organized in all of the towns. In fact in most of them more than one union bargains collectively with employers. These organizations vary in political affiliation and negotiating style; at Talara in 1968, for example, union "Number 1" was Aprista and moderate whereas "Number 2" was socialist and aggressive. Both had obrero and empleado divisions and together included more than 80 percent of the workforce. As for the haciendas, a single union was organized at Cartavio and four at Paramonga; the Cartavio group had strong ties with APRA whereas the Paramonga leaders were divided between APRA and AP. No less than twenty-four unions bargained with Cerro de Pasco at the company's various sierra operations at this time; in La Oroya they tended to be weak and apolitical, but at Cerro de Pasco militant and Aprista. One empleado union and one obrero union each operated at San Juan, Pueblo Nuevo, and Toquepala; none was particularly aggressive and none had direct political affiliations.[15]

Extensive interviewing of various community leaders in all eight towns yielded the impression that these unions are at least independent of company control. Their officers are elected freely by union memberships and a highly developed body of labor law protects union independence. Collective bargaining is spirited and strikes quite frequent; wage increases and other benefits are won frequently, and by Peruvian standards the workers of these companies are well paid.

Yet this does not mean the unions were effective politically. With respect to local elections when they occurred, the unions generally did not attempt to mobilize their memberships to vote for favored parties or candidates. Only in the town of Cerro de Pasco was this done, to my knowledge, and even there formal endorsements were not made. In direct relationships with management, effective union power was often undermined by the leaders' habit of demanding the impossible to appease the membership and then accepting modest compromises arbitrated by the government. Labor violence occurs now and then both as a sporadic phenomenon and as a conscious tool of union policy. Bargaining takes on the air of personalistic, somewhat irresponsible histrionics in which valiant speeches are made, but rather limited increments of progress are achieved.

Furthermore—and this is perhaps the most important point here—the union leaders take little interest in community issues. Their concern is the type of question that is most tangibly meaningful to memberships: wage rates, work schedules, dismissals, and such inconveniences as time clocks. Matters such as the quality of housing, maintenance of the towns, the availability of recreation facilities, and activities of the town government are ignored.[16]

The Roman Catholic clergy has quite different potentialities as an independent pressure group. Priests are resident in all eight towns, performing parish duties and also running schools and medical posts. As is true elsewhere in Peru and Latin America, many are foreign; among our eight towns native clergy was dominant only in Talara, Paramonga, and Toquepala. At Cartavio, La Oroya, and San Juan American priests predominated, most of them very young. Whereas the older, Peruvian priests tended to identify with corporate interests, the younger foreigners sympathized with the workers and sometimes became militantly antimanagement. As a result in half the towns, Cartavio, La Oroya, San Juan, and Pueblo Nuevo, the priesthood was a force with which management had to reckon. Since clergymen are not employees and their property is usually church-owned, economic independence is possible. And, of course, the priests are hierarchically responsible to their bishop and order rather than to management.[17]

As a result political fireworks break out now and then between clergy and company. But the priests can seldom agitate efficaciously enough to create a truly explosive political situation. As a result the corporation is merely harassed and perhaps its conscience pricked. To illustrate, in June 1966 a young Irishman, Father Patrick Brannon, brought his strong sense of social justice and inexhaustible energies to the San Juan mining camp. He saw that not all workers had free housing, that the población flotante lived in bad slums, and that the unions were divided and ineffective as a political force. "Father Pat" insisted that the company build more housing; he also urged formation of a housing cooperative and community action group. To reach his goals he circulated petitions, pled from the pulpit, and incessantly pressed Marcona managers. A temporary halt was called in the campaign when the company agreed to form a liaison committee that would supposedly work out specific actions. But this never materialized and the struggle between Father Pat and Marcona resumed. In December 1967 it was suddenly over, however: the young priest had been reassigned by his superiors back to the United States. Marcona executives admit that they had strongly urged church officials in Lima to have Brannon removed and that the conservative papal nuncio, Monsignor Romolo Carboni, had intervened in the case.

With the unions preoccupied with labor matters and the priests without much real power, the company managements do, then, remain the predominant political force in these towns. They dominate the communities economically and control some mass communications. The authority of town officials is weakened by company displacement of governmental functions and control of some governmental resources. Ample means of company leverage over individual officeholders exist. Many paternalistic practices toward workers are required by law and hence do not constitute "favors"; but they may add to an atmosphere of dependence and create restive frustration as well. Some companies have attempted to depaternalize and even experiment in community development, but that, too, may actually heighten management's political power. IPC's Club de Niños may have been more of an indoctrination center for Standard Oil than a class in self-government. Self-help projects at Laraos, Barriada John F. Kennedy, and Cabo Blanco not only served corporate interests by getting a specific job done but, apparently, added to the local popularity of Cerro, SPCC, and IPC, respectively. At Cabo Blanco, where I personally interviewed, the fishermen's respect for and gratitude to Dr. Gorbitz and other IPC personnel was in great evidence.

As a final step in assessing corporate political influence in the towns a variety of inhabitants of each was asked what conflicts or controversies had occurred in the community in recent years and what the outcomes had been. The intention was to determine whether management "won" community battles in which it became engaged or whether any such conflicts occurred at all. The general finding was that controversies involving the company definitely occur but that usually they involve quite minor matters which do not threaten vital corporate interests. Often they constitute dramatic confrontations between managers and flamboyant persons who joust company windmills in Don Quixote fashion. The result is nagging embarrassment to the company and perhaps a few concessions. Marcona's fight with Father Pat is one example. At Talara Father Pat's counterpart was the president of union Number 2; although a gifted orator, he was more of a thorn than blade in IPC's flesh and had nothing to do with the company's expropriation.[18]

At La Oroya the Cerro de Pasco Corporation has little difficulty in maintaining basic control because much of the population consists of Indians or cholos who are emotionally attached to their home villages and view La Oroya as merely a place to work. Generally the atmosphere is passive politically. But occasionally someone attempts to stir things up, as was done by the mayor elected in 1966, Daniel Florencio Lovarra Ramírez. This individual spent council funds—made ample by the electricity resale arrangement—to purchase land for a town coliseum despite the fact that Cerro had given another parcel of land for this purpose. Lovarra also led a successful campaign to expropriate the company's soccer stadium. The property was fully paid for, although the company remained unsatisfied in view of the fact that it was owed a large amount in back electricity payments. On top of all this the mayor was implicated in the disappearance of substantial official funds and found it convenient to be at unknown locations for months at a time. These matters caused many headaches in the Cerro industrial relations and public relations departments, but they did not affect the industrial activities of La Oyora and were not considered of major moment by the company.

The local politics of Cerro de Pasco have been somewhat more of a problem to Cerro. The "Pasqueños" are not as passive as the workers at La Oroya but are actually quite "fiesty," to use an adjective employed by management itself. Mining has gone on in the area for hundreds of years and the people carry with them accumulated generations of resentment against exploitation by successive Spanish, Peruvian, and American mine operators. Local politicians and labor leaders vie for the most complete anticompany position on local issues in order to capitalize on this animosity. Although APRA is the strongest party in the area, the far Left attracts much support.

A wide variety of conflict arises in this atmosphere. A case that illustrates how the company can be greatly inconvenienced in small matters involved a local judge who seemed to enjoy twitting the company's nose. Once he issued an arrest warrant on the Cerro superintendent of mines on the technical charge of closing a company road; theoretically all roads are public ways in Peru, including those on concession property. The company hurriedly hospitalized the superintendent for protection and succeeded in keeping him out of the arms of the law by transfers from one company clinic to another for several months.

Nevertheless the judge had his opportunities to get even. Given privileges in the staff social center, Club Esperanza, he was in the habit of consuming large quantities of alcoholic beverages in the bar each night and thereupon abusing verbally company personnel and their female companions. Although many a Cerro engineer swore to "get" the judge, all personnel were warned that instant dismissal would follow any attack on him—verbal or physical. The company was anxious to avoid other arrest warrants and dropping his club privileges was out of the question. Cerro attempted to bring political pressure to bear in Lima to have the individual dismissed, but to no avail.

In this cold, forlorn, Andean community of Cerro de Pasco it is possible for conflicts to emerge where more is involved than inconvenience. The major substantive issue of recent years in the town has been its substantial relocation. This question, involving the vital interests of almost everyone, is the outstanding illustration of a deep-seated political clash to occur within an American company town in Peru in recent years. That there was only one such fight (of which I am aware) is itself indicative of the degree to which these communities are dominated.[19]

The company's interest in moving Cerro de Pasco stems from the great tonnage of rich polymetallic ores that lie under much of the old town—perhaps the world's most valuable ore body of this kind. The minerals there had been known to exist for decades and, in fact, had long been reached by lateral tunneling. As early as 1909 some houses of the town had been weakened or made uninhabitable by the digging. When in recent years it was determined that only open-pit mining could economically reach the minerals, the company decided it would be most expeditious to raze much of the old city and replace it with a new one. A plan was drawn up which to company executives seemed fair and reasonable: The owners of buildings to be demolished would be given new structures of comparable size or compensating cash payments. Company employees to be displaced—a minority of the affected population—would be given standard, new quarters free of charge as the law required. Others would be moved to homes they would eventually purchase, with the company in effect holding the mortgage. Payments for these would be less than $10 monthly and the corporation would charge no interest. Additionally Cerro said it would construct public structures such as plazas, civic buildings, schools, a church, and even a university. The new town would be built on lands both owned by the city and held in concession by the company and would be known as "San Juan Pampa." It was to be a totally new city built de novo, with detached, cement buildings, inside plumbing, and modern architecture.

From the beginning the project confronted ardent opposition, led by local Communists but by no means confined to them. Much of the feeling against San Juan Pampa no doubt stemmed from the universal reluctance on the part of settled people to move at all. Businessmen fought the change because of fear of losing customers. Landlords did not want to lose renters. Many feared that the company could not be trusted to live up to its promises.

Cerro went ahead anyway. As the new structures took shape their appearance intensified the opposition. The first houses built were neatly uniform in design, a far cry from the ancient hodgepodge of the old city. When they were attacked as being too "camp-like" several house plans were used in mixed fashion. The new Roman Catholic church, designed by a Swiss architect, consisted essentially of two inclined walls meeting at the top. Although the design was considered "modern" by management a veritable storm of community protest arose when the edifice was completed. The lack of steeples, bells, and other traditional accouterments of Peruvian churches was decried; also it was likened to a "chosa" or Indian house. Popular feeling on the matter intensified when, without warning in the dead of night, the Guardia Civil cordoned off the beloved old church for demolishment. Military units had to be called in to keep order. The company was forced to do nothing short of constructing a second new church in San Juan Pampa that was an exact replica of the one destroyed.

But even with this controversy and bitter opposition, the important point is that Cerro de Pasco went ahead with relocation anyway and the ore was made available. True, San Juan Pampa is many times more attractive than the old town by almost any conceivable standard of material welfare, but it had been imposed on its people.

Eight   Aspects of National Integration

The present chapter differs from the preceding six in that instead of dealing with the political *power* implications of American business in Peru, it considers possible impacts for national political *integration*.

As noted in Chapter Two, Peru is a country of great geographical and social divisions. The nation's modern, metropolitan life is centered along the coast, particularly at Lima. The desert coastline is bordered by the spectacular Andean mountain ranges in which live most of the millions of unassimilated Indians. To the east is the vast selva or thinly settled Amazon basin. Although a great many Indians have made the transition to "cholo" or "mestizo" status—that is, they have been acculturated to the Hispanic way of life in successive degrees—one-third or more of "Peruvians" remain culturally and spatially cut off from national life. Vast portions of the sierra and selva are to this day virtually inaccessible from the coast.

Hypothesis III states that certain activities of American corporations in Peru have had, over time, the effect of lessening the spatial and cultural separateness of Peru. Surely any such impact would have to be unintentional, for no profit-seeking business deliberately fosters an intangible, societal goal such as national integration. However, American entrepreneurs and investors have, over the years, been significantly involved in various aspects of transportation in Peru. This involvement includes engaging in transportation service as a business enterprise and the construction of transportation infrastructure either under contract or for industrial purposes. It is recognized that these activities could make unimportant or even negative contributions to Peruvian transportation, but the hypothesis states that the net effect is improvement of the network.

Another relevant activity of American corporations is establishment and operation of remote mining and petroleum centers. To the extent that Indians are attracted to these points for employment and are subsequently exposed to the national Hispanic culture, these places could function latently as cultural assimilation centers. Location of enterprises along important migratory routes to the coast could also lead to an assimilationist role. Again, the hypothesized impact could be minimized or obverted under certain conditions, for example if the communities were sealed, foreign enclaves.

Pioneers of Peruvian Transportation

Three of the most dramatic instances of American involvement in Peruvian transport have technically not concerned corporate U.S. business but rather individual American business entrepreneurs. These individuals, all native-born Americans, employed primarily British and Peruvian capital to take notable, pioneering steps in the development of the country's transportation services and facilities. The men are William Wheelwright (1798-1873), Henry Meiggs (1811-1877), and Elmer J. Faucett (1891-1960).

William Wheelwright is known as a great nineteenth-century builder of railroads with respect to that part of his career spent in Chile and Argentina. In Peru his role was that of founder of coastal steam navigation.

After residing in Guayaquil and later Valparaiso as a young man, Wheelwright in 1835 began to seek concessions from the governments of the West Coast of South America for establishment of a steamer service that would link Panama with Valparaiso. By 1837 some of the necessary agreements had been secured and the entrepreneur was in London seeking capital. Although denounced as a wild visionary by some, English financiers were receptive to Wheelwright's proposal in view of the great interest at that time in steamboat transportation, plus recognition of the practical benefits such a service would have for British trade in the area.[1]

Soon the "Pacific Steam Navigation Company" was formed. Two 180-foot, 700-ton coppered-wood steamers were built in England, the "Chile" and the "Peru." The latter arrived at Callao in November 1840, greeted by cheering throngs and elaborate celebrations. In its early trips up and down the Peruvian coast the smoke-belching paddle-wheeler created a sensation, causing official alarm at some points; in one reported instance local port authorities dispatched a rowed rescue vessel to save what was perceived as a burning ship, but it could not be reached and the smoke gradually disappeared. According to the recorder of the incident, "The affair was dismissed by commending the victims to the mercy of God."[2]

In its early years the "P.S.N.C." was beset by difficulties such as accidents, a shortage of coal, and managerial upheavals. But eventually the line prospered. A succession of larger and more advanced ships was put into service down through the decades, carrying passengers, mail,* and freight. The line was international, but regular calls were made at the Peruvian ports of Paita, Salaverry, Callao, Pisco, and Mollendo. In 1965 the company celebrated its 125th anniversary as the world's oldest steamship line.[3]

---

*The P.S.N.C. actually prepared the first postage stamps to be issued in Peru, in 1857. The Peruvian government subsequently recognized the practicality of adhesive-backed stamps and issued its own the following year. Henry Harman de Izcue, "The Postage Stamps of Peru," *Peruvian Times*, November 12, 1971.

The contribution of Wheelwright to Peruvian transportation was limited but specific: although his steamers were primarily for international communication and although they duplicated the service provided by existing sailing ships, they increased the reliability and eventually speed of Peruvian cabotage transportation. The currents and winds along the Pacific coast of South America are unusually tricky and unpredictable, thus the introduction of steam propulsion was a definite step ahead. The domestic ports serviced were (and are) of great economic significance to the coastal population of the country; until deep into the twentieth century the "natural" ocean highway of Peru was the principal means of internal communication.

A rival of Wheelwright in Chilean railroad construction was another American entrepreneur, Henry Meiggs. Known to history both as a fantastic organizer and extraordinary scoundrel, Meiggs arrived in South America in 1855 under the most questionable circumstances. After making a fortune in lumber and real estate in San Francisco following the gold rush, he overextended himself and engaged in fraudulent financial practices in an attempt to recover. When he was discovered, Meiggs and his family fled the country by boat in the middle of one night in 1854, narrowly evading capture. After sailing in the South Pacific for some months he landed in Chile, where he eventually assumed responsibility for completing a railroad construction project linking Valparaiso and Santiago that had been unsuccessfully underway for a decade. In a pattern that was to be repeated later, Meiggs said he could complete the road in three years and then proceeded to finish it in two. In so doing he pocketed one million dollars, much of it from bonuses for early completion.[4]

In 1868 Meiggs shifted his base of operations to Peru, where railroading was in its infancy. Since the 1850's very short railroads had linked Lima with Callao, Lima with Chorillos, and Tacna with Arica (now in Chilean territory). But as yet no lines penetrated inland toward the Andes, clearly the challenge of any railroad dreamer.

When Meiggs arrived in Lima in January 1868, the presidency was temporarily in the hands of General Pedro Diez Canseco, a native of Arequipa. One of Diez's aspirations was to build a railroad from his home city to the sea. Contract proposals were solicited for this approximately 100-mile project with the expectation that it would be financed by British loans secured by future guano sales. Within four months Meiggs had beaten off all rival contractors and had signed a contract that was suspiciously inflated in price and loose in its terms. Evidence gathered by the Meiggs biographer, Watt Stewart, indicates that enormous personal bribes had been paid by "Don Enrique" Meiggs to the state engineers and ministers responsible. Apparently Meiggs simply made allowance in his construction estimates for these added expenses of doing business.

Shortly after the Arequipa contract was signed José Balta was elected president. Even more infected with railroad fever than his predecessor, Balta was obsessed with the vision of crisscrossing Peru with bands of steel, believing that the iron horse was the key to the country's unification and progress. All of this was to be paid for by guano income. The situation was made-to-order for the promoter Meiggs, who fanned Balta's railroad ardor by propaganda and personal theatrics. By the end of 1868 the American had secured two more rail contracts. These provided for extension of the Arequipa line further inland to Puno and construction of an ambitious link up into the Andes from Callao to La Oroya. During the remaining years of the Balta administration—for which Meiggs became an éminence grise—the Yankee builder signed four more railroad contracts; these called for Juliaca-Cuzco and Ilo-Moquegua connections in the south and lines inland from Pacasmayo and Chimbote in the north. Altogether 1042 miles of track were envisioned by the seven Meiggs contracts, anticipating an expenditure of nearly 120 million soles— a huge sum for the time.

From the standpoint of sheer organizational ability the confidence placed in Meiggs was justified. He was nothing short of a genius in marshaling resources and coordinating efforts on a grand scale. Equipment and materials were imported mostly from the United States, where construction of the transcontinental roads was producing the most advanced technology. Only the best materials were used, regardless of cost. For manpower he drew upon Peruvian, Bolivian, and Chilean Indians, plus Chinese coolies; this combination of labor was highly volatile but performed adequately on the whole inasmuch as Meiggs usually paid and treated his laborers well by contemporary standards. Extreme care was taken in selection of key engineers and superintendents; these were recruited from wherever they could be found at whatever cost was necessary.

The most telling indicator of Meiggs's abilities is the La Oroya railroad, operating still today. Although he laid only 87.5 of the 138 miles of track, Meiggs designed the entire route and graded most of it. The track ascends the Andes by means of the Rimac River canyon, utilizing more than sixty bridges and sixty tunnels, often in immediate conjunction with each other. The ascent is extraordinarily steep; gradients of 4.9 percent are occasionally reached and numerous switchbacks are employed including five of double design. The greatest altitude attained by the main track is 15,848 feet, making the line the highest regularly used in the world. Experts consider its construction as one of the most notable feats in the history of railroad building.[5] (See Figure 2 for the location of this and other railroads.)

Not all of Meiggs's projects were carried out during his lifetime. But in view of the grandiose scope of his proposals the record of completion was not bad. By the time construction was generally suspended in 1875, four of the seven projects were completed. More than 700 miles of track had

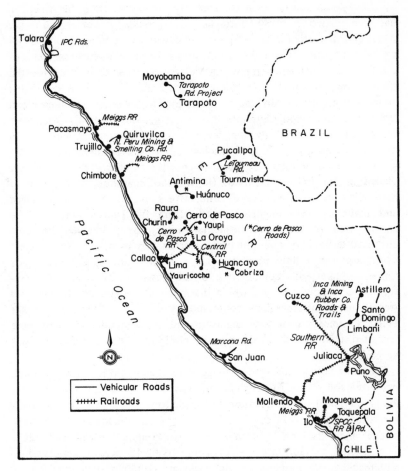

Figure 2. Roads and Railroads Associated with U.S. Entrepreneurs or Corporations

been laid. Mollendo, Arequipa, and Puno were linked by one continuous line. The Ilo-Moquegua connection was finished, as were the Pacasmayo lines. The other projects were either well started or near completion.

The suspension of operations was initially the result of declining guano income. By the mid-1870's it was barely covering the annual service charge on Peru's accumulated foreign debt and new capital was not being attracted. By 1872 Balta was dead and the next president, Manuel Pardo, was interested in education rather than railroads. Meiggs himself died in 1877.

Subsequent events led to delivery of the completed railroads to foreign hands. In the War of the Pacific with Chile (1879-1883) Peru was defeated with a consequent occupation of Lima and loss of southern territory. When the Chileans withdrew, the track that had been laid was either destroyed or in a state of serious deterioration. The European holders of Peruvian bonds—of which more than 50 million pounds sterling was outstanding—sought to make the most of what had turned out to be an investment disaster. In 1889 an agreement was made with the bondholders whereby they would take possession of what was left of all state railroads for sixty-six years. This arrangement, called the "Grace contract" after the Michael A. Grace who had arranged it, also awarded the investors guano deliveries, 80,000 pounds cash annually, a grant of five million acres of selva land, and exclusive rights to navigate Lake Titicaca. In return Peru was excused from its debt obligation and the bondholders agreed to rebuild and complete the railroads. In 1890 a company named the Peruvian Corporation was formed to manage the bondholders' interests.[6]

But the investors lost out in the end. The Peruvian Corporation repaired and completed the Callao-La Oroya line by 1893 and it forms the backbone of today's Central Railway (now extending to Huancayo). By 1907 the Puno road was linked through Juliaca to Cuzco, forming most of the Southern Railway. But over a period of eighty years the corporation was unable to make enough profits to afford a single dividend payment to stockholders, and beginning in 1967 it began to default on loan payments. By 1971 the firm was bankrupt and its railroads had been nationalized.[7]

An evaluation of the legacy of Don Enrique Meiggs for Peru must be mixed. On the one hand, he was a brilliant organizer and builder whose handiwork can still be seen. Without him the La Oroya line might never have been built although the other, less-demanding roads could probably have been constructed. Certainly the arrival of significant railroad transportation in Peru was greatly hastened by his presence. The importance of this development can be overlooked today because in most instances vehicular roads parallel the tracks. But for roughly half a century this was not true; railroads essentially came to Peru before motor roads. As late as 1928 the only access from the coast to the Mantaro River region in the central sierra was the Central Railway. Its existence was indispensable to development of the mining industry. In the south, for half a century the main link between Lima and such cities as Cuzco, Puno, and Arequipa was via ship and the Southern Railway. These were major, new communication lines to important parts of the interior.

On the other hand, however, Meiggs's great promotional ability helped to push Peru to a condition of serious financial overextension in the later nineteenth century. Other capital needs were ignored and the country was economically weakened prior to war. The American's apparent propensity for large-scale bribery did nothing to improve the moral climate of the time.

Furthermore the Meiggs lines did not form a unified transportation network that could assist the full integration of the country. With the exception of the Puno-Cuzco connection (now extended beyond Machu Picchu), the roads penetrated inland from the sea at different points along the coast. This improved communication between the coast and the sierra but did not unite the nation laterally. Cerro de Pasco and Huancavelica were later linked but Meiggs was not involved. No border-to-border railroad was built and still has not been. Neither was the selva penetrated.

Elmer J. Faucett is the third notable American pioneer in Peruvian transportation history. Unlike Wheelwright and Meiggs, whose contributions were to surface transport, Faucett's was in aviation. The emergence of this twentieth-century mode of travel was of great significance to Peru, as to the rest of South America. Great mountain ranges and vast jungles could be crossed quickly and at comparatively low financial investments in infrastructure. Whereas railroads are economically a poor choice of transportation mode for a low-income country with difficult terrain, aviation has great possibilities.

When the youthful Faucett arrived in Peru in June 1920, considerable aviation activity was already underway in the country. Experimental and irregular flying had been going on for about a decade. President Leguía was interested in aviation and in 1919 had induced a French military air mission to come to Peru to help establish a Peruvian naval air service, which was accomplished the following year.[8]

Faucett's own appearance in Peru was occasioned by the delivery of some Curtiss aircraft to a new and short-lived Peruvian aviation firm, Cía. Nacional Aeronáutica. Faucett was the Curtiss mechanic sent to assemble the planes after their shipment to Callao by sea. As the young American soon realized, the potentialities for civil aviation in Peru were enormous and as yet almost untapped: Scheduled commercial flying along the coast had not been established and, as for the interior, no pilot crossed the Andes or landed in the Amazon basin.[9]

After completing assembly of the delivered planes Faucett became a pilot for the company that had acquired them. In this job he perfected his ability as a pilot (for which he was never trained) and decided to establish his own flying service. Lacking the funds to do so, he approached President Leguía and suggested that a prize of 5000 soles be offered to the first pilot to fly from Lima to Iquitos (note location in Figure 2), whom Faucett obviously intended to be. After much cajoling Leguía agreed, although he insisted that to try for the money Faucett would have to sign a declaration absolving the Peruvian government of responsibility in case he was killed. On September 11, 1922, Faucett flew a borrowed Curtiss "Oriole" from a Lima race track to Chiclayo. On October 5 the trans-Andean hop to Iquitos was attempted; Faucett managed to take the small craft through a narrow pass and find the Marañón River as a guide to the Amazon, but a mere seventy-five air miles short of his destination the weather forced him to land on a sand bar. Unhurt but his propeller broken, Faucett caught a ride on a passing boat to Iquitos. A replacement was ordered by telegraph and it arrived two months later in December. After installing it a takeoff was attempted but during it the new propeller broke. A second replacement was ordered and finally arrived three months later. Finally on May 9 Faucett succeeded in taking off from the river bank and he landed two hours later at Iquitos. This made him the winner of the prize, but the now-cautious Faucett shipped the plane to Lima via the Panama Canal rather than fly it home.

The American invested the prize money in the Oriole he had borrowed and proceeded to establish a one-man flying business. For the next five years odd jobs were done such as delivering payrolls to remote haciendas and making chartered passenger flights. Supplementing his income by automobile and motorcycle racing, "Slim" Faucett became a colorful and well-known figure in Peru.

In 1928 a group of Peruvian investors decided to back Faucett in establishing a regular commercial air service. Together with the American's personal savings, 100,000 soles ($40,000) was assembled to found Cía. de Aviación Faucett S.A. Operations commenced in September of that year, using two six-seater Stinson "Detroiters." One hundred passengers were carried in the remaining months of 1928, and almost four hundred in 1929. Within five years 10,000 passengers were being carried annually, plus more than seventy tons of mail and cargo. Regular flights were scheduled up and down the coast, with irregular trips into the interior and also to Quito, La Paz, and Santiago.[10]

As the company prospered Faucett was faced with the problem of appropriate equipment. U.S. plane manufacturers in the 1930's were converting from single-engine craft to twin-engined and tri-motor machines, which not only cost more than simpler planes but required longer landing strips. Faucett's meager capital and Peru's limited airfields were not suited to this development.

To solve the equipment problem the former aircraft mechanic decided to build his own planes in Peru in accord with the country's specific needs.

The services of two U.S. aeronautical engineers were obtained to design a plane that would operate at unusually high altitudes, land and take off in short compass, and at the same time carry economical payloads. Engines, instruments, propellers, and a few other items were ordered from American suppliers. The rest of the plane was constructed in shops that Faucett built near the Lima Country Club. The resulting aircraft, nicknamed "El Chico," boasted one Pratt & Whitney engine, a 140 mph cruising speed, and a ceiling of 20,000 feet; it carried eight passengers and was painted a brilliant orange. A total of thirty were built, the last in 1947. Two of them are still extant, housed in Faucett hangers at the Lima-Callao airport.

With its own equipment and, later, Catalina flying boats, surplus World War II aircraft, and modern jets, Cía. de Aviación Faucett became and has remained the clear leader in domestic Peruvian air transportation. Faucett's own mechanic background led him to insist on the highest maintenance standards for his aircraft, and the company has enjoyed an excellent safety record. All major cities and towns in Peru with adequate landing strips are served on a regular basis; more than 400,000 passengers and 20,000 tons of mail and cargo were carried annually by the late 1960's.

Although, as we shall see later, Panagra purchased a minority bloc of Faucett stock in the 1930's, the company is Peruvian in every other respect, including the nationality of top management and pilots. As a national firm it suffers none of the hostility encountered by U.S. enterprises in Peru. The fact that "Slim" was a North American seems to make no difference; when he died after a painful illness in 1960, the principal avenue leading to the Lima airport was immediately renamed "Avenida Elmer J. Faucett." The aviator's sizable estate was left to a foundation that grants aviation scholarships to young Peruvians.

Faucett's contribution to Peruvian transportation was that, together with others,* he opened the era of commercial flying. He dramatized the feasibility of air penetration of the selva, produced a specialized Peruvian aircraft, and established what was to become Peru's leading domestic air carrier. The arrival of commercial aviation meant that as airfields were built even isolated communities could be reached quickly and comfortably. Although the masses were left unaffected by this development, the elites of the country now knew that Peru consisted of more than a desert coastal strip a few miles wide. It is not much of an exaggeration to say that governance of the entire country from Lima became at least a possibility for the first time.

*Two other Americans active in early Peruvian aviation were Harold B. Grow and Harold R. Harris. Grow came to Peru in 1923 as a member of the U.S. Naval Mission and made several exploratory surveys for air routes in the sierra and selva. Also he drafted the first civil aviation regulations and helped to organize what was later to become the Peruvian air force. Harris, whose career is discussed below, initiated the founding in 1928 of what later became Panagra.

Transportation and the Corporations

We turn now from the contributions of individual American entrepreneurs to relevant activities of U.S. business firms. In several instances American companies have been deeply involved in Peruvian transportation—in fact half of the twelve top firms of 1968 may be so described.

One such area of involvement has been port development. For decades W.R. Grace & Co. provided tug and lighterage services at many Peruvian ports. Although this may seem inconsequential, it is important because ships for many years had to anchor at open roadsteads at several of the country's thirty or so ports.[11]

The extractive industries, because of their need to export, invested in permanent port facilities. IPC built fairly extensive facilities at Talara, which has one of the most attractive natural harbors in Peru. In 1925 the Talara port had one of the few reinforced-concrete piers in the country. The port investments left by IPC when it was expropriated in 1968 were of course inherited by Petróleos del Perú and are, for the most part, usable for general cargo.

In the 1950's the two big U.S. mining companies then launching operations in Peru constructed significant port facilities. SPCC built a 550-foot pier near Ilo as the necessary first step in the construction of the Toquepala project; it was used first to bring construction equipment in and later to ship copper out. Similarly, Marcona built port facilities at San Juan to permit construction of the company town and exportation of iron ore. In 1962 Marcona supplemented its San Juan facility with a second port at San Nicolás which included a 1000-foot dock designed especially for bulk pellet and slurry loading of benefacted iron ore.

In evaluating the contributions of these port investments one finds a mixed picture. The Talara port was quite important in that it preceded the age of coastal road transportation in Peru and was vital to cabotage as well as international shipping. The SPCC and Marcona investments never had comparable value for Peru, however; Ilo already had a pier before SPCC arrived and the area surrounding San Juan was serviced from existing ports. The San Nicolás facilities were designed for industrial purposes and may never see generalized use. As mentioned earlier, Marcona gave its San Juan pier and warehouses to the Peruvian navy, but as of 1968 even they were not in use.

Grace and the extractive companies were involved in railroad construction as well. In 1906, a 6-mile, narrow-gauge system was built at Cartavio. In its early years IPC constructed approximately 100 miles of narrow-gauge track between its Talara-area camps and various points in the La Brea y Pariñas oil fields.[12] But these roads were exclusively for company use and neither exists today. The most recent railroad construction is by SPCC; in the late 1950's the corporation built more than 120 miles of standard-gauge track to accommodate daily ore trains between Toquepala and Ilo. SPCC is now connecting this line to Cuajone, largely by tunnel. No passengers or noncompany freight are carried.

In only one instance of which I am aware was a company-built railroad to become of generalized importance to Peruvian transportation. This is the Cerro de Pasco Railway. Constructed mostly in 1902-1904 by the Haggin Syndicate for purposes of ore and coal shipment, the line has always served primarily company needs. But it was the first means of mechanized transportation established between the two key sierra communities of La Oroya and Cerro de Pasco. Between these two centers lie a number of connecting towns, including Junín and Carhuayamo, and the track linking them was laid long before the motor road that today parallels the track.

From the very beginning the Cerro de Pasco Railway operated as a common carrier between La Oroya and Cerro de Pasco, and still today operates daily passenger trains along this 82-mile run. Although the trip is very slow (it takes about seven hours) and uncomfortable because of the ancient rolling stock in use, it is inexpensive and well used by local cholos. Because La Oroya is on the Central Railroad connecting to Lima, the Cerro de Pasco line has for seventy years constituted a main communication link between the central sierra and coast (see Figure 2). The entire Cerro system consists of 170 miles of track, the *lowest* point of which is 11,573 feet above sea level. About half the trackage is used for public carriage; the remainder is for industrial use only.[13]

In a third mode of transportation, aviation, we find W.R. Grace & Co. once again involved. But in this field, unlike shipping and railroading, the contribution is more than of marginal importance. Grace owned half of Pan American-Grace Airways—or "Panagra"—which for years was South America's leading international airline but which also affected internal Peruvian aviation.

In a sense Panagra had its own "Slim Faucett." This was Harold R. Harris, who came to Peru for the first time in 1926 to combat an infestation of army worms that had seriously damaged the cotton crop of the Cañete Valley. Pedro Beltrán, representing the valley's growers, had sought relief from the problem in the United States and was directed to a cotton-dusting company which employed Harris. The American's subsequent flying experience in Peru led him to consider the future of commercial aviation in that country and elsewhere in South America. After his dusting job was over Harris traveled in much of the continent, surveying the aviation potential. Before returning home in 1927 he was satisfied that an airline based at Lima and serving primarily the West Coast of South America would be a sound business venture. At that time two German airlines were operating in the area, but their flights were confined to Colombia and Bolivia. Faucett had not yet organized his airline, although this was not many months away.[14]

Harris took the idea to New York and there confronted the extraordinarily ambitious and aggressive Juan Trippe. At this time Trippe, only in his late twenties, was buying up any and all airline properties he could find, including the fledgling Pan American Airways—then without any equipment but in possession of a mail contract between Key West and Havana. Dreaming of expanding his operations into a Latin American aviation monopoly, Trippe was immediately attracted to Harris's plans and financed creation of the Peruvian Airways Corporation, with Harris as vice-president in charge of operations. The company commenced service on September 13, 1928, with a flight from Lima to Talara. This flight, by a single-engine Fairchild carrying four passengers, constituted the beginning of scheduled airline service in Peru.[15]

Trippe's aspiration of creating a hemispheric aviation monopoly led him inevitably to a showdown with the Grace organization. The latter was not prepared to see its domination of international sea transportation along the West Coast of South America injured by a competitive airline. Although chary of each other, both Trippe and Grace recognized the advantages of cooperation: Pan American possessed connecting routes to the lucrative U.S. market and Grace had general commercial experience in Latin America plus Grace Line steamers that could supply weather reports along air routes. The two formed an uneasy alliance in January 1929 by creating Pan American-Grace Airways, Inc., on a 50-50 ownership basis. Peruvian Airways and a small airline Trippe had set up in Chile were absorbed into it.[16]

Harris was in the Panagra management from the start and guided its rapid growth. Within a few months scheduled service included not just the northern run to Talara but a southern flight to Mollendo. By 1935 Trujillo, Chiclayo, Arequipa, and Tacna were also receiving regular service, with occasional flights to Huancayo and Cuzco. Conceived from the beginning as primarily an international air carrier, Panagra soon instituted flights as far north as Panama and as far south as Santiago, with intermediate stops in Cali, Quito, and La Paz. Service between Santiago and Buenos Aires was established, the first scheduled trans-Andean commercial air service in history. To make these flights—quite daring for the day—Panagra used Ford Tri-Motors and lighter single-engine aircraft over land and Sikorsky amphibians over water.[17]

Although international in scope, Panagra's role in the development of Peruvian aviation was notable. As explained, its flights were between Peruvian cities as well as to foreign cities; in fact until 1934 Panagra had a larger share of the Peruvian domestic market than Faucett. In 1938, apparently to forestall competition between the two, Panagra purchased 25 percent of Faucett stock (later reduced to 20), thus giving it two seats on the Faucett board of directors.

More than this, Panagra considered Peru as the center of its South American operations and located its headquarters in Lima. The quality of

Lima airport facilities was thus of great consequence to the company. When it was realized that Lima's original airport, Las Palmas, would be inadequate for expanding traffic, Panagra built—beginning in 1934—the Limatambo airport. This field, located in the Lima suburb of San Isidro, served as the country's main air facility until 1962, when the present Jorge Chávez airport in Callao was finished. Limatambo was built entirely with company funds and included not only landing field and hangers but a major building, passenger facilities, radio and meteorological stations, maintenance shops, power and water systems, and access roads. The aerodrome's main structure, now used as government offices, can still be seen in San Isidro.

Panagra contributed to Peru's aviation infrastructure outside Lima. During the 1930's the company embarked on an ambitious landing-strip construction program up and down the coast. This activity was under the direction of Bill Peper Nicolas van Meurs, a Dutch immigrant to Peru who eventually became a naturalized Peruvian. Van Meurs's job was to make his way personally to wherever Panagra wanted a ground facility, which in some cases meant going in on foot or muleback. Once at the site van Meurs would survey the terrain for a suitable landing strip and hire local labor, oftentimes Indian women. The Dutchman then placed stakes in the ground to which were attached red or white flags; the women were told to dig at the red flags and fill at the white flags and use their petticoats to carry the material in between. In this manner unpaved landing strips were built at Talara, Paita, Piura, Chiclayo, Pacasmayo, Trujillo, Paramonga, Huacho, Cerro-Azul, Pisco, Ica, Nazca, Arequipa, Ilo, and Tacna. Later the more important strips were paved and facilities such as passenger buildings and radio, power, and weather stations were added.[18] As late as 1952 the company was still contributing to Peruvian airports, which by this time were owned and operated exclusively by the government. In that year Panagra financed and installed an instrument landing system and high-intensity approach lights at Limatambo.[19] Although obviously the company's own planes could then operate more safely, all aircraft benefited. In 1967 Panagra's corporate existence ended when it merged with Braniff Airways.*

A final element of Peruvian transportation in which American companies have been involved is vehicular roads. The Incas and other ancient peoples before them had constructed magnificent networks of Andean foot trails, but a modern road system was not built in Peru until comparatively late and in fact is still far from complete. In 1925 the country possessed about

*Mention might be made of another international airline associated with Peru, Aerolineas Peruanas S.A. or APSA. This carrier was founded in 1956 by the late Cornell Newton "Connie" Shelton, an American aviation tycoon who at one time flew for Chiang Kai-shek. Supposedly APSA was entirely Peruvian-owned, but Shelton and his associates controlled it. Although the carrier experienced a perfect safety record, it went into receivership in 1971 and ceased operations.

2,500 miles of roads of which only 250 were classified as "fairly good" for motor vehicles. In that year only a single completed paved concrete road existed, a 4-mile thoroughfare from Lima to Miraflores (today Avenida Arequipa). By 1964 Peru had some 41,500 miles of road, a tenth of which were paved.[20]

In general, as is true in most countries, Peru's roads have been constructed at government initiative and with public funds. But in some notable instances private businesses, including American firms, have built roads for their own purposes with their own funds. As we have seen, all Peruvian roads are open to the public, hence such privately built roads can be of significance to public transportation.

In the early years of the century IPC built many miles of graded dirt roads between Talara and Negritos and from Negritos to Lagunitos.[21] In the 1950's Marcona constructed a twenty-four-mile paved road from the Pan American Highway to its concession on the sea coast; similarly SPCC built a forty-six-mile link from the Pan American Highway inland to Toquepala. These roads led only to the property of the companies involved, however, and probably had next to no significance for general geographic mobility.

In certain other instances, however, new hinterland areas have been opened up to surface communication with the coast because of American capital. An interesting historical case involves the Inca Mining Company, a U.S.-owned enterprise which in 1896 acquired a gold mining concession in an extremely remote area of the selva. This was on the upper Inambari River in the Puno Department. To get materials in and gold out, the company improved a crude trail that extended more than 100 miles from the Southern Railway track at Tirapata to the town of Limbani (see Figure 2). A mule trail was then laid out between Limbani and the mining site, located at what is today the town of Santo Domingo.[22]

With both good ore and transport routes, Inca Mining subsequently became Peru's most successful gold producer. Impressed with the company's performance, the government granted it a huge rubber-harvesting concession on condition that it build another mule trail, this time between Santo Domingo and Astillero, a port on the Tambopata River to the north. This was completed by 1908, establishing what at the time was the main and practically only transportation link between the sierra and selva in southern Peru. After a Road Conscription Act was passed in 1920 the government improved the trail. Today this route is usable by motor vehicles as far as Limbani.

In at least one recorded instance, road construction was undertaken by the government with public funds but apparently to serve American commercial interests. Favoritism if not corruption must have been involved, for the road benefited primarily the Northern Peru Mining & Smelting Company, to whose mining concession in La Libertad Department it led. The time was Leguía's oncenio; Northern Peru was then owned by Guggenheim interests and today is an affiliate of ASARCO. The sixty-mile road went through no large population settlements and connected the Quiruvilca copper deposit with a railroad leading to the sea. Six meters wide with mild gradients, it constituted the most sophisticated highway project of its time in Peru. The public expenditure involved was rationalized on grounds that taxes from ore trucked on it would cover costs, but in view of the rampant public works bribery of the 1920's one is inclined to suspect the sincerity of that explanation.[23]

Down through the years the Cerro de Pasco Corporation has built several roads in and around its extensive mining operations in the sierra. Between 1945 and 1968 five major projects were completed which together constitute more than 200 miles of new road, in many cases carved out of incredibly difficult terrain (see Figure 2). All five roads connect Cerro industrial sites with existing thoroughfares. In 1945 the company completed a road to the Yauricocha mine from the La Oroya-Huancayo highway near Jauja. In 1953 a penetration road from the Central Highway at Carhuamayo was built to the company hydroelectric plant at Yaupi. Four years later a link was completed between the Central Highway near Huánuco to the Antimina metal mine. Then in 1960 a road between Churín—already linked to the coast by road—and the Raura mine was completed. In all of these instances extremely high and extremely remote areas were penetrated by vehicular road for the first time.[24]

The most recent road to be built by Cerro is the access link to the Cobriza copper mine, opened in 1968. This required construction of or improvement to more than 100 miles of road. Although the mine is located at a comparatively low altitude (7,500 feet) on the Mantaro River, access to it required construction work at altitudes in excess of 14,000 feet. In addition to providing access to the mine, the road has for the first time opened some thirty-five Indian villages to motor transportation that had previously been reachable only on foot or horseback.[25]

In one case road construction for which U.S. enterprise was responsible grew out of a selva land colonization project. In December 1953 the Odría government signed a contract with the LeTourneau organization, a Texas-based manufacturer of enormous earth-moving and land-clearing equipment. The contract stipulated that a large concession of jungle land would be ceded to LeTourneau south of Pucallpa in exchange for construction of a thirty-one mile road from the existing Central Highway to the Pachitea River, a navigable tributary of the Amazon system. The government, which for years had attempted to promote colonization of sections of the selva, hoped that the venture would result in permanent new settlement. LeTourneau saw in the deal an opportunity to test out its heavy equipment under the harshest of conditions. Furthermore the firm's founder and president, the late Robert G. LeTourneau, was an ardent

Christian evangelist who hoped the undertaking would spread the gospel to the Peruvian jungle.[26]

But the project did not realize much success. Much land was cleared by the great machines, but the cost turned out to be greater than by using hand labor. A town called "Tournavista" was built, complete with power and sewer systems, schools, a church, store, clinic, two airfields, and a water treatment plant (the only one for hundreds of miles). But only a mere handful of families were enticed to settle down; in fact most of the inhabitants were LeTourneau workers. In 1970, after having invested $8 million in the project, LeTourneau voluntarily withdrew, giving up the concession and accepting expropriation of its installations.

Two accomplishments were achieved, however. First, it had been proven that cleared jungle land could be profitably employed to raise beef cattle; an excellent herd of about 5000 animals had been developed over the sixteen years of the project. Second, the access road was driven through, although the difficulties encountered in doing so were unexpectedly great. The route, as it turned out, was thirty-eight instead of thirty-one miles long. Because of impassable mud during the rainy season, construction was possible only part of the year. Each year's torrential rains would wash out sections of road completed the previous year. Although the road became passable in 1958, even today it is not in satisfactory condition; moreover, unlike the sierra road projects described above, this road opened up an empty area for future settlement and did not provide external communication for already existing populations (see location in Figure 2).

The last involvement of American business in Peruvian road-building to be mentioned concerns a section of Belaúnde's visionary *Carretera Marginal*. This highway was projected as an international thoroughfare that would link, at a minimum, Colombia, Ecuador, Peru, and Bolivia along the eastern slopes of the Andes. It was Belaúnde's dream that such a road would open up the vast Amazon basin for development. Peru's section was to consist of 1500 miles of almost entirely new road from the Ecuadorian border (at its southernmost point) to the Bolivian frontier near Puerto Maldonado.[27]

As it turned out, the only section of the road to be worked on during the Belaúnde administration was a northern stretch intended to link an existing road leading to the Pan American Highway with the isolated towns of Moyobamba and Tarapoto in the San Martín Department. These communities were highly inaccessible; in fact the entire Department of San Martín had no usable roads of penetration from the coast whatever. The Department's population, estimated at 170,500 in 1961, was almost entirely cut off from the rest of Peru.

It was contemplated that an army civic action battalion would construct the segment from the connecting outer highway (at Ingenio) over the mountain pass to the Nieva River. The route from this point to Tarapoto, a distance of 146 miles, would be built by a consortium of construction companies headed by Constructora Emkay, which has already been identified as the Peruvian subsidiary of the Morrison-Knudsen Company. Another American construction firm, Brown & Root, Inc., was to survey and design the road and then supervise its construction on behalf of the Peruvian government. Associated with the project from the very beginning, the U.S. government provided most of the funds for the Nieva-Tarapoto section; of the anticipated $46 million required, the Export-Import Bank was lending 60 percent and the Agency for International Development 16 percent. Because of the "tied" nature of U.S. economic assistance, American contractors had to be used.[28]

The undertaking got off to an excellent start after the contract was signed in 1965. Equipment was shipped to the area from the United States via the Amazon. The existing road from Yurimaguas was improved so that materials could be trucked to Tarapoto, where the main construction camp was built. By early 1968, with 1050 Peruvian laborers and 50 American supervisors on the job, more than twenty miles of road were completed and open, and advance work on other sections was well along.[29]

Soon relationships between the Peruvian government and the U.S. contractors began to deteriorate, as did progress on the road. It was discovered that a Brown & Root official, Bert W. Donelson, had channeled labor and materials from the project to the building of a private residence for himself. The company fired Donelson after this came to light and reimbursed the Peruvians to the extent of $13,000. Yet it was Brown & Root that was supposedly acting as the government's consultant in overseeing the job. The relationship between consultant and client became further strained when Brown & Root began authorizing payment to Morrison-Knudsen for costs incurred in repairing landslides on completed stretches of road. For some time the Brown & Root field engineer had refused to permit such payments on grounds that Emkay had in effect caused the landslides by improper blasting and placement of access roads. After a top-level meeting between executives of the two companies the policy had suddenly changed. The Peruvian government, by now headed by General Velasco, abruptly discharged Brown & Root as consulting engineers and halted further payments to Morrison-Knudsen.[30]

By mid-1969 Emkay had stopped all work. Its staff was withdrawn from the sites and all heavy equipment was left behind. The Peruvian government sent in its own personnel to resume the job, which at this point was about 40 percent complete. The Peruvians then rescinded the original contract, sued the two companies for $23 million in damages, and brought criminal charges against Donelson. The American government, disappointed to see a prime aid project crumble, tried to save the situation but was unable to do so. Thus, unfortunately for the isolated Department of San Martín, about sixty miles of new (and now deteriorating) road exists between Tarapoto and Moyobamba but does not connect to the coast. It constitutes the principal monument to Belaúnde's now abandoned road dream.

Cultural Assimilation and the Corporations

We turn now to cultural assimilation as a potential by-product of long-term American business involvement in Peru. In discussing this matter we shall consider first the degree of access to company towns and industrial sites by unassimilated Indians, and second whether the character of the American communities is such as to promote genuinely *national* integration.

Some U.S. communities can be dismissed immediately as noncontributory. The La Brea y Pariñas oil field has always been worked by mestizo labor. Even when British oilmen first arrived in the 1860's, the population of the area was mestizo. Talaraños are not Indian at all and in recent years Talara has attracted few outsiders; in 1958 Richard Patch found that 73 percent of its residents were native-born.[31] Similarly, Pueblo Nuevo is populated exclusively by mestizos, since as a matter of policy SPCC will not employ there persons who migrate directly from the sierra; the explanation given is that *serranos* unacclimatized to sea level are highly susceptible to tuberculosis.

Yet companies such as Cerro employ laborers in the sierra itself, as does SPCC at Toquepala. In addition to the major company towns of La Oroya, Cerro de Pasco, and Toquepala, a number of secondary settlements are involved; Cerro alone has six metal mines, a coal mine, and numerous other facilities at which workers live. In assessing the exposure of Indians to these sites, it would appear that at least some assimilation must occur prior to employment; both Cerro and SPCC require all hired labor to know enough Spanish to be able to read signs and understand orders. Yet this requirement may act as an incentive to learn some Spanish in order to qualify for employment.

The SPCC management has collected some precise data on its Toquepala workers that are relevant here. As of 1966, 30.4 percent of them were born in the Puno Department, 25.8 percent in the Arequipa Department, 20.9 percent in the Moquegua Department, and 14.0 percent in the Tacna Department.[32] These figures are meaningful in two respects: first, most workers are from departments other than that in which the mine is located (Tacna); second, the heavily Indian department of Puno is the most important single source. In short, Toquepala attracted workers from far away and some of them could have been very "Indian" upon arrival. This conclusion is supported by informal comments of veteran SPCC field personnel.

Migration to sierra work sites is not merely unidirectional and one-time. Workers frequently return to their villages for fiestas or temporary periods and then journey back to the place of employment once again. I was told at La Oroya that 80 percent of the mine workers there commute back and forth frequently and that strong roots are retained in the home village.[33] In his study of Muquiyauyo, a town located on the La Oroya-Huancayo road near Jauja, anthropologist Richard Adams found that villagers worked intermittently at mines in the area and that this relationship constituted an important external influence. The principal mines involved were French-owned mines near Huaron and Cerro de Pasco's Morococha facility. Adams believes that the mobile Muquiyauyiños brought home with them knowledge of construction and medical techniques plus the idea of installing a power plant in the town. Muquiyauyiños working at Morococha had organized a social club and this group helped finance the plant and arranged for a Cerro engineer to come to the town to install it.[34]

At the coastal plantations workforces have typically been quite stable in recent years. Commercially oriented haciendas such as Cartavio and Paramonga need fewer and fewer workers as technology advances. Scarce, permanent jobs are not given up by their holders lightly to make room for newcomers. Yet not many decades ago the reverse was true; patrónes faced a shortage of manpower and needed to import Indian labor from the sierra. This was done by sheer impressment on the part of labor contractors or by a system of *engancho* whereby Indians were given cash advances for wages and thereby drawn into a type of debt peonage. As late as 1940 workers were brought to Cartavio and Paramonga this way, creating a forced confrontation by unassimilated Indians of the coastal culture.[35]

But even after forced recruitment ended, Paramonga, in particular, continued to be a terminus of Indian migration. The hacienda population grew much more rapidly than fertility levels would account for; recorded at 4,985 in 1940, the population was 9,765 by 1949 and 18,487 by 1960 (the growth rate has since leveled off—about 22,000 lived there in 1968). The principal reason for this expansion was completion of a road from the Callejón de Huaylas section of the sierra to the coast. This intersects the Pan American Highway almost directly across from the entrance gate to Paramonga. The Callejón is a beautiful but poor Andean valley containing a large mestizo and Indian population. According to Eduardo Soler, a student of this subject, the road became a major migration route for the Indian seeking work or escape from home-village problems. At Paramonga he would engage in trade with the residents or take temporary work. The recent migrant would typically return to his home village several times but would eventually settle more permanently at the hacienda. As evidence for this explanation of the growth of Paramonga, a study conducted in 1958 showed that 56 percent of community residents were born off the hacienda and that 34 percent came from the Department of Ancash, which is not Paramonga's department but is the locale of the Callejón.[36]

What happens to the compartively unassimilated Indian after he arrives at a sierra mine or coastal plantation?

It is known that he is exposed to at least some features of industrial civilization. He becomes familiar with the rules, tools, and values of modern productive enterprise. The fact that large American companies have a penchant for on-the-job training courses adds to the impact. Most firms also send workers to vocational-technical schools in Lima and elsewhere.

We also know that the new arrival is subject to status pressures within the community. According to Richard Patch, the Indians arriving at Paramonga—where they are called *paisanos*—attempt deliberately to rise to what is perceived as a superior social class, that of the *acriollados*.

They soon learn the rudiments of Spanish—it is difficult to find a person in Paramonga who does not speak at least a partially understandable version—but among themselves they continue to speak Quechua. Their clothing is no longer the homespun wool of the native communities, but is not as yet the apparel worn on the coast. Most often it is the clothing of purchased muslin and drill worn by Indians living in the mestizo towns of the sierra. They still chew coca, especially during work.

After arriving at this intermediate level, Patch continues, an effort is made to reach the next highest class, the *criollo* or mestizo:

They served their apprenticeship as paisanos, and now demonstrate their affiliation with the criollos by rejecting the paisanos and the Indian culture which they represent. They speak Spanish, even among themselves, and to an outsider they will deny they can also speak Quechua, or that they were born in the sierra. Their dress is completely and typically coastal. They make a point of referring to the Indians' dirtiness and their own cleanliness, so that—as one put it—"There will be no confusion." As is typical of a mobile group, they do not make friends aimlessly but in order to be accepted into a group which was previously closed to them. They "study" their friendships.

Seldom, Patch believes, is criollo or mestizo status actually achieved by the Paramonga worker who has come to the hacienda as a young Indian. But, he says, the children of the acriollado group will normally be considered mestizos.[37]

What about *American* cultural influences at these centers? To this vital question a mixed answer must be given. On the one hand the communities have many features indistinguishable from other Peruvian towns. Architecture and dress are the same for all practical purposes. Usually not enough foreigners are present to make them more than marginally visible. Public schools operate with the same curricula, teaching methods, and student uniforms as elsewhere in Peru. Many priests are foreign but this is true throughout the country. Most radio and all television broadcasts are from indigenous sources; this is true for newpapers as well, except for the company house organ. The dominant sport in all communities is soccer, not basketball or baseball. The dominant language is of course Spanish, and several companies conduct free literacy classes for residents who cannot read or write it. When cultural events are brought in under company auspices—as was done by Grace at Paramonga—the performers are usually Peruvian.

On the other hand one cannot help but notice some American or at least non-Peruvian elements at the communities.* The first self-service grocery store to be established in Peru was the IPC mercantile at Talara. English-speaking schools operate for the benefit of staff children at La Oroya and Pueblo Nuevo; the latter is accredited by the state of Texas. The annual soccer championship competition between Cerro's camps is known as the "Koenig Cup" after the corporation's former president.[38] At Marcona an intensive birth control program was begun under company auspices in 1962, contrary to government policy and Catholic doctrine.[39]

In the last chapter we saw how Americans were in charge of all eight major company towns save the Grace plantations. Thus the economic and political domination described in that chapter means that even slight Americanizing tendencies at the top have widespread effect. At Toquepala, the most authoritarian and paternalistic of the towns, U.S. cultural influences were in particular abundance. Motion pictures shown in company theaters tend to be from Hollywood; "Radio Cultura Toquepala" transmitted not only Peruvian music but recordings of Lawrence Welk and Billy Vaughn. In a program shown to me of "charlas" or informal conversations operated by the SPCC Department of Welfare, topics were discussed such as human relations, sex education, venereal disease, and the church's social function in the community. These are not traditional subjects for open discussion in a Latin American society.[40]

It is quite natural that American and European managers and technicians and their families associate socially with one another in these towns. Thus defined, foreign colonies exist to some extent. Often these groups are socially and even physically segregated from the mass of the Peruvian work force—they, together with Peruvian staff, have their own clubs and

---

*Just as the American towns exhibit signs of American culture, the same is true with other industrial communities with a foreign origin. The hacienda Casa Grande, founded by the Gildemeister family, has a distinct German flavor. The old British oil camp of Lobitos north of Talara features an Anglican chapel and staff houses with wide verandahs as one might expect to see in India.

schools. At Cerro de Pasco even the company hospital is segregated: separate wards exist for obreros, empleados, and staff. Staff houses, as Grant found in Guyana, tend to be separated from the rest of the community by the industrial plant or natural land curvature. In view of this segregation the local cultural impact of resident foreigners is probably somewhat contained. Of course, social distinctions are nothing new to Peru or any other Latin country; the segregation itself is not "foreign." One of the more curious aspects of staff privileges in the towns is that the supposedly egalitarian Americans quite faithfully perpetuate hierarchical class structures that to them are "foreign."

Recapitulation

Wheelwright significantly increased the efficiency of coastwise shipping by introducing steam. Meiggs played a decisive role in the construction of most of Peru's railroads, but some of these lines were unintegrated fragments and the builder encouraged a railroad mania that contributed to national bankruptcy. Faucett helped to open the era of commercial flying by demonstrating the feasibility of air penetration of the selva, building a specialized aircraft for the region, and founding the country's leading domestic airline.

In the distant past Grace and IPC contributed to public cabotage shipping, but the more recent port construction by SPCC and Marcona benefited the corporations alone. Grace, IPC, and SPCC built various railroad links, but these were not open to common carriage; Cerro's railroad, however, has served as an important common carrier in the sierra for seventy years. Panagra, although an international air carrier, contributed to internal Peruvian aviation by the construction of numerous airfields and related installations, including the Limatambo airport.

Vehicular roads built by IPC, Marcona, and SPCC served immediate industrial interests; only the firm's own extractive activity made them of value. At the turn of the century the Inca Mining Company and its subsidiary constructed significant penetration roads and trails into the southern selva. A road built by the Leguía administration in the 1920's to the Quiruvilca mine was an apparent outright subsidy to the Northern Peru Mining & Smelting Company. Between 1945 and 1968 Cerro de Pasco constructed five mine access roads, some of which opened up remote villages to modern transport for the first time. LeTourneau built a difficult selva road, but because of the failure of a colonization project it ended up going nowhere important. Two U.S. construction companies were engaged in building a link of the Carretera Marginal, but prior to completion they withdrew amid charges of malfeasance and corruption.

Although Talara and Pueblo Nuevo had no role in assimilation of the Indian, several other U.S. installations and communities probably did. The sierra mines of Cerro and SPCC attracted comparatively unassimilated workers. In past decades the Grace plantations did as well, Paramonga in particular because of its location. Hispanic acculturation is said to occur at these centers; although some American cultural influences are present, they may be of secondary importance, in part because of self-imposed isolation by foreigners. The communities are not, and most probably never were, sealed foreign enclaves.

Part IV   **Conclusions**

Nine   Summation and Comment

In this concluding chapter we review and synthesize the findings of the book. In doing so both generalizations and variations are noted with regard to American corporate involvement in Peruvian politics. A brief comment is also made with respect to what this study implies for other developing countries vis-à-vis foreign investment.

The Hypotheses Reexamined

The normative perspective of this study has been the interests of Peruvians. Is their national independence challenged by American business and its allies? Is their political system vitally affected at certain points or as a totality? Certainly Peruvians are well disposed to consider these questions, for since the 1920's American rather than British capital has predominated in the country's foreign investment sector. More than 300 American business firms are resident on Peruvian soil and they include the biggest private enterprises in the country. The parent corporations of these firms are among the largest multinational corporations in existence. By conservative estimates U.S. private, direct investments in Peru are worth around $700 million; more liberal estimates would place their value close to $1 billion.

An attempt has been made to assess a number of potential political consequences of foreign investment. In most of the study the focal concept is political power. In examining power relationships, assessment was made of capacities of the corporations to possess influence, behavior of the corporations (and other actors) that would suggest on-going effort to secure influence, and effects or outcomes of relevant activity or controversy that might point to exercise of influence. In Chapter Eight an exploratory study was conducted of possible impacts of American business activity on Peruvian national integration. This was done by examining transportation activities and possible cultural effects of remote industrial sites.

The first hypothesis explored was taken from the literature of economic imperialism. This school of thought views the foreign capitalist, and today the American multinational corporation in particular, as dominating the political life of underdeveloped countries. I applied the point of view to Peru as follows:

Hypothesis I. American corporations in Peru participate actively and directly in Peruvian politics. By means of bribes and favors, control of the mass media, and intervention by the American government, the corporations are able to control Peruvian public policies pertinent to their interests. Basic to their influence is an alliance with conservative Peruvian elites and an economic dependence on the companies by Peru.

The hypothesis is sustained in part but refuted in part.

Certainly most of the corporations do not shy away from politics; they do not hesitate to involve themselves when their interests require it. The most common form of involvement is direct lobbying; high-ranking executives systematically seek out and exploit contacts at pertinent points in the Peruvian political and governmental structure. They utilize pressure groups as well, although as an avenue of access the groups are of secondary importance to direct corporate action.

Most corporate political involvement consists of a variety of exchange-making behaviors. On a bureaucratic level petty venality is ubiquitous. On the policy level large-scale bribery was practiced by certain companies at various times in the past, but it does not appear to be a commonplace tool of influence today. Rather, nonmonetary favors of both a personal and "institutional" type are used; these do not carry the stigma and risk of bribes and yet can lead to reciprocal obligation. Occasionally campaign contributions are made to the political parties—when there are elections, that is.

The companies do not "control" the Peruvian mass media. American investments in broadcasting and publishing are minor. The corporations are among the largest advertisers in the country, however, and advertising expenditures probably lead to some influence over editorial policy. Informal payments to sympathetic journalists are not unknown.

The American government definitely intervenes in Peruvian affairs on behalf of the companies but not in errand-boy fashion, at least today. In past decades Washington supported U.S. business flagrantly and aggressively on more than one occasion. In recent years economic sanctions have been threatened or applied against Peru several times in support of business interests, but not necessarily when and in the way wanted by the businessmen. Diplomatic protection of U.S. business is generally a rather routine series of inquiries, protests, and the arrangement of negotiations. The businessmen communicate with the American ambassador on a regularized basis but do not rely on him for most political dealings.

With respect to the central question of whether the companies "control" public policies pertinent to their interest, it must be noted that many examples can be cited of policy outcomes which seem to reflect corporate desires quite faithfully. Often this took time, and a price had to be paid, but the eventual outcome was accommodation to the foreign investors.

Illustrations can be given from both the historic and recent past. In

1903-1908 the Haggin Syndicate was able to overcome all opposition in establishing what later became the Cerro de Pasco Corporation. In 1915-1922 Standard Oil was able to force upon the Peruvians an extraordinarily favorable status for La Brea y Pariñas. In later years these same interests were again able to mold public policy to their liking— Cerro's impact on the Mining Code of 1950, Koenig's dictation of mining contracts, and IPC's ability to obtain an eventual gasoline price increase. As recently as the Belaúnde administration, the mining companies were able to secure a liberalized Article 56 of the Mining Code, ITT was able to obtain tariff increases, SPCC was able to divert an antipollution campaign against its copper smelter, and Goodyear was able to lead a successful drive to retain import duty exonerations.

When one turns to the regime of Juan Velasco Alvarado, however, an unmistakable shift is perceived in the treatment of American business enterprise. The Revolution's first act was expropriation of La Brea y Pariñas. The Grace sugar properties were later expropriated and General Motors, Anderson Clayton, and Morrison-Knudsen were forced from the country in varying ways and degrees. All unworked mining concessions held by U.S. corporations were seized without compensation and the government entered the fields of mineral refining and marketing. Far-reaching decree-laws were issued in the realms of profit-sharing, exchange control, and governmental regulation and enterprise. Eventual termination of majority foreign ownership of industry was even called for.

It is true that, beginning about two years after the Revolution, the generals began to communicate more freely with the business community. Draft decrees were circulated for comment and some adjustments were made in deadlines, tax policy, and credit and exchange regulations. But the basic reforms of the Revolution—the most radical in Peruvian history— were left unscathed in their major thrust. U.S. capital was most unhappy to say the least; although the investors obtained minor concessions in the application of the new policies they were unable to emasculate or compromise them. For a time, at least, the Peruvian government was in "control," not the corporations.

The Revolution damaged not only U.S. economic interests in Peru but domestic Peruvian interests associated with land, finance, and industry. Although American business and traditionalist Peruvian elites have many values and goals that overlap, it would be a mistake to characterize their relationship as a close alliance. Ties with such bastions of conservatism as the National Agrarian Society and the Club Nacional definitely exist, but for functional rather than ideological purposes. U.S. business executives in Peru tend in attitude to be on the Right side of the political spectrum but not at its extreme end. They are pragmatists, as are most businessmen, and are capable of adjusting to a stabilized revolution if profits can be made under it.

Peru's degree of economic dependence on U.S. investments is moderate but not overwhelming. A significant but limited percentage of total investment, production, jobs, and revenues are accounted for by American corporations. However the operations of individual enterprises, namely, Cerro, SPCC, Marcona, Goodyear, and—prior to the Revolution—ITT, IPC, and Grace—are sufficiently critical to the economy in one way or another to constitute considerable basis for leverage. Ultimately this leverage protected all companies quite well except IPC; the explanation for Standard Oil's downfall is partly an image left over from an exploitationist past and partly a deliberate attempt by Peruvian politicians to discredit the corporation for their own purposes.

As noted at the beginning of this volume, a great "gap of opinion" exists between the economic imperialism school and another conception of foreign-investor political impact articulated by some students of the multinational corporation. The latter argue that the companies avoid active political involvement, concentrate on being corporate good citizens, and engage in hardheaded, bilateral investment bargaining—a practice that would not be necessary if the investors were domineering imperialists. The hypothesis that incorporates this point of view follows:

Hypothesis IA. American corporations in Peru avoid active participation in Peruvian politics and do not seek important intervention from U.S. authorities. Instead they attempt to minimize their local visibility or improve their image. Public policies unfavorable to corporate interests are possible but, because of the economic importance of U.S. capital, the corporations are able to bargain effectively over investment terms. Corporate bargaining strength is greater with respect to new capital than existing capital.

This alternative view, like the first one, is verified to some extent but not totally by the evidence presented. We have already noted in this summation that the corporations often *are* active participants in the Peruvian political process, and that sometimes they *do* seek diplomatic intervention of consequence. We also found public relations strategies of both the low visibility and promotional types. The second strategy is more common than the former and can become quite amazingly multifaceted. Public-opinion polls indicate that PR campaigns can be highly ineffective, however; poll results in Lima show, in fact, a steep downward trend in the popularity of American business generally between 1958 and 1966.

Furthermore it is clear that the corporations do engage in investment bargaining. We traced in detail how IPC, ITT, Cerro, and other mining companies sought policy quid pro quos with the Peruvian government that involved new or existing capital. Offers of new investment were generally the most efficacious bargaining tactic, although IPC employed operational-curtailment tactics with success. But over time the bargaining outcomes seemed to favor the companies less and less until, under Velasco, they were quite balanced rather than one-sided. Indeed, under the Revolution corporate bargaining goals seemed to be not so much special privilege as in earlier years but simply survival under viable conditions. A tacit bargain may have been struck with the regime about 1971 in which the business-men and generals "agreed" to cooperate with each other more fully; if so, this may be viewed as a political consequence of subtle but powerful economic pressures generated by mutual self-interest rather than imperialism.

With respect to the challenge posed to Peru's national independence by U.S. investments, then, I do not perceive either grossly imperialistic domination or politically innocent negotiation. American capital is not sufficiently critical to the economy to bring the country forcibly to its knees and it is not sufficiently in control of public opinion to manipulate Peruvian desires. Yet some enterprises possess individual economic leverage. They do not hesitate to bargain hard with it, nor do they hesitate to apply aggressively a full range of lobbying and PR techniques. The consequence prior to 1968 was frequent but not inevitable modification of established or pending public policies in the investors' favor. The Velasco Revolution, however, demonstrated that such accommodation to foreigners *can* be cut off, a possibility that does not comport with imperialist theory. In short, Hypothesis I is essentially right about political behavior (except for alliance with the oligarchy) but is essentially wrong on total economic dependence and policy control. Hypothesis IA is largely right in acknowledging the nonabsolute nature of dependence and control and in predicting economic bargaining behavior; but it is largely wrong in expecting political noninvolvement.

Thus the corporations frequently act like imperialists, but they cannot always achieve imperialistic results. They do not render Peru's national independence meaningless but they constitute a potent and self-seeking foreign force within the national polity that must be adequately contained. The lesson of the Velasco regime is that this *is* possible.

In its wide-ranging search for all significant political consequences of American corporations in Peru this book considered impacts on the community and society. Those deemed worthy of exploration were the political power structure of the company town and implications for national political integration.

Because of the economic domination of the towns connotated by the phrase "company town" itself, and also because of the potential for control of communications, the reasoning of economic imperialism was employed to construct a hypothesis of political domination. Also introduced was the possibility, taken from literature on the industrial town and community development, that attempts to reduce paternalism were possible but that the consequence may not be a lessening of domination.

Hypothesis II. In Peruvian communities where American corporations are the principal employer, company management dominates local political life. This is achieved by means of economic dependence, bribes and favors, worker benefits and services, and control of mass media. Attempts to reduce or replace paternalism are made, but they result in augmenting as well as reducing company political influence.

The hypothesis is largely confirmed. Because of the corporation's control of most of the jobs and real estate in the community, and because of its great capacity to issue valuable favors to individuals and groups, it is in a position to offer attractive exchanges in return for cooperation and subservience. A mass communications monopoly does not exist, but nevertheless most companies control local cinemas and all of them publish house organs. The companies are required by law to provide free housing and services and some managements go beyond the minima. It is doubtful that this paternalism creates loyalty to the corporate patrón but it may leave barren soil for the growth of initiative. At Toquepala, SPCC owns, operates, and controls virtually everything; armed guards at the gates supervise movement in and out of the site like sentries at national frontiers. Some companies have made valiant efforts to lessen paternalism, usually for the very practical reason that it is both costly and bothersome. This activity has included promotion of worker-owned housing, independent commercial enterprises, and self-help community projects. Some of these undertakings have met with apathy, others with enthusiastic success; the net result probably has been no reduction in management control and possibly a gain. Although antimanagement attitudes and political forces are prevalent in the communities, the corporation's preeminent position remains unchallenged. Management must endure many harassments but it gets its way on all important issues and probably keeps many from arising in the first place. The communities are definitely "company towns" in the political as well as economic sense.

The final hypothesis of the study focuses on the Peruvian political system as a whole. A very tentative formulation, it draws upon relationships hypothesized by others between political integration and variables of proximity, transaction, and homogeneity. When these variables are operationalized as the quality of national transportation and the opportunity for cultural unification, the activity of foreign business enterprise is potentially relevant.

Hypothesis III. The activity of some American entrepreneurs and corporations has had the unintended, long-term, net effect of adding to the political integration of Peru. This has resulted from contributions to the internal transportation network and the operation of remote or strategically located enterprises which accelerate assimilation of the Indian.

It is impossible to evaluate with certainty the evidence bearing on this hypothesis because of incomplete knowledge of linkages between company activities and effects regarding transportation, assimilation, and integration. Other forces than foreign investment are obviously at work in shaping Peru's transportation system and the Indian's Hispanization.

Yet, over the course of Peruvian history, U.S. business has been involved in building and operating transportation facilities to perhaps a surprising degree. Ocean shipping, railroads, vehicular roads, and aviation have been affected significantly. Surely the degree of integration of this spatially and culturally divided country has to some degree been touched. The impact has been both negative and positive: some transport facilities have been for company use only, of temporary value, unintegrated themselves, wasteful, or associated with corruption and conflict of interest. Other undertakings have represented innovative, lasting improvements to public transportation that might not have come about for some time if it were not for U.S. business involvement. My impression is that on balance Peruvian transportation benefited moderately but not optimally.

As for the cultural aspect of the hypothesis an initial point is that some of the transportation developments probably contributed to assimilation by opening up new routes for cultural contact and migration. The construction activities of Meiggs, Inca Mining, and Cerro come particularly to mind. With respect to the impact of strategically located mines and plantations, we have the views of several anthropologists that these have, in fact, led to the spread of coastal culture into the sierra and, conversely, the attraction of serranos to the coast. What we have added to this finding is the results of a limited survey of the cultural environment of all major U.S. company towns. They are basically "Peruvian" in the coastal sense but with an overlay of American influence that varies in depth. The effect of this foreign element is mitigated by the communities' class system, however, which isolates the elite from the mass.

I speculate, then, that Hypothesis III is mildly confirmed. Before concluding that the Peruvian political system has thus been made more integrated by the corporations, we need to recall that the findings of Hypotheses I and II are pertinent to this subject. If foreign businessmen are allied with and reinforce an indigenous oligarchy a national elite-mass gap could be widened, which in a sense is disintegrative. Or, if company towns are so management-dominated that the national political jurisdiction stops at the community's perimeter, that too would be counterintegrative. We have found, in this book, that the corporations do not today identify intimately with national oligarchs but that they do run their towns in relatively tight fashion. Local government, which in centralized Peru is an extension of the national government, is essentially subverted. This point, then, adds a countercontributory element to the equation. In the final analysis it seems clear that whatever their net value for integration, the corporations have helped both to bring the country together and to divide it up. Economic imperialism reigns in these selected local polities, but since they are open to migratory flow and exhibit essentially the national culture their effect is ambivalent upon the political system.

Variation and a Plea

These conclusions constitute the principal contribution of this book. Yet as an important postscript variety among individual corporations with respect to political consequence must be stressed. Generalizations on a complex subject such as this, so necessary to the formulation of opinion, have a way of hiding important differences. Consider, for example, the fact that a Cerro or SPCC possesses a degree of economic importance in Peru that is on a different order of magnitude than a Sears or IBEC. Or, the point that some firms necessarily operate in remote areas for access to minerals or oil and are hence potential contributors to integration whereas others must be confined to urban places for the sake of manpower and markets.

Beyond these unavoidable differences are interesting distinctions in behavior. Grace promotes Peruvians to high management levels but SPCC does not. Cerro invites local capital participation but most companies do not. The managers of some enterprises are politically reactionary, whereas the executives of others are quite liberal. ITT and, at one time, IPC engaged in high-handed pressure tactics while SPCC and Goodyear played a more private and subtle game. Not all firms run to Washington when in trouble as did ITT and Grace; not all firms renegotiate contracts periodically in favor of the government as did Marcona; not all firms were evicted from the country under charges of malfeasance as was Morrison-Knudsen; not all companies rebuilt their towns completely as did IPC.

Aside from stressing this diversity for the sake of honestly coming to terms with reality, it lays bare a feature of the politics of foreign investment that can be of assistance to host-government policy-makers. They should, I believe, take careful heed of the differences in political behavior and effect that various corporations may bring to their shores.

It has already been stated that the political threat embodied in foreign investment is believed to be real but controllable, at least in Peru. Foreign capital can, conceivably, even be beneficial to the political system (in the sense of integration). Under certain circumstances the dangers could loom intolerably large, however—for instance, when a country is very small or its economy is based on a single commodity. But aside from such cases the risk may be worth taking; the question then is how to minimize it.

My plea is that host-country leaders discard all stereotypes of the foreign corporation as to its political conduct and significance and instead develop an ability to distinguish between managements. A firm's political reputation and record elsewhere is not unknowable; it should be ascertained prior to admittance to the country. In other words political as well as economic factors should enter into assessments of benefits and costs of individual investment projects. As for corporations already in the country, distinctions in political conduct should be noted and remembered so that they can become matters to be considered when concessions or informal privileges are distributed. The corporations must be made to realize that it is in their long-term interest to avoid crass attempts to manipulate. Moreover, bargaining over expanded investments should incorporate not only ratios of income-division and other economic benefits but, say, the openness of company towns. By recognizing that the political consequences of foreign investment are variable the policy-makers can, in time, seek to minimize and mold them. Viewing the investors flatly and without exception as either economic imperialists or corporate good citizens forecloses any attempt to discriminate among them and apply selective counterpressures.

Appendix

Selected Bibliography

Notes

Index

Appendix

Appendix. Information Related to Interviews.

Interviews conducted					
Place of interview	Number	Year	Number	Year	Number
Peru	167	1966	12	1969	7
United States	53	1967	59	1970	8
	220	1968	107	1971	27

Respondents interviewed			
Nationality of respondent	Number	Occupation of respondent	Number
American	91	**Business**	
Peruvian	75	Executive, U.S. parent company	25
Other	16	Head or deputy head, U.S. subsidiary	22
	182	Department head, U.S. subsidiary	33
		Staff of U.S. subsidiary	22
		Executive, Peruvian firm	6
			108
		Government	
		Former president of Peru	1
		Peruvian ambassador to United States	1
		Former U.S. ambassador to Peru	1
		Head, Peruvian government agency	4
		Member, Peruvian Congress	2
		Peruvian local official	6
		Staff, U.S. government agency	6
		Staff, U.S. Embassy in Peru	7
			28
		Other	
		Peruvian professor or scholar	2
		American professor or scholar	4
		Member, Peruvian press	2
		Staff, business interest group	7
		Staff, American foundation	3
		Company town union official	9
		Company town clergy	14
		Company town merchant	5
			46

Selected Bibliography

Adams, Richard N. *A Community in the Andes: Problems and Progress in Muquiyauyo*. Seattle, Wash., University of Washington Press, 1959.

———— ed. *Social Change in Latin America Today*. New York, Harper & Brothers, 1960.

Adelman, Irma, and Cynthia Taft Morris. *Society, Politics, and Economic Development: A Quantitative Approach*. Baltimore, Md., Johns Hopkins University Press, 1967.

Ake, Claude. *A Theory of Political Integration*. Homewood, Ill., Dorsey Press, 1967.

Alberdi, J.B. *The Life and Industrial Labors of William Wheelright in South America*. Boston, A. Williams & Co., 1877.

Allred, Wells M. "System of Government in Peru," *Philippine Journal of Public Administration*, 4 (January 1960), 46-60.

Astiz, Carlos A. *Pressure Groups and Power Elites in Peruvian Politics*. Ithica, N.Y., Cornell University Press, 1969.

Baer, Werner, and Mario Henrique Simonsen. "American Capital and Brazilian Nationalism," *The Yale Review*, 53 (1963), 192-198.

Banco Central de Reserva del Perú. *Plan nacional de desarrollo económico y social del Perú, 1962-1971*, vol. 1, Lima, 1962.

Baum, Daniel J. "The Global Corporation: An American Challenge to the Nation-State?" *Iowa Law Review*, 55 (1969), 410-437.

Behrman, Jack N. *National Interests and the Multinational Enterprise: Tensions Among the North Atlantic Countries*. Englewood Cliffs, N.J., Prentice-Hall, 1970.

Belaúnde Terry, Fernando. *Peru's Own Conquest*. Lima, American Studies Press, 1965.

Benavides Correa, Alfonso. *Oro negro del Perú: La Brea y Pariñas: Problema para la IPC y solución para el Perú*. Lima, 1963.

Bernstein, Marvin D., ed. *Foreign Investment in Latin America: Cases and Attitudes*. New York, Knopf, 1966.

Biddle, William W. *The Community Development Process: The Rediscovery of Local Initiatives*. New York, Holt, Rinehart & Winston, 1965.

Bonilla, Frank. "Invisible Elites," *Studies in Comparative International Development*, 6 (1970-71), 139-155.

Bourricaud, François. *Power and Society in Contemporary Peru*. New York, Praeger, 1970.

Bravo Bresani, Jorge. "Mito y realidad de la oligarquía Peruana," *Revista de Sociología*, 3 (1966), 43-71.

———— "Gran empresa y pequeña nación," *Perú Problema*. Lima, Francisco Moncloa Editores, 1968, pp. 119-152.

Broehl, Wayne G., Jr. *The International Basic Economy Corporation.* Washington, D.C., National Planning Association, 1968.

Brown, Wilson B. "Governmental Measures Affecting Exports in Peru, 1945-1962: A Study in Policy and Its Making," unpub. diss., Fletcher School of Law and Diplomacy, Tufts University, 1965.

Burgess, Eugene W., and Frederick H. Harbison. *Casa Grace in Peru.* New York, National Planning Association, 1954.

Carey, James C. *Peru and the United States, 1900-1962.* Notre Dame, Ind., University of Notre Dame Press, 1964.

Castro Bastos, Leonidas. *Geohistoria del Perú: Ensayo económico-político-social.* Lima, 1962.

Champlin, John R., ed. *Power.* New York, Atherton Press, 1971.

Chaplin, David. *The Peruvian Industrial Labor Force.* Princeton, N.J., Princeton University Press, 1967.

_____ "Peru's Postponed Revolution," *World Politics,* 20 (1968), 393-420.

Clark, Terry N., ed. *Community Structure and Decision-Making: Comparative Analysis.* San Francisco, Calif., Chandler Publishing Company, 1968.

Cohen, Alvin. "The Technology/Elite Approach to the Developmental Process: Peruvian Case Study," *Economic Development and Cultural Change,* 14 (1966), 323-333.

_____ "Externalities in the Displacement of Traditional Elites," *Economic Development and Cultural Change,* 17 (1968), 65-76.

Collado, Emilio, and Jack F. Bennett. "Private Investment and Economic Development," *Foreign Affairs,* 35 (1957), 631-645.

El Comercio (Lima).

Committee for Economic Development. *Economic Development Issues: Latin America.* Supplementary Paper No. 21. New York, Committee for Economic Development, 1967.

Cotler, Julio. "The Mechanics of Internal Domination and Social Change in Peru," *Studies in Comparative International Development,* 3 (1968), 229-246.

_____ "Political Crisis and Military Populism in Peru," *Studies in Comparative International Development,* 6 (1970-71), 95-113.

Coutu, Arthur J., and Richard A. King. *The Agricultural Development of Peru.* New York, Praeger, 1969.

Cox, Oliver C. *Capitalism as a System.* New York, Monthly Review Press, 1964.

Davenport, John. "Why Peru Pulls Dollars," *Fortune* (November 1956), pp. 130-136, 140-141.

Dew, Edward. *Politics in the Altiplano: The Dynamics of Change in Rural Peru.* Austin, Texas, University of Texas Press, 1967.

Dobyns, Henry, and Mario C. Vásquez, eds. *Migración e integración en el Perú.* Lima, Editorial Estudios Andinos, 1963.

_____ et al., eds. *Peasants, Power, and Applied Social Change: Vicos as a Model.* Beverly Hills, Calif., Sage Publications, 1971.

Doughty, Paul L. *Huaylas: An Andean District in Search of Progress.* Ithaca, N.Y., Cornell University Press, 1968.

Drewes, Wolfram U. *The Economic Development of the Western Montaña* of Central Peru as Related to Transportation: A Comparison of Four Areas of Settlement. Lima, Peruvian Times, 1958.

Dunn, Robert W. American Foreign Investments. New York, B.W. Huebsch, 1926.

Einaudi, Luigi R. The Peruvian Military: A Summary Political Analysis. Santa Monica, Calif., Rand Corporation, 1969.

_____Peruvian Military Relations with the United States. Santa Monica, Calif., Rand Corporation, 1970.

_____ et al. Latin American Instutitional Development: The Changing Catholic Church. Santa Monica, Calif., Rand Corporation, 1969.

Erasmus, Charles J. "Community Development and the 'Encogido' Syndrome," Human Organization, 27 (1968), 65-74.

Evans, John C.W. "Grace Machine Inaugurated, One of Three New in S.A. for 1968," Paper Trade Journal, July 29, 1968, pp. 44-50.

Evans, Peter B. "National Autonomy and Economic Development: Critical Perspectives on Multinational Corporations in Poor Countries," International Organization, 25 (1971), 675-692.

Fann, K.T., and Donald C. Hodges, eds. Readings in U.S. Imperialism. Boston, Porter Sargent, 1971.

Fawcett, Brian. Railways of the Andes. London, George Allen & Unwin Ltd., 1963.

Fayerweather, John. Facts and Fallacies of International Business. New York, Holt, 1962.

Felix, David. "United States Investment in Latin America: Problems and Prospects," Journal of International Affairs, 14 (1960), 140-151.

Ferrero, Rómulo A. "Economic Development of Peru," Economic Development Issues: Latin America. New York, Committee for Economic Development, 1967, pp. 211-259.

Feuerlein, Willy, and Elizabeth Hannan. Dollars in Latin America: An Old Problem in a New Setting. New York, Council on Foreign Relations, 1941.

Fieldhouse, D.K. The Theory of Capitalist Imperialism. New York, Barnes & Noble, 1967.

Ford, Thomas R. Man and Land in Peru. Gainesville, Fla., University of Florida Press, 1955.

Frank, André Gunder. Capitalism and Underdevelopment in Latin America: Historical Studies of Chile and Brazil. New York, Monthly Review Press, 1967.

_____ Latin America: Underdevelopment or Revolution. New York, Monthly Review Press, 1969.

Fritsch, William R. The Sears, Roebuck Story in Peru: Progress and Profits. Washington, D.C., Action Committee for International Development, 1962.

Furlong, William L. "Peruvian Local Government: Structures, Functions, and Style," unpub. diss., University of Florida, 1967.

Gall, Norman. "Peru: The Master is Dead," Dissent, 18 (1971), 281-320.

General Bureau of Information [Government of Peru], Petroleum in Peru: For the World to Judge: The History of a Unique Case. Lima, 1969.

Gerassi, John. The Great Fear in Latin America, rev. ed. New York, Collier Books, 1965.

Gerbi, Antonello. *Caminos del Perú*. Lima, Banco de Crédito del Perú, n.d.

Gibb, George Sweet, and Evelyn H. Knowlton. *The Resurgent Years, 1911-1927*. New York, Harper & Brothers, 1956.

Goodman, Bernard. "The Political Economy of Private International Investment," *Economic Development and Cultural Change*, 15 (1957), 263-276.

Goodwin, Richard N. "Letter from Peru," *The New Yorker*, May 17, 1969, pp. 41-110.

Gordon, Lincoln, and Engelbert L. Sommers. *United States Manufacturing Investment in Brazil: The Impact of Brazilian Government Policies*. Boston, Harvard Business School, 1962.

Gordon, Wendell C. *The Political Economy of Latin America*. New York, Columbia University Press, 1965.

Grace, J. Peter, Jr. *W.R. Grace (1832-1904) and the Enterprises He Created*. New York, Newcomen Society, 1953.

Grant, C.H. "Company Towns in the Caribbean: A Preliminary Analysis of Christianburg-Wismar-Mackenzie," *Caribbean Studies*, 11 (1971), 46-72.

Grunwald, Joseph. "Foreign Private Investment: The Challenge of Latin American Nationalism," *Virginia Journal of International Law*, 11 (1971), 228–245.

Guzmán Marquina, Oscar. *Reivindicación de la Brea y Pariñas*. Lima, n.d.

Hamilton, Stanley Kerry. "Factors Influencing Investment and Production in the Peruvian Mining Industry, 1940-1965," unpub. diss., University of Wisconsin (Madison), 1967.

Hannifin, Rieck B. "Expropriation by Peru of the International Petroleum Company: A Background Study." Washington, D.C., Library of Congress, Legislative Reference Service, 1969.

Hayter, Teresa. *Aid as Imperialism*. Harmondsworth, England, Penguin Books, 1971.

Hilliker, Grant. *The Politics of Reform in Peru: The Aprista and Other Mass Parties of Latin America*. Baltimore, Md., Johns Hopkins University Press, 1971.

Hobsbawm, E.J. "Peru: The Peculiar 'Revolution,' " *New York Review*, December 16, 1971, pp. 29-36.

Hobson, J.A. *Imperialism: A Study*. London, George Allen & Unwin, 1902.

Huizer, Gerrit. "Resistance to Change and Radical Peasant Mobilization: Foster and Erasmus Reconsidered," *Human Organization*, 29 (1970), 303-313.

International and Comparative Law Center. *Selected Readings on Protection by Law of Private Foreign Investments*. Albany, N.Y., Matthew Bender & Co., 1964.

International Petroleum Company. *The La Brea y Pariñas Controversy: A Resumé*. 1972.

Ismodes Cairo, Aníbal. *Bases de una sociología del Perú*. Lima, Editorial Minerva, 1967.

Jacob, Philip E., and Henry Teune. "The Integrative Process: Guidelines for Analysis of the Bases of Political Community," *The Integration of*

Political Communities, ed. Jacob and James V. Toscano. Philadelphia, Pa., J.B. Lippincott, 1964, pp. 1-45.

James, Daniel. "Sears, Roebuck's Mexican Revolution," *Harper's*, June 1959, pp. 65-71.

Johnson, Harry G., ed. *Economic Nationalism in Old and New States.* Chicago, Ill., University of Chicago Press, 1967.

Johnson, Leland L. *U.S. Private Investment in Latin America: Some Questions of National Policy.* Santa Monica, Calif., Rand Corporation, 1964.

———— "U.S. Private Investment in Latin America Since the Rise of Castro," *Inter-American Economic Affairs*, 18 (1964), 53-75.

Josephson, Matthew. *Empire of the Air: Juan Trippe and the Struggle for World Airways.* New York, Harcourt, Brace & Co., 1943.

Kantor, Harry. *The Ideology and Program of the Peruvian Aprista Movement.* Washington, D.C., Savile Books, rev. ed., 1966.

Kautsky, John, ed. *Political Change in Underdeveloped Countries: Nationalism and Communism.* New York, Wiley, 1962.

Keohane, Robert O., and Joseph S. Nye, Jr., eds. *Transnational Relations and World Politics.* Cambridge, Harvard University Press, 1972.

Kindleberger, Charles P. *American Business Abroad: Six Lectures on Direct Investment.* New Haven, Conn., Yale University Press, 1969.

———— ed. *The International Corporation.* Cambridge, Mass., The MIT Press, 1970.

Kling, Merle. "Towards a Theory of Power and Political Instability in Latin America," *Western Political Quarterly*, 9 (1956), 21-35.

Koo, Anthony Y.C. "A Short-Run Measure of the Relative Economic Contribution of Direct Foreign Investment," *Review of Economics and Statistics*, 31 (1961), 269-276.

Kuhn, Gary Glen. "The History of Aeronautics in Latin America," unpub. diss., University of Minnesota, 1965.

Larson, Larry. "Labor, Social Change and Politics in Peru," unpub. diss., University of North Carolina, 1968.

Larson, Magali Sarfatti, and Arlene Eisen Bergman. *Social Stratification in Peru.* Berkeley, Calif., Institute of International Studies, University of California, 1969.

Lauterbach, Albert. *Enterprise in Latin America: Business Attitudes in a Developing Economy.* Ithaca, N.Y., Cornell University Press, 1966.

LaValle, Hernando de. *A Statement of the Laws of Peru in Matters Affecting Business*, 3rd ed. Washington, D.C., Pan American Union, 1962.

Lenin, V.I. *Imperialism: The Highest Stage of Capitalism.* New York, International Publishers, 1939.

Levin, Jonathan V. *The Export Economies: Their Pattern of Development in Historical Perspective.* Cambridge, Mass., Harvard University Press, 1960.

Lewis, Cleona. *America's Stake in International Investments.* Washington, D.C., The Brookings Institution, 1938.

_____ *The United States and Foreign Investment Problems*. Washington, D.C., The Brookings Institution, 1948.

Lewis, Sherman. "The International Petroleum Company vs. Peru: A Case Study in Nationalism, Management, and International Relations." Reproduced, California State College at Hayward, 1972.

McLaughlin, Donald H. "Origin and Development of the Cerro de Pasco Copper Corporation," *Mining and Metallurgy*, November 1945, pp. 509-511.

McMillan, Claude, Jr., Richard F. Gonzalez, with Leo H. Erickson. *International Enterprise in a Developing Economy: A Study of U.S. Business in Brazil*. East Lansing, Mich., Michigan State University Graduate School of Business Administration, 1964.

Magdoff, Harry. *The Age of Imperialism: The Economics of U.S. Foreign Policy*. New York, Monthly Review Press, 1968.

Malpica, Carlos. *Los dueños del Perú*, 3rd ed. Lima, Ediciones Ensayos Sociales, 1968.

Mann, Charles K. "Sears, Roebuck de México: A Cross-Cultural Analysis," *Social Science*, 40 (1965), 149-157.

Mariátegui, José Carlos. *Siete ensayos de interpretación de la realidad Peruana*. Lima, Biblioteca Amauta, 1928.

Matos Mar, José. "Dominación, desarrollos desiguales y pluralismos en la sociedad y cultura Peruana," *Perú Problema*. Lima, Francisco Moncloa Editores, 1968.

May, Herbert K. *The Effects of United States and Other Foreign Investment in Latin America*. New York, The Council for Latin America, 1970.

Mayer, Dora. *The Conduct of the Cerro de Pasco Mining Company*. Lima, Impresa El Progreso, 1913.

Maynard, Eileen A. *Patterns of Community Service Development in Selected Communities of the Mantaro Valley, Peru*. Ithaca, N.Y., Cornell University Press, 1964.

Mikesell, Raymond F. *Foreign Investments in Latin America*. Washington, D.C., Pan American Union, 1955.

_____ et al. *Foreign Investment in the Petroleum and Mineral Industries: Case Studies of Investor-Host Country Relations*. Baltimore, Md., Johns Hopkins University Press, 1971.

_____ ed. *U.S. Private Investment Abroad*. Eugene, Ore., University of Oregon Books, 1962.

Miller, Solomon. "Hacienda to Plantation in Northern Peru: The Processes of Proletarianization of a Tenant Farmer Society," *Contemporary Change in Traditional Societies*, Julian H. Stewart, ed., vol. 3, Urbana, Ill., University of Illinois Press, 1967, pp. 133-225.

Millikan, Max, and Donald L.M. Blackmer, eds. *The Emerging Nations: Their Growth and United States Policy*. Boston, Little, Brown, 1961.

Morris, Earl W., et al. *Coming Down the Mountain: The Social Worlds of Mayobamba*. Ithaca, N.Y., Department of Anthropology, Cornell University, 1968.

Mullins, Richard H. "Principal Manufacturing Industries in Peru," *Overseas*

Business Reports. Washington, D.C., U.S. Department of Commerce, August 1965.

Multinational Investment in the Economic Development and Integration of Latin America. Washington, D.C., Inter-American Development Bank, 1968.

Nearing, Scott, and Joseph Freeman. *Dollar Diplomacy: A Study in American Imperialism*. New York, Monthly Review Press, reprinted ed., 1966.

Needler, Martin. "Cabinet Responsibility in a Presidential System: The Case of Peru," *Parliamentary Affairs*, 18 (1965), 156-161.

Nehrt, Lee Charles. *The Political Climate for Private Foreign Investment: With Special Reference to North Africa*. New York, Praeger, 1970.

Nelson, Eastin. "A Revolution in Economic Policy: An Hypothesis of Social Dynamics in Latin America," *The Southwestern Social Science Quarterly*, 34 (1953), 3-16.

The New York Times.

Nieves Ayala, Arturo. *Legislación sobre compañias e instituciones extranjeras*. Lima, 1962.

Nolan, Louis Clinton. "The Diplomatic and Commercial Relations of the United States and Peru, 1826-1875," unpub. diss., Duke University, 1935.

North, Liisa. *Civil-Military Relations in Argentina, Chile and Peru*. Berkeley, Calif., Institute of International Studies, University of California Press, n.d.

Palacio, Gustavo. "El laudo de la Brea y Pariñas," *Revista de la Facultad de Ciencias Económicas y Comerciales* (Cuzco), 1 (1963-1964), 31-54.

Patch, Richard W. "An Oil Company Builds a Town," *American Field Universities Staff Reports*, West Coast of South America, vol. 5, no. 2 (March 12, 1958).

_____ "The Role of a Coastal Hacienda in the Hispanization of Andean Indians," *American Universities Field Staff Reports*, West Coast of South America, vol 6, no. 2 (March 15, 1959).

Payne, Arnold. *The Peruvian Coup d' Etat of 1962: The Overthrow of Manuel Prado*. Washington, D.C., Institute for the Comparative Study of Political Systems, 1968.

Payne, James L. *Labor and Politics in Peru: The System of Political Bargaining*. New Haven, Conn., Yale University Press, 1965.

Pareja Paz-Soldán, José. *Derecho constitucional Peruano*, 3d ed. Lima, Ediciones del Sol, 1963.

Peeler, John Allen. "The Politics of the Alliance for Progress in Peru," unpub. diss., University of North Carolina, 1968.

Peruvian Times (Lima). (Full Masthead: *Andean Air Mail & Peruvian Times*.)

Pike, Frederick B. *The Modern History of Peru*. New York, Praeger, 1967.

Pinelo, Adalberto J. *The Multinational Corporation as a Force in Latin American Politics: A Case Study of the International Petroleum Company in Peru*. New York, Praeger, 1973.

Plank, John N. "Peru: A Study in the Problems of Nation-Forming," unpub. diss., Harvard University, 1958.

La Prensa (Lima).

Purser, W.F.C. *Metal-Mining in Peru, Past and Present*. New York, Praeger, 1971.

Quijano, Aníbal. *Nationalism and Capitalism in Peru: A Study in Neo-Imperialism*. New York, Monthly Review Press, 1971.

Ramírez Novoa, E. *Recuperación de la Brea y Pariñas: Soberanía nacional y desarrollo económico*. Lima, 1964.

Reinaga, Cesar Augusto. *La fisonomía económica del Perú*. Cuzco, Editorial Garcilaso, 1957.

Riencourt, Amaury de. *The American Empire*. New York, Dial Press, 1968.

Rippy, J. Fred. *British Investments in Latin America, 1822-1949: A Case Study of the Operations of Private Enterprise in Retarded Regions*. Minneapolis, Minn., University of Minnesota Press, 1959.

Robinson, David A. *Peru in Four Dimensions*. Lima, American Studies Press, 1964.

Rockefeller, David. "What Private Enterprise Means to Latin America," *Foreign Affairs*, 44 (1966), 403-416.

Rodríguez del Valle, Antonia. *El problema de Brea y Pariñas*. Arequipa, Universidad Nacional de San Agustín, 1965.

Roel Pineda, Virgilio. *Problemas de la economía Peruana*. Lima, Gráfica Popular, 1959.

Roemer, Michael. *Fishing for Growth: Export-led Development in Peru, 1950-1967*. Cambridge, Mass., Harvard University Press, 1970.

Rogers, William D. "United States Investment in Latin America: A Critical Appraisal," *Virginia Journal of International Law*, 11 (1971), 246-255.

Romero, Emilio. *Geografía económica del Perú*. Lima, 1961.

Root, Franklin R. "Foreign Government Constraints on U.S. Business Abroad," *Economic and Business Bulletin*, 20 (1967), 28-37.

Salazar Bondy, Augusto. "La cultura de la dominación," *Perú Problema*. Lima, Francisco Moncloa Editores, 1968.

Salera, Virgil. *Multinational Business*. Boston, Houghton Mifflin, 1969.

_____ "Beneficent Investment: The Department of Commerce Survey," *Inter-American Economic Affairs*, 10 (1957), 71-77.

Schelling, Thomas C. "Bargaining, Communication, and Limited War," *Journal of Conflict Resolution*, 1 (1957), 19-36.

Schiller, Herbert I. "The Multinational Corporation as International Communicator" (1970).

Schrickel, Clyde Calvin. "Personnel Practices of United States Manufacturing Firms Operating in Colombia, Ecuador, Peru, and Venezuela," unpub. diss., Ohio State University, 1966.

Servan-Schreiber, J.-J. *The American Challenge*. New York, Atheneum, 1968.

Sharp, Daniel A., ed. *U.S. Foeign Policy and Peru*. Austin, Texas, University of Texas Press, 1972.

Shea, Andrew B. *Panagra: Linking the Americas During 25 Years*. New York, Newcomen Society, 1954.

Shea, Donald R. *The Calvo Clause: A Problem of Inter-American and International Law Diplomacy*. Minneapolis, Minn., University of Minnesota Press, 1955.

Shearer, John C. *High-Level Manpower in Overseas Subsidiaries: Experience in Brazil and Mexico*. Princeton, N.J., Princeton University Press, 1960.

Sociedad Geográfica de Lima. *Anuario Geográfico del Perú*. Lima, 1962.

Staley, Eugene. *The Future of Underdeveloped Countries: Political Implications of Economic Development*. New York, Harper & Brothers, 1954.

———— *War and the Private Investor: A Study in the Relations of International Politics and International Private Investment*. New York, Howard Fertig, 1967.

Stephens, Richard H. *Wealth and Power in Peru*. Metuchen, N.J., Scarecrow Press, 1971.

Stevens, Carl M. *Strategy and Collective Bargaining Negotiation*. New York, McGraw-Hill, 1963.

Stewart, Watt. *Henry Meiggs: Yankee Pizarro*. Durham, N.C., Duke University Press, 1946.

Stokes, William S. "Economic Anti-Americanism in Latin America," *Inter-American Economic Affairs*, 11 (1957), 3-22.

Taylor, Milton C. "Problems of Development in Peru," *Journal of Inter-American Economic Studies*, 9 (1967), 85-94.

———— "Taxation and Economic Development: A Case Study of Peru," *Inter-American Economic Affairs*, 21 (Winter 1967), 43-54.

Thomas, Ann Van Wynen, and O.J. Thomas, Jr. *Non-Intervention: The Law and Its Import in the Americas*. Dallas, Tex., Southern Methodist University Press, 1956.

Turner, Louis. *Invisible Empires: Multinational Companies and the Modern World*. London, Hamish Hamilton, 1970, and New York, Harcourt Brace Jovanovich, 1971.

UN Department of Economic and Social Affairs. *Analysis and Projections of Economic Development VI, The Industrial Development of Peru*. Mexico, D.F., 1959.

———— *External Financing in Latin America*. New York, 1965.

———— *Foreign Capital in Latin America*. New York, 1955.

———— *United Nations Statistical Yearbook 1968*. New York, 1969.

U.S. Department of the Army. *U.S. Army Area Handbook for Peru*. Washington, D.C., 1965.

U.S. Department of Commerce. *Investment in Peru: Basic Information for United States Businessmen*. Washington, D.C., 1957.

———— *Market for U.S. Products in Peru*. Washington, D.C., 1961.

———— *The Multinational Corporation: Studies on U.S. Foreign Investment*, vol. 1. Washington, D.C., 1972.

———— *Peru: A Commercial and Industrial Handbook*. By W.E. Dunn. Washington, D.C., 1925.

_____ *Survey of Current Business.*

_____ *U.S. Business Investments in Foreign Countries.* Washington, D.C., 1960.

_____ *U.S. Investments in the Latin American Economy.* Washington, D.C., 1957.

U.S. Department of Labor. *Labor Law and Practice in Peru.* Washington, D.C., 1968.

U.S. Department of State. *Resources Survey for Latin American Countries.* Washington, D.C., 1965.

Urquidi, Victor L. *The Challenge of Development in Latin America.* New York, Praeger, 1964.

Vernon, Raymond, ed. *How Latin America Views the U.S. Investor.* New York, Praeger, 1966.

_____ "Saints & Sinners in Foreign Investment," *Harvard Business Review,* 41 (May-June 1963), 146-161.

_____ *Sovereignty at Bay: The Multinational Spread of U.S. Enterprises.* New York, Basic Books, 1971.

Wall Street Journal.

The Washington Post.

Weiner, Myron. "Political Integration and Political Development," *Annals of the American Academy of Political and Social Science,* 358 (March 1965), 52-64.

Werlich, David Patrick. "The Conquest and Settlement of the Peruvian Montaña," unpub. diss., University of Minnesota, 1968.

Whitman, Marina von Neumann. *Government Risk-Sharing in Foreign Investment.* Princeton, N.J., Princeton University Press, 1965.

Whyte, William F., and Allan R. Holmberg. "Human Problems of U.S. Enterprise in Latin America," *Human Organization,* 15 (1956), 1-40.

Wimpfen, Sheldon P. "How the Toquepala Project Runs," *Mining Congress Journal,* April 1969, pp. 42-50.

Winkler, Max. *Investments of United States Capital in Latin America.* Boston, World Peace Foundation, 1928.

Wionczek, Miguel S. "United States Investment and the Development of Middle America," *Studies in Comparative International Development,* 5 (1969-70), 3-17.

Wolf, Charles, Jr. "The Political Effects of Economic Programs: Some Indications from Latin America," *Economic Development and Cultural Change,* 14 (1965), 1-20.

Wood, Richardson, and Virginia Keyser. *Sears, Roebuck de México, S.A.* Washington, D.C., National Planning Association, 1953.

Wythe, George. *Industry in Latin America.* New York, Columbia University Press, 1945.

Yglesias, José. "The Reformers in Brass Hats," *New York Times Magazine,* Dec. 14, 1969.

Zimmermann Zavala, Augusto. *La historia secreta del petróleo.* Lima, 1968.

Notes

Chapter One, Foreign Investment and Politics

1. *The Great Fear in Latin America*, rev. ed. (New York, Collier Books, 1965), p. 380.
2. "Oil: Source of Arab Wealth and Friction," *New York Times*, January 4, 1970.
3. "The Global Corporation: An American Challenge to the Nation-State?" *Iowa Law Review*, 55 (November 1969), 410.
4. Behrman, Kindleberger, Mikesell, and Vernon are the leading American students of the multinational corporation, and note should be taken of their several works mentioned in the bibliography. They are all economists, but political analysis is particularly strong in Behrman's *National Interests and the Multinational Enterprise: Tensions among the North Atlantic Countries* (Englewood Cliffs, Prentice-Hall, 1970); ch. 2 of Mikesell's *Foreign Investment in the Petroleum and Mineral Industries: Case Studies of Investor-Host Country Relations* (Baltimore, Johns Hopkins Press, 1971); ch. 6 of Vernon's *Sovereignty at Bay: The Multinational Spread of U.S. Enterprise* (New York, Basic Books, 1971); and Vernon's article "Multinational Enterprise & National Sovereignty," *Harvard Business Review*, 45 (March-April 1967), 156-172. A British view is found in Turner's *Invisible Empires: Multinational Companies and the Modern World* (New York, Harcourt Brace Jovanovich, 1971).
5. Brief analyses are found in works of the following, all cited in the bibliography: Baer and Simonsen, Bonilla, P.B. Evans, Goodman, W.C. Gordon, Grunwald, L.L. Johnson, and Rogers. Frankly probusiness statements are made in works by Collado and Bennett, Rockefeller, Salera, and Staley, and in case studies by Broehl, Burgess and Harbison, Fritsch, James, Mann, and Wood and Keyser. Antibusiness comments are made by Cox, Frank, Gerassi, Kautsky, Kling, Nearing and Freeman, Magdoff, and Riencourt. Readers on foreign investment are edited by Bernstein, Fann and Hodges, H.G. Johnson, Kindleberger, Mikesell, and Vernon.
6. Comments on the politics of American business in Peru are made in Astiz, Carey, Cotler (1971), Guzmán Marquina, Hannifin, Hayter, Hobsbawm, Malpica, Matos Mar, Mayer, Patch, Pike, Pinelo, Quijano, Ramírez Novoa, Reinaga, Roel Pineda, and Salazar Bondy (see Bibliography).
7. John Gerassi, "Our Good Neighbors," *Book Week*, July 3, 1966.
8. "United States Investment and the Development of Middle America," *Studies in Comparative International Development*, vol. 5, no. 1 (1970), p. 4.

9. U.S. Congress, Joint Economic Committee, Subcommittee on Inter-American Economic Relationships, Hearings, *Private Investment in Latin America*, 88th Cong., 2nd Sess., January 1964, p. 31.

10. "Towards a Theory of Power and Political Instability in Latin America," *Western Political Quarterly*, 9 (March 1956), 29-30.

11. U.S. Department of Commerce, *U.S. Business Investments in Foreign Countries* (Washington, D.C., 1960), p. 92, and *Survey of Current Business*, October 1969, p. 28, October 1970, p. 28, and October 1971, p. 32.

12. Behrman, *National Interests and the Multinational Enterprise*, p. 10.

13. Vernon, *Sovereignty at Bay*, p. 7; *New York Times*, January 16, 1970, and June 6, 1971.

14. See Teresa Hayter, *Aid as Imperialism* (Harmondsworth, Eng., Penguin Books, 1971) and Marina von Neumann Whitman, *Government Risk-Sharing in Foreign Investment* (Princeton, Princeton University Press, 1965).

15. See Behrman, *National Interests and the Multinational Enterprise*, chs. 3, 4, and 5.

16. For a survey of incentives and restrictions on foreign investment by host countries, see Franklin R. Root, "Foreign Government Constraints on U.S. Business Abroad," *Economic and Business Bulletin*, 20 (September 1967), 28-37.

17. For greater detail, see the works cited in note 5. A concise survey of Latin American literature on this subject is William S. Stokes, "Economic Anti-Americanism in Latin America," *Inter-American Economic Affairs*, 11 (1957), 3-22.

18. Reviews of this complex situation are found in Behrman, "Economic Effects of Private Investment," in Mikesell, ed., *U.S. Private and Government Investment Abroad* (Eugene, University of Oregon Books, 1962); Vernon, *Sovereignty at Bay*, ch. 5, and "Saints & Sinners in Foreign Investment," *Harvard Business Review*, 41 (May-June 1963), 146-161; and Mikesell, *Foreign Investment in the Petroleum and Mineral Industries*, chs. 1, 6, 10, and 16. An interesting attempt to construct a rank-order of Latin countries in terms of benefits received from U.S. investments is described in Anthony Y.C. Koo, "A Short-Run Measure of the Relative Economic Contribution of Direct Foreign Investment," *Review of Economics and Statistics*, 31 (August 1969), 269-276. Peru is given the second lowest rank, interestingly enough, using aggregate U.S. Department of Commerce data from the 1950s.

19. John R. Champlin, ed., *Power* (New York, Atherton Press, 1970), p. 3.

20. See Champlin, *Power*, for various viewpoints on these issues. A recent essay on the intention question is D.M. White, "Power and Intention," *American Political Science Review*, 65 (1971), 749-759.

21. Note the dialogue in the following pages of the *American Political Science Review*: Seymour Martin Lipset, "Some Social Requisites of Democracy: Economic Development and Political Legitimacy," 53 (1959), 69-105; Karl Deutsch, "Social Mobilization and Political Development,"

55 (1961), 493-514; Donald McCrone and Charles Cnudde, "Toward a Communication Theory of Democratic Political Development," 61 (1967), 72-79; Deane Neubauer, "Some Conditions of Democracy," 61 (1967), 1002-1009; and Martin Needler, "Political Development and Socioeconomic Development: The Case of Latin America," 62 (1968), 889-897. Other pertinent literature is noted in these articles.

22. James O'Connor, "The Meaning of Economic Imperialism," in K.T. Fann and Donald C. Hodges, eds., *Readings in U.S. Imperialism* (Boston, Porter Sargent, 1971), pp. 23-68.

23. An excellent summary of the evolution of this theory is D.K. Fieldhouse, *The Theory of Capitalist Imperialism* (New York, Barnes & Noble, 1967).

24. *The Age of Imperialism: The Economics of U.S. Foreign Policy* (New York, Monthly Review Press, 1969), p. 14.

25. This point is admirably made by Robert O. Keohane and Joseph S. Nye, Jr. in *Transnational Relations and World Politics* (Cambridge, Harvard University Press, 1972), pp. xix-xx.

26. *The Military-Industrial Complex* (Philadelphia, Pilgrim Press and National Catholic Reporter, 1970), p. 29.

27. John Kautsky, ed., *Political Change in Underdeveloped Countries: Nationalism and Communism* (New York, Wiley, 1962), pp. 22-23.

28. "Dependency and Imperialism: The Roots of Latin American Underdevelopment," in Fann and Hodges, *Readings in U.S. Imperialism*, pp. 155-181.

29. "Madison Avenue Imperialism," in Richard L. Merritt, ed., *Communication in International Politics* (Urbana, University of Illinois Press, 1972), pp. 319, 337.

30. *Dollar Diplomacy: A Study in American Imperialism* (New York, Heubsch and the Viking Press, 1925; Monthly Review Press, 1966), pp. 17-18.

31. Amaury de Riencourt, *The American Empire* (New York, Dial Press, 1968). Riencourt sees the "empire" as oriented toward presidential rather than business interests, however.

32. "Dominación, desarrollos desiguales y pluralismos en la sociedad y cultura Peruana," *Perú Problema* (Lima, Francisco Moncloa Editores, 1968), pp. 21, 23. Translation by this author.

33. *Problemas de la economía peruana* (Lima, Gráfica Popular, 1959), p. 91. Translation by this author.

34. *Peru 1965: Notes on a Guerrilla Experience* (New York, Monthly Review Press, 1969), p. 27.

35. "La cultura de la dominación," *Perú Problema*, pp. 57-82.

36. Magali Sarfatti Larson and Arlene Eisen Bergman, *Social Stratification in Peru* (Berkeley, Institute of International Studies, University of California, 1969), p.270.

37. Béjar, *Peru 1965*, pp. 25, 42.

38. *Los dueños del Perú*, 3rd ed. (Lima, Ediciones Ensayos Sociales, 1968), pp. 37-39. All Malpica quotes are translated by this author.

39. *Los dueños del Perú*, pp. 41-42.

40. Malpica, *Los dueños del Perú*, pp. 62-63.

41. *National Interests and the Multinational Enterprise*, p. 4.

42. *Invisible Empires*, p. 62.

43. *Foreign Investment in the Petroleum and Mineral Industries*, p. 432.

44. *American Business Abroad: Six Lectures on Direct Investment* (New Haven, Yale University Press, 1969), p. 198.

45. "Multinational Enterprise & National Sovereignty," p. 163.

46. *Sovereignty at Bay*, pp. 208-209, 213.

47. Kindleberger, *American Business Abroad*, pp. 150-159.

48. Carl M. Stevens, *Strategy and Collective Bargaining Negotiation* (New York, McGraw-Hill, 1963), pp. 57-58.

49. *Foreign Investment in the Petroleum and Mineral Industries*, pp. 33-44, 54.

50. "Company Towns in the Caribbean: a Preliminary Analysis of Christianburg-Wismar-Mackenzie," *Caribbean Studies*, 11 (April 1971), 50, 55.

51. Terry N. Clark, ed., *Community Structure and Decision-Making: Comparative Analyses* (San Francisco, Chandler Publishing Company, 1968), pp. 94, 102.

52. "The Role of a Coastal Hacienda in the Hispanization of Andean Indians," *American Universities Field Staff Reports*, West Coast of South America, vol. 6, no. 2 (March 15, 1959), pp. 5, 11.

53. "Human Problems of U.S. Enterprise in Latin America," *Human Organization*, 15 (Fall 1956), 22-26.

54. Solomon Miller, "Hacienda to Plantation in Northern Peru: The Processes of Proletarianization of a Tenant Farmer Society," *Contemporary Change in Traditional Societies*, vol. 3, ed. Julian H. Stewart (Urbana: University of Illinois Press, 1967), pp. 138-142 ff.

55. "Changing Community Attitudes and Values in Peru: A Case Study of Guided Change," ch. 2 in Richard N. Adams, ed., *Social Change in Latin America Today* (New York, Harper & Brothers, 1960). See also "Human Problems of U.S. Enterprise in Latin America," pp. 15-18, and Henry F. Dobyns, et al., *Peasants, Power, and Applied Social Change: Vicos as a Model* (Beverly Hills, Sage Publications, 1964, 1971).

56. See, e.g., William W. Biddle, *The Community Development Process: The Rediscovery of Local Initiative* (New York, Holt, Rinehart & Winston, 1965).

57. "Community Development and the 'Encogido' Syndrome," *Human Organization*, 27 (Spring 1968), 65-74.

58. "Resistance to Change and Radical Peasant Mobilization: Foster and Erasmus Reconsidered," *Human Organization*, 29 (Winter 1970), 303-313.

59. *A Theory of Political Integration* (Homewood, Ill., Dorsey Press, 1967).

60. Lucian W. Pye, *Aspects of Political Development* (Boston, Little, Brown and Company, 1966), pp. 65-66.

61. Myron Weiner, "Political Integration and Political Development," *Annals of the American Academy of Political and Social Science*, 358 (March 1965), 52-64.

62. "The Integrative Process: Guidelines for Analysis of The Bases of Political Community," *The Integration of Political Communities*, ed. Jacob and James V. Toscano (Philadelphia, J.B. Lippincott, 1964), p. 4.

63. Ibid., pp. 11-12.

64. Jacob and Tuene, "The Integrative Process," pp. 16-18, 23-26.

65. *The Future of Underdeveloped Countries: Political Implications of Economic Development* (New York, Harper, 1954), pp. 296, 299.

66. `The Peruvian Industrial Labor Force* (Princeton, Princeton University Press, 1967), p. 25.

67. "The Integrative Process," pp. 18-23.

68. Earl W. Morris, et al., *Coming Down the Mountain: The Social Worlds of Mayobamba* (Ithaca, Cornell Department of Anthropology, 1968). See also José Matos Mar, "Dominación desarrollos desiguales y pluralismos en la sociedad y cultura Peruana," pp. 41-48, and Henry Dobyns and Mario C. Vásquez, eds., *Migración e integración en el Perú* (Lima, Editorial Estudios Andinos, 1963).

69. "The Role of a Coastal Hacienda," pp. 3-4.

70. *A Community in the Andes: Problems and Progress in Muquiyauyo* (Seattle, University of Washington, 1959), ch. 6.

71. Paul L. Doughty, *Huaylas: An Andean District in Search of Progress* (Ithaca, Cornell University Press, 1968), pp. 82-83.

72. William Mangin, "The Indians," in Daniel A. Sharp, ed., *U.S. Foreign Policy and Peru* (Austin, University of Texas Press, 1972), pp. 229-235 ff.

73. On this matter, see Peter Bachrach and Morton S. Baratz, "Decisions and Nondecisions: An Analytical Framework," *American Political Science Review*, 57 (September 1963), 632-642.

Chapter Two, Peru and American Business

1. Wolfram U. Drewes, *The Economic Development of the Western Montaña of Central Peru as Related to Transportation: A Comparison of Four Areas of Settlement* (Lima, *Peruvian Times*, 1958), pp. 10-16.

2. *Society, Politics, & Economic Development: A Quantitative Approach* (Baltimore, Johns Hopkins Press, 1967), pp. 54-56. For additional sources on Peruvian "separateness," consult Emilio Romero, *Geografía económica del Perú* (Lima, 1961); Leónidas Castro Bastos, *Geohistoria del Perú: Ensayo económico-político-social* (Lima, 1962); Thomas R. Ford, *Man and Land in Peru* (Gainesville, University of Florida Press, 1955); David A. Robinson, *Peru in Four Dimensions* (Lima, American Studies Press, 1964); and Arthur J. Coutu and Richard A. King, *The Agricultural Development of Peru* (New York, Praeger, 1969).

3. Earl W. Morris, et al., *Coming Down the Mountain: The Social Worlds of Mayobamba* (Ithaca, Cornell Department of Anthropology, 1968), pp. 149-150. This small village should not be confused with the much larger city of Moyobamba, located in the Department of San Martín.

4. *Pressure Groups and Power Elites in Peruvian Politics* (Ithaca, Cornell University Press, 1969), p. 87. For more on Peruvian social

structure, see Astiz; François Bourricaud, *Power and Society in Contemporary Peru* (New York, Praeger, 1970); Julio Cotler, "The Mechanics of Internal Domination and Social Change in Peru," *Studies in Comparative International Development*, vol. 3, no. 12; Magali Sarfatti Larson and Arlene Eisen Bergman, *Social Stratification in Peru* (Berkeley, University of California, 1969); Jorge Bravo Bresani, "Mito y realidad de la oligarquía Peruana," *Revista de Sociología*, 3 (1966), 43-71; David Chaplin, *The Peruvian Industrial Labor Force* (Princeton, Princeton University Press, 1967) and "Peru's Postponed Revolution," *World Politics*, 20 (April 1968), 393-420; and Henry Dobyns and Mario C. Vásquez, eds., *Migración e integración en el Perú* (Lima, Editorial Estudios Andinos, 1963). A study of Indian revolts specifically is F. LaMond Tullis, *Lord and Peasant in Peru: A Paradigm of Political and Social Change* (Cambridge, Harvard University Press, 1970).

5. *The Politics of Reform in Peru: The Aprista and Other Mass Parties of Latin America* (Baltimore, Johns Hopkins Press, 1971), pp. 34, 39.

6. See the works cited in note 4, this chapter, particularly by Astiz, Bourricaud, and Cotler.

7. Note in this regard Norman Gall, "Peru: The Master is Dead," *Dissent*, 18 (1971), 281-320; E.J. Hobsbawm, "Peru: The Peculiar 'Revolution,'" *New York Review*, December 16, 1971, pp. 29-36; José Yglesias, "The Reformers in Brass Hats," *New York Times Magazine*, December 14, 1969, pp. 58-59, 128-142. For a view that claims a traditional Peruvian upper class is still in control, see Richard H. Stephens, *Wealth and Power in Peru* (Metuchen, N.J., Scarecrow Press, 1971).

8. Additional material on the Peruvian military is found in Luigi R. Einaudi, *Peruvian Military Relations with the United States* (Rand Corporation, June 1970) and *The Peruvian Military: A Summary Political Analysis* (Rand Corporation, May 1969). See also Liisa North, *Civil-Military Relations in Argentina, Chile, and Peru* (Berkeley, University of California Press, n.d.).

9. Luigi R. Einaudi, et al., *Latin American Institutional Development: The Changing Catholic Church* (Rand Corporation, October 1969). Astiz, *Pressure Groups and Power Elites in Peruvian Politics*, contains a chapter on the church and one on the military as well.

10. *Labor and Politics in Peru: The System of Political Bargaining* (New Haven, Yale University Press, 1965).

11. A government crackdown in November 1971 led to a violent confrontation at one of the American-owned mining centers (Cobriza) which encouraged new antagonism between the regime and the CGTP and leftists in general. For added background in Peruvian unionism, see U.S. Department of Labor, *Labor Law and Practice in Peru* (Washington, D.C., GPO, 1968); and Larry Larson, "Labor, Social Change and Politics in Peru," unpub. Ph.D. diss., University of North Carolina, 1968.

12. Astiz, *Pressure Groups and Power Elites in Peruvian Politics*, p. 196.

13. See Astiz, *ibid.*, pp. 191-204; U.S. Department of Labor, *Labor Law and Practice in Peru*, pp. 29-30; Robert E. Scott, "Political Elites and Political Modernization: The Crisis of Transition," *Elites in Latin America*,

ed. Seymour M. Lipset and Aldo Solari (New York: Oxford University Press, 1967), p. 138.

14. On the structure of Peruvian government, see José Pareja Paz-Soldán, *Derecho constitucional Peruano*, 3rd ed. (Lima, Ediciones del Sol, 1963); Wells M. Allred, "System of Government in Peru," *Philippine Journal of Public Administration*, 4 (January 1960), 46-60; and Martin Needler, "Cabinet Responsibility in a Presidential System: The Case of Peru," *Parliamentary Affairs*, 18 (1965), 156-161.

15. An excellent discussion of Peruvian coups, as well as Peruvian politics and history generally, is found in Arnold Payne, *The Peruvian Coup d' Etat of 1962: The Overthrow of Manuel Prado* (Washington, D.C., Institute for the Comparative Study of Political Systems, 1968).

16. Added material on the parties generally is found in Astiz, *Pressure Groups and Power Elites in Peruvian Politics*, ch. 6. For studies of APRA, with extremely varied viewpoints, note Hilliker, *The Politics of Reform in Peru*; Harry Kantor, *The Ideology and Program of the Peruvian Aprista Movement*, rev. ed. (Washington, D.C., Savile Books, 1966); and the last two chapters of Frederick B. Pike, *The Modern History of Peru* (New York, Praeger, 1967).

17. Note the interpretation of Julio Cotler in his "Political Crisis and Military Populism in Peru," *Studies in Comparative International Development*, 6 (1970-71), 99-101.

18. See J. Fred Rippy, *British Investments in Latin America, 1822-1949* (Minneapolis, University of Minnesota, 1959), pp. 19-21; Jonathan V. Levin, *The Export Economies: Their Pattern of Development in Historical Perspective* (Cambridge, Harvard University Press, 1960), ch. 2.

19. Louis Clinton Nolan, "The Diplomatic and Commercial Relations of the United States and Peru, 1826-1875," unpub. diss., Duke University, 1935, p. 229. According to Nolan, one Dr. Charles Easton of the United States owned a mine and mill in Andahuaylas in 1851 (pp. 241-242).

20. Cleona Lewis, *America's Stake in International Investments* (Washington, D.C., The Brookings Institution, 1938), pp. 583-584, 588, 590, 603.

21. On the Oncenio in general see Pike, *The Modern History of Peru*, ch. 8.

22. Lewis, *America's Stake in International Investments*, p. 655.

23. James C. Carey, *Peru and the United States, 1900-1962* (Notre Dame, University of Notre Dame Press, 1964), ch. 5.

24. An extensive discussion of the controls of the Bustamante period and their subsequent dismantlement by Odría is given in Wilson B. Brown, "Governmental Measures Affecting Exports in Peru, 1945-1962: A Study in Policy and Its Making," unpub. diss., Fletcher School of Law and Diplomacy, Tufts University, 1965.

25. For the text of these laws, see Arturo Nieves Ayala, *Legislación sobre compañias e instituciones extranjeras* (Lima, 1962). They are described generally in Hernando de LaValle, *A Statement of the Laws of Peru in Matters Affecting Business*, 3rd. ed. (Washington, D.C., Pan American Union, 1962), pp. 86-104.

26. Payne, *The Peruvian Coup d' Etat of 1962*, ch. 3. The Industrial Promotion Law 1959 is analyzed in Romulo A. Fererro, "Economic Development of Peru," *Economic Development Issues: Latin America* (New York, Committee for Economic Development, 1967), pp. 239, 257-259.

27. No full treatments of the Belaúnde period yet exist. See, however, Cotler, "Political Crisis and Military Populism in Peru," pp. 99-101, and Astiz, *Pressure Groups and Power Elites in Peruvian Politics*, ch. 12. See also Belaúnde's own *Peru's Own Conquest* (Lima, American Studies Press, 1965).

28. The following discussion of the Velasco government is based on interviews in Peru and contemporary reports in the Peruvian press. The best summaries of the regime I have seen in English are cited in note 7.

29. For an example of Leftist attack, see Aníbal Quijano, *Nationalism and Capitalism in Peru: A Study in Neo-Imperialism* (New York, Monthly Review Press, 1971). Rightist and business criticism will be described in Chapter Three.

30. U.S. Department of Commerce, *U.S. Business Investments in Foreign Countries* (Washington, D.C., 1960), p. 122.

31. U.S. Department of Commerce, *Survey of Current Business*, November 1972, p. 28.

32. *Survey of Current Business*, October 1969, p. 28.

33. *Fortune*, May 15, 1969, pp. 166-202.

34. A thorough exposition on technical aspects of Peruvian mining is found in W.F.C. Purser, *Metal-Mining in Peru, Past and Present* (New York, Praeger, 1971), pt. II.

35. The historical information on Cerro is from: Donald H. McLaughlin, "Origin and Development of the Cerro de Pasco Copper Corporation," *Mining and Metallurgy*, November 1945, pp. 509-511; Golden Anniversary issue of *El Serrano* (Cerro de Pasco house organ), February 1952; and Stanley K. Hamilton, "Factors Influencing Investment and Production in the Peruvian Mining Industry, 1940-1965," unpub. diss., University of Wisconsin (Madison), 1967, pp. 72-109.

36. Data on Cerro's recent operations are from company annual reports for 1966-1971 and various brochures published by it.

37. "Programa de expansión de la Southern Peru Copper Corporation," *Ingeniero Andino* (Lima), September 1965; "La era del cobre," *La Prensa* (supplement), October 22, 1967; Sheldon P. Wimpfen, "How the Toquepala Project Runs," *Mining Congress Journal*, April 1969, pp. 42-50.

38. Hamilton, "Factors Influencing Investment and Production in the Peruvian Mining Industry," pp. 109-130.

39. *Business Latin America*, August 31, 1967; *Engineering & Mining Journal*, January 1968, p. 114; *Peruvian Times*, December 24, 1971.

40. J. Peter Grace, Jr., *W.R. Grace (1832-1904) and the Enterprises He Created* (New York, Newcomen Society, 1953).

41. Eugene W. Burgess and Frederick H. Harbison, *Casa Grace in Peru* (New York, National Planning Association, 1954), pp. 3-4.

42. For more elaborate discussions on IPC, see Rieck B. Hannifin,

"Expropriation by Peru of the International Petroleum Company: A Background Study," Library of Congress Legislative Reference Service, 1969; "Chronological History of 'La Brea y Pariñas Oilfields of the International Petroleum Company, 1826-1963," *Peruvian Times*, July 28, 1967; "The International Petroleum Company in Peru," Harvard Business School, 1970; Richard N. Goodwin, "Letter from Peru," *New Yorker*, May 17, 1969, pp. 41-110; Sherman Lewis, "The International Petroleum Company vs. Peru," California State College at Hayward, reproduced, 1972; and Adalberto J. Pinelo, *The Multinational Corporation as a Force in Latin American Politics: A Case Study of the International Petroleum Company in Peru* (New York, Praeger, 1973). For IPC's version, see its own publication "The La Brea y Pariñas Controversy: A Resumé," September 1972. The Peruvian government's view is contained in *Petroleum in Peru: For the World to Judge, the History of a Unique Case* (Lima, General Bureau of Information, 1969). Other anti-IPC publications include: Alfonso Benavides Correa, *Oro negro del Perú* (Lima, 1963); Oscar Guzmán Marquina, *Reivindicación de la Brea y Pariñas* (Lima, n.d.); Gustavo Palacio, "El laudo de la Brea y Pariñas," *Revista de la Facultad de Ciencias Económicas y Comerciales* (Cuzco), 1 (1963-1964), 31-54; E. Ramírez Novoa, *Recuperación de la Brea y Pariñas: Soberanía nacional y desarrollo económico* (Lima, 1964); Antonio Rodríguez del Valle, *El problema de Brea y Pariñas* (Arequipa, Universidad Nacional de San Agustín, 1965); and Augusto Zimmermann Zavala, *La historia secreta del petróleo* (Lima, 1968).

43. For laudatory treatments, note William R. Fritsch, *The Sears, Roebuck Story in Peru: Progress and Profits* (Washington, D.C., Action Committee for International Development, 1962) and Marion Baldwin, "Sears Roebuck in Lima: A How-To-Do-It Success Story," *Peruvian Times*, September 29, 1967. For Sears's Mexican experience, see Daniel James, "Sears, Roebuck's Mexican Revolution," *Harper's*, June 1959, pp. 65-71; Charles K. Mann, "Sears, Roebuck de México: A Cross-Cultural Analysis," *Social Science*, 40 (June 1965), 149-157; and Richardson Wood and Virginia Keyser, *Sears, Roebuck de México, S.A.* (Washington, D.C., National Planning Association, 1953).

44. On IBEC generally, see Wayne G. Broehl, Jr., *The International Basic Economy Corporation* (Washington, D.C., National Planning Association, 1968).

45. On this episode, see "The Helpful Americans: In Peru 'No,' " *New York Times*, August 23, 1970.

46. It should be added that newer parts of both hacienda towns are physically very attractive, however. For an attempt to put Cartavio in the best possible light, see Burgess and Harbison, *Casa Grace in Peru*, pp. 73-77.

47. Note the following description in Brian Fawcett, *Railroads of the Andes* (London, George Allen & Unwin, 1963): "Cerro de Pasco itself is a nondescript town at 14,208 feet, notable for its coldness, wetness and general unattractiveness. It is ancient, hollow underneath with a myriad old mine shafts, some dating back to the start of mining there in 1630,

surrounded by the newer and organized workings of later years. A writer of 1871 described it as a town of 10,000 people, lacking order and design in every part—the streets crooked and uneven—the houses stuck about anywhere—everything filthily dirty. The town, he asserted, looked as though it were built on the back of one huge lode—lode-stuff everywhere—what Cornish miners call an 'iron gossan.' Well, the town of today has obviously improved greatly, but the truth of the above description is still recognizable" (p. 177).

48. This and the following paragraph are based on George Sweet Gibb and Evelyn H. Knowlton, *The Resurgent Years, 1911-1927* (New York, Harper & Brothers, 1956), pp. 400-403.

49. "Industrial and Social Study: Talara-Peru," internal IPC document dated September 15, 1945, p. 25. As part of its study the committee had considered the condition of other company towns in Peru: "In our discussions throughout Peru a number of concerns, such as Casa Grande, Cerro de Pasco Copper Corporation and the Santa Corporation, have already realized the changing conditions [in Peru] and have been giving a great deal of thought as to how they can keep pace with the modern trend. . . . It was interesting to note that certain other companies, notably Grace and Company, which had not been cognizant of changing conditions, had the most antiquated living conditions and social arrangements for their employees and workmen" (p. 22).

50. *La Prensa*, August 8, 1967. For the views of Richard W. Patch on this subject, see "An Oil Company Builds a Town," *American Universities Field Staff Reports*, West Coast of South America, vol. 5, no. 2 (March 12, 1958).

Chapter Three, Control, Dependence, Attitudes

1. List obtained from American Republics Division Office of International Regional Economics, Bureau of International Commerce, U.S. Department of Commerce.

2. Interview with Paul Boswell, Cerro de Pasco Corporation, Lima, July 30, 1968.

3. See Hernando de LaValle, *A Statement of the Laws of Peru in Matters Affecting Business*, 3rd ed. (Washington, D.C., Pan American Union, 1962), p. 13. For a comparison of four countries on this point, see Clyde Calvin Schrickel, "Personnel Practices of United States Manufacturing Firms Operating in Colombia, Ecuador, Peru, and Venezuela," unpub. diss., Ohio State University, 1966, p. 114.

4. The 1956 figure is calculated from John C. Shearer, *High-Level Manpower in Overseas Subsidiaries: Experience in Brazil and Mexico* (Princeton, Princeton University Press, 1960), pp. 54-55. The 1957 percentage is calculated from U.S. Department of Commerce, *U.S. Business Investments in Foreign Countries* (Washington, D.C., 1960), p. 122.

5. Shearer, *High-Level Manpower in Overseas Subsidiaries*, p. 61. However, a survey of U.S. Enterprises in Brazil between 1950 and 1970

showed that as of 1970, 64 percent of the top 450 management positions were occupied by Brazilians. Reported in Raymond Vernon, *Sovereignty at Bay: The Multinational Spread of U.S. Enterprises* (New York, Basic Books, 1971), p. 149.

6. Similar findings for U.S. companies in Brazil are described in Lincoln Gordon and Engelbert L. Sommers, *United States Manufacturing Investment in Brazil: The Impact of Brazilian Government Policies* (Boston, Harvard Business School, 1962), pp. 110-112, and in Claude McMillan, Jr., Richard F. Gonzalez, with Leo G. Erickson, *International Enterprise in a Developing Economy: A Study of U.S. Business in Brazil* (East Lansing, Michigan State University School of Business, 1964), pp. 98-105.

7. McMillan, et al., *International Enterprise in a Developing Economy*, p. 73; Shearer, *High-Level Manpower in Overseas Subsidiaries*, pp. 27-31; Vernon, *Sovereignty at Bay*, pp. 132-134.

8. Interview with Norman Carignan, W.R. Grace & Company, New York, September 5, 1969.

9. Interview with Robert P. Koenig, Cerro Corporation, New York, September 3, 1969.

10. Instituto Nacional de Planificación, "Mid-Term Development Policy Basic Guidelines (summary)" (Lima, April 1970), p. 1.

11. David Felix, "United States Investment in Latin America: Problems and Prospects," *Journal of International Affairs*, 14 (1960), 14.

12. Newsletter of Society for International Development, *Survey of International Development*, April 15, 1969.

13. Virgilio Roel Pineda, *Problemas de la economía Peruana* (Lima, Gráfica Popular, 1959), p. 92.

14. *Plan nacional de desarrollo económico y social del Perú, 1962-1971*, I (Lima, Banco Central de Reserva del Perú, 1962), 98.

15. "Mid-Term Development Policy Basic Guidelines," p. 7.

16. Humberto Espinoza Uriarte, "La inversión privada Norteamericana en el Perú (informe preliminar)" (Lima, Universidad Nacional Federico Villarreal, 1968), p. 18.

17. U.S. Department of Commerce, *U.S. Investments in the Latin American Economy* (Washington, 1957), pp. 17, 181. The calculation of 10.8 percent is obtained on the basis of a total 1955 revenue of 4,124.0 million soles (19.27 to the dollar then) given in Milton C. Taylor, "Taxation and Economic Development: A Case Study of Peru," *Inter--American Economic Affairs*, 21 (Winter 1967), 46.

18. Vernon, *Sovereignty at Bay*, p. 52; Herbert K. May, *The Effects of United States and Other Foreign Investment in Latin America* (New York, Council for Latin America, 1970), p. 5.

19. See, e.g., John R. Moore and Frank A. Padovano, *U.S. Investment in Latin American Food Processing* (New York, Praeger, 1967), p. 13.

20. *El Peruano*, June 27, 1968.

21. *Peruvian Times*, June 5 and 26, 1970, February 19, 1971, August 6 and 13, 1971.

22. *Peruvian Times* 1970 Fisheries Supplement, July 24, 1970, p. 57. Cf. Michael Roemer, *Fishing for Growth: Export-led Development in Peru, 1950-1967* (Cambridge, Harvard University Press, 1970), pp. 153-154.

23. May, *The Effects of United States and Other Foreign Investment in Latin America*, p. 1.

24. "Survey of Peru and International Development Finance," *Peruvian Times*, May 7, 1971.

25. *Peruvian Times*, January 2, 1970. For a quite complete description of Peruvian manufacturing in the mid-1960's, see Richard H. Mullins, "Principal Manufacturing Industries in Peru," U.S. Department of Commerce, *Overseas Business Reports*, August 1965.

26. Data furnished by Goodyear and Grace.

27. This and following paragraph based on *Peruvian Times*, September 6, 1968, January 3, 1969, August 28, 1970, September 4, 1970, December 24, 1971.

28. For a provocative categorization of factors that determine the "climate" or perceived attractiveness of host countries to foreign investors, see Lee Charles Nehrt, *The Political Climate for Private Foreign Investment: With Special Reference to North Africa* (New York, Praeger, 1970), pp. 1-3.

29. *New York Times*, October 26, 1969.

30. Interview with Wallace Life, Goodyear del Perú, Lima, July 5, 1971.

31. Interview with Enrique R. East, Marcona Mining Company, Lima, July 1, 1971.

Chapter Four, Corporate Political Behavior

1. Interview with Paul Benner, Constructora Emkay, Cerro de Pasco, August 2, 1968.

2. U.S. Department of Labor, *Labor Law and Practice in Peru* (Washington, D.C., 1968), p. 29.

3. W.F.C. Purser, *Metal-Mining in Peru, Past and Present* (New York, Praeger, 1971), pp. 100-101.

4. *Pressure Groups and Power Elites in Peruvian Politics* (Ithaca, Cornell University Press, 1969), pp. 199-203.

5. Interview with George B. Olbert, Goodyear del Perú, Lima, July 24, 1968.

6. *Peruvian Times*, December 17, 1971.

7. U.S. Congress, House Agriculture Committee, Hearings, *Extension of the Sugar Act*, 92nd Cong., 1st Sess., 1971, p. 232.

8. The Council's formation in 1964 was accomplished by merging the Business Group for Latin America, the United States Inter-American Council, and the Latin American Information Committee. Its central offices are at 680 Park Avenue, New York.

9. Taken from notes on the meeting prepared by Enno Hobbing, Staff Director of the Council (reproduced, February 9, 1971).

10. George Sweet Gibb and Evelyn H. Knowlton, *The Resurgent Years, 1911-1927* (New York, Harper & Brothers, 1956), pp. 99-101.

11. A May 1969 issue of the Peruvian magazine *Oiga* displayed a picture of Jones on its cover with this caption.

12. *Peruvian Times*, November 15, 1969.

13. See Albert Lauterbach, *Enterprise in Latin America: Business Attitudes in a Developing Economy* (Ithaca, Cornell University Press, 1966), ch. 1, and William F. Whyte and Allan R. Holmberg, "Human Problems of U.S. Enterprise in Latin America," *Human Organization*, 15 (Fall 1956), 19.

14. Interview with Fernando Belaúnde Terry, Chicago, March 6, 1970.

15. On this practice in Brazil, see Werner Baer and Mario Henrique Simonsen, "American Capital and Brazilian Nationalism," *Yale Review*, 53 (December 1963), 196.

16. *La Prensa*, February 8, 1969.

17. See Robert O. Tilman, "Emergence of Black-Market Bureaucracy," *Public Administration Review*, 28 (September-October 1968), 437-444.

18. For relevant comments on administrative corruption in Peru and Latin America, see Aníbal Ismodes Cairo, *Bases de una sociología del Perú* (Lima: Editorial Minerva, 1967), pp. 172-174; David Chaplin, *The Peruvian Industrial Labor Force* (Princeton, Princeton University Press, 1967), pp. 15-16; and Whyte and Holmberg, "Human Problems of U.S. Enterprise in Latin America," pp. 19-20.

19. Watt Stewart, *Henry Meiggs: Yankee Pizarro* (Durham, Duke University Press, 1946), pp. 47-48.

20. *Peru and the United States, 1900-1962* (Notre Dame, University of Notre Dame Press, 1964), pp. 58-59, 73-75.

21. For background on the Mantaro affair see the *Peruvian Times*, December 17 and 24, 1965; February 4, March 4, and August 26, 1966; January 23, 1970; and December 10, 1971. See also *Ingeniero Andino*, May-July 1969. According to Teresa Hayter, the World Bank had urged the Peruvian government to retain the British contractors. *Aid As Imperialism* (Harmondsworth, Eng., Penguin Books, 1971), p. 147.

22. Interview with Robert P. Koenig, Cerro Corporation, New York, June 14, 1968.

23. Interview with Pedro A. Pessoa, General Motors del Perú, Lima, July 10, 1968.

24. A theoretical discussion of this point is found in Ralph H. Turner, "The Navy Disbursing Officer as a Bureaucrat," *American Sociological Review*, 12 (June 1947), 342-348.

25. See James L. Payne's discussion of patronage and influence in his *Labor and Politics in Peru: The System of Political Bargaining* (New Haven, Yale University Press, 1965), pp. 233-234.

26. Gibb and Knowlton, *The Resurgent Years*, p. 100.

27. Raymond F. Pelissier, "The Contribution of Certain American Business Firms to the Development of Mexico since World War II," unpub. diss., American University, 1958, p. 292.

28. Authorized by Law No. 11953, January 9, 1953.

29. Interview with Pessoa, July 11, 1968.

30. Interview with Robert Helander, IBEC, Lima, July 18, 1968.

31. Interview with James Freeborn, W.R. Grace & Company, Lima, June 29, 1971. See also *Peruvian Times*, November 21, 1969.

32. Interview with Pessoa, July 10, 1968.

33. *El Comercio*, November 3, 1967. This and the following quotations are my translations.

34. *El Comercio*, November 4, 1967.

35. *El Comercio*, November 7, 1967.

36. *El Comercio*, November 9, 1967.

37. *El Comercio*, November 10, 1967.

38. *Peruvian Times*, November 17, 1967.

39. Interview with Belaúnde, March 6, 1970.

40. This text, translated by me, was obtained from a Lima radio station.

41. *Peruvian Times*, October 18, 1968.

42. *Peruvian Times*, October 18, 1968.

43. Interview with Donald Griffiths, *Peruvian Times*, Lima, June 30, 1971.

44. *New York Times*, December 22, 1970.

45. On the potential impact of films, see Louis Turner, *Invisible Empires: Multinational Companies and the Modern World* (New York, Harcourt Brace Jovanovich, 1971), pp. 63-66.

46. See William Bollinger, "Advertising in Peru," *Peruvian Times*, May 15, 1970.

47. In early 1972 Beltrán was forced by the government to relinquish ownership of *La Prensa* on grounds that he had not resided in Peru six months of a year.

48. Interview with Pessoa, July 11, 1968.

49. A number of other studies of U.S. business in Latin America report, somewhat in contrast to my findings here, a lack of interest in institutional advertising or other public relations activities. Baer and Simonsen say that foreign firms in Brazil almost never engage in noncommercial advertising. The explanation they suggest is merely neglect. "American Capital and Brazilian Nationalism," p. 194. Similar comments are found in Claude McMillan, Jr., Richard F. Gonzalez, with Leo G. Erickson, *International Enterprise in a Developing Economy: A Study of U.S. Business in Brazil* (East Lansing, Michigan State School of Business, 1964), pp. 62-63, and Pelissier, "The Contribution of Certain American Business Firms to the Development of Mexico since World War II," pp. 256-257.

50. U.S. Department of State, *Resources Survey for Latin American Countries* (Washington, D.C., November 1965), p. 515.

51. "Peruvian Institute for the Promotion of Education" and other documents furnished by the Instituto.

52. *Peruvian Times*, June 12, 19, and 26, 1970; July 10, 1970; October 31, 1970.

53. It is something of a historical oddity that in 1868, 102 years before, Henry Meiggs allegedly endeared himself to the Peruvian government by

donating $50,000 for relief to victims of an earthquake of August 16 that laid Arequipa flat. This act may have helped Meiggs get his first big railroad contract in Peru. Brian Fawcett, *Railways of the Andes* (London, George Allen & Unwin, 1963), p. 151.

Chapter Five, Behavior of the U.S. Government

1. See Louis C. Nolan, "The Diplomatic and Commercial Relations of the United States and Peru, 1825-1875," unpub. diss., Duke University, 1935, chs. 4 and 7. Nolan says that after 1862 the incessant pressures on damage claims abated greatly.

2. Nolan, pp. 193-210. On U.S. efforts to open up Brazil's rivers at this time, see Percy A. Martin, "The Influence of the United States on the Opening of the Amazon to the World's Commerce," *Hispanic-American Historical Review*, 1 (1918), 146-162.

3. *Richardson's Messages and Papers of the Presidents*, vol. 4, p. 2619. The message is dated December 2, 1850. See also Jonathan Levin, *The Export Economies: Their Pattern of Development in Historical Perspective* (Cambridge, Harvard University Press, 1960), pp. 54-55, 62-63, 73-75.

4. Nolan, "Diplomatic and Commercial Relations," pp. 155-177.

5. James C. Carey, *Peru and the United States, 1900-1962* (Notre Dame, University of Notre Dame Press, 1964), pp. 22–23.

6. U.S. Department of State, *Papers Relating to the Foreign Relations of the United States, 1930*, vol. 3, pp. 724, 728, 729, 750-755. Regarding the prospects of W.R. Grace & Co., at this time, Ambassador Dearing cabled that "I am reliably informed that Sánchez Cerro told the manager of the Grace Company that he was entirely satisfied with the company and it could expect his support as it had never dabbled in politics."

7. Adalberto J. Pinelo, *The Multinational Corporation as a Force in Latin American Politics: A Case Study of the International Petroleum Company in Peru* (New York, Praeger, 1973), pp. 13-14.

8. Government of Peru, *Petroleum in Peru* (Lima, 1969), p. 37.

9. This and the following paragraphs on IPC are based on George Sweet Gibb and Evelyn H. Knowlton, *The Resurgent Years, 1911-1927* (New York, Harper & Brothers, 1956), pp. 102-105, 366-369.

10. Copies of the Award and associated documents are found in Rieck B. Hannifin, "Expropriation by Peru of the International Petroleum Company: A Background Study" (Washington, D.C., Legislative Reference Service, 1969), pp. 106-126. Copies of all major legal documents associated with the controversy are reprinted also in a two-volume edition published by IPC entitled, *The La Brea y Pariñas Controversy: A Resumé*. A third source of most of the documents is *International Legal Materials*, 7 (1968), 1201-1264.

11. Information on these meetings was obtained from a number of business and diplomatic sources, including discussions with Ambassador Jones in Chicago, November 3, 1969. I attempted to obtain access to the staff summaries but was unable to do so.

12. U.S. Department of State, *Foreign Affairs Manual*, vol. 10, "Economic Affairs," secs. 911 and 912 (1961).

13. See B.T. Colley, "The Haciendas of the Cerro de Pasco Copper Corporation," *Mining and Metallurgy,* 26 (1945), 568-571.

14. Interview with Alberto Benavides, Cerro de Pasco Corporation, Lima, July 6, 1967.

15. *Peruvian Times,* May 9, 1969.

16. Interview with Robert P. Koenig, Cerro Corporation, New York, September 3, 1969.

17. *Peruvian Times,* November 8, 1968, and September 26, 1969.

18. Letter to the author from Ambassador Jones, May 20, 1970.

19. Interview with President Belaúnde, Chicago, March 6, 1970.

20. This and the following paragraph are based on reports in the *Peruvian Times,* August 13 and 27, 1965, December 3, 1965; September 30, 1966, December 23, 1966; January 13, 1967, and February 17, 1967.

21. The date of the cable is "probably" February 2 because the day is not known directly but is inferred from the telegram's content, where at one point it is said that "The President has until midnight tomorrow February third to act." The message is not in its original English text but has been retranslated from Spanish by me. As will be explained below, the cable's content has become known because of its publication in Spanish in the Peruvian press and at least one book. See *El Comercio,* February 16, 1967, p. 1, and Carlos Malpica, *Los dueños del Perú,* 3rd ed. (Lima, Ediciones Ensayos Sociales, 1968), pp. 53-55.

22. Except where otherwise cited, my sources for the following discussion of the IPC case are: a variety of informants; executives of Standard Oil and officials of the State Department; Richard Goodwin, "Letter from Peru," *New Yorker,* May 17, 1969; U.S. Senate, Subcommittee on Western Hemisphere Affairs of the Committee on Foreign Relations, Hearings, *United States Relations with Peru,* April 14-17, 1968; and IPC, *The La Brea y Pariñas Controversy.*

23. *Washington Post,* September 5, 1965, February 11, 1966; *New York Times,* September 28, 1965, February 10, 1966.

24. These figures were obtained from Agency for International Development *Operations Reports* covering the affected years. The "Summary of U.S. Government Financed Foreign Assistance to Peru: FY 1946-FY 1967" (AID, 1967) shows development loans to Peru (by signature dates) as FY 1964, $16.2 million; FY 1965, $14.6 million; FY 1966, $2.0 million. It is impossible to explain the discrepancy between the two sets of figures; yet both show drastic declines in the period concerned.

25. Interview with Howard C. Kauffmann, Esso Inter America, Coral Gables, Fla., June 23, 1967.

26. Comments of Belaúnde, March 6, 1970.

27. See Goodwin, "Letter from Peru," p. 102, and Hearings, *United States Relations with Peru,* p. 92.

28. *Oiga* (Lima), May 1969.

29. U.S. Congress, P.L. 87-565, August 1, 1962, sec. 620 (e), 76 Stat. 260.

30. P.L. 89-331, November 8, 1965, sec. 409 (c), 79 Stat. 1280.

31. *New York Times*, October 26, 1968, December 14, 1968; *Peruvian Times*, December 7 and 27, 1968.

32. *Peruvian Times*, January 31, 1969, February 7, 1969. *New York Times*, March 5, 1969.

33. *New York Times*, April 8, 1969.

34. According to a *Wall Street Journal* dispatch published January 8, 1969, "The company [IPC] said that under terms of the Hickenlooper Amendment to U.S. foreign aid legislation, the U.S. could cut off economic and military aid to Peru if 'meaningful negotiations' about the expropriation don't begin by early April." In Lima the government's information office circulated reports alleging an IPC campaign to influence President Nixon to act against the Peruvian government. See *La Prensa*, February 11, 1969.

35. For a full discussion of the background and issues of the dispute, consult David C. Loring, "The Fisheries Dispute," in Daniel A. Sharp, ed., *U.S. Foreign Policy and Peru* (Austin, University of Texas Press, 1972), pp. 57-118.

36. *Peruvian Times*, March 28, 1969; *New York Times*, January 30, 1971.

37. P.L. 680, August 27, 1954, 68 Stat. 883; P.L. 90-482, August 12, 1968, 82 Stat. 729-730.

38. P.L. 89-171, September 6, 1965, sec. 620 (o), 79 Stat. 660.

39. P.L. 90-629, October 22, 1968, sec. 3 (b), 82 Stat. 1322.

40. P.L. 90-224, December 26, 1967, 81 Stat. 729.

41. *The American Fisherman and Cannery Worker* (New York, February 1969.

42. *New York Times*, May 25, 1969, June 15, 1969; *Peruvian Times*, May 23 and 30, 1969.

43. *New York Times*, February 15 and 26, 1969.

44. *Peruvian Times*, January 21, 1972.

45. The Grace position is spelled out by James P. Freeborn in testimony before the U.S. House Agriculture Committee on April 20, 1971. See Hearings, *Extension of the Sugar Act*, 1971, pp. 233-238, 259-260, 264-265.

46. Hearings, *Extension of the Sugar Act*, pp. 233-234, 265.

47. Interview with James P. Freeborn, W.R. Grace & Co., Lima, June 29, 1971.

48. For the House bill see House Report No. 92-245, June 5, 1971.

49. See Senate Report No. 92-302, July 24, 1971.

50. P.L. 92-138, October 14, 1971, sec. 17 (c), 85 Stat. 389.

51. Interview with Koenig, June 21, 1971.

52. Interview with Frank Archibald, SPCC, New York, June 22, 1971.

53. Interview with Wallace Life, Goodyear del Perú July 5, 1971.

54. Reprinted in House Agriculture Committee, Hearings, *Extension of the Sugar Act*, p. 232, and Senate Finance Committee, Hearings, *Sugar Act Amendments of 1971*, June 16-22, 1971, pt. 2, pp. 958-959.

55. *Peruvian Times*, April 23, 1971.

56. Interviews at U.S. Embassy, Lima, June 30, 1971.

57. Hearings, *Extension of the Sugar Act*, p. 228.
58. *Peruvian Times*, December 3, 1971.

Chapter Six, Bargaining over Investments

1. The source for this and the following two paragraphs is George Sweet Gibb and Evelyn H. Knowlton, *The Resurgent Years, 1911-1927* (New York, Harper & Brothers, 1956), pp. 101-105, 366-369.

2. Discussion of the price negotiations of the 1950's is largely dependent upon "The International Petroleum Company in Peru," Harvard Business School case study (reproduced, 1964; revised 1970), pp. 5-10.

3. See his *Oro negro del Perú: La Brea y Pariñas: Problema para la IPC y solución para el Perú* (Lima, 1963).

4. For IPC's negotiations with the Belaúnde administration, I have drawn heavily on Rieck B. Hannifin, "Expropriation by Peru of the International Petroleum Company: A Background Study" (Washington, D.C., Legislative Reference Service, 1969); Richard N. Goodwin, "Letter from Peru," *New Yorker*, May 17, 1969; IPC, *The La Brea y Pariñas Controversy* (February 1969); and interviews. Additional details are available in Sherman Lewis, "The International Petroleum Company vs. Peru," 1972 and Adalberto J. Pinelo, *The Multinational Corporation as a Force in Latin American Politics: A Case Study of the International Petroleum Company in Peru* (New York, Praeger, 1973).

5. Most of the material for the period 1930-1960 is from an interview with Roger Conklin, Cía. Peruana de Teléfonos, Lima, July 1, 1968. For a brief survey, see "Since 1888: Regaining Time Lost in Telephone Communications," *Peruvian Times*, April 11, 1969.

6. For events of 1960-1964, reliance has been placed on a speech by Francis J. Tracy, ITT official and later general manager of Cía. Peruana de Teléfonos. This address, delivered July 13, 1964, is reprinted in the *Peruvian Times*, August 7, 1964.

7. Based on average common equity. This and other profit information mentioned for the period 1960-1966 is from a consultant report furnished me by ITT officials in New York: Henry S. Bloch and James W. Whittaker [consulting economists for E.M. Warburg & Co., New York], "An Analysis of the Earnings Performance of PERUTELCO (Compañia Peruana de Teléfonos Limitada)," January 30, 1967, chart 3 and table 9.

8. A reproduced copy of this letter was given to me by officials of ITT-New York. It is not dated, although from the context it appears to have been written in the 2nd quarter of 1963.

9. In 1965 the number of telephones per hundred persons was less in Peru than in any of the other South American countries in which ITT had telephone concessions. For Peru the figure was 1.15, compared to 1.58 for Brazil, 2.83 for Chile, and 6.64 for Argentina. *Statistical Abstract for Latin America, 1966* (Los Angeles, University of California Latin American Center, 1967), p. 154.

10. On the events of 1965-1967, see the *Peruvian Times*, August 27,

1965, December 3, 1965; April 15, 1966, September 23 and 30, 1966, December 2, 9, 16, and 23, 1966; February 17, 1967, and September 8, 1967.

11. The letter is reprinted in full in the *Peruvian Times*, December 24, 1965.

12. The statement is reprinted in the *Peruvian Times*, January 13, 1967.

13. Details of the 1967 contract are found in the Cía. Peruana de Teléfonos annual report for 1967.

14. *Peruvian Times*, March 15, 1968.

15. *La Prensa*, May 17, 1969.

16. *Peruvian Times*, July 11, 1969, and August 15, 1969.

17. For information concerning the sale, see the *Peruvian Times*, August 29, 1969; January 30, 1970, March 27, 1970, and April 10 and 17, 1970.

18. Quoted in the *Peruvian Times*, October 31, 1969.

19. *New York Times*, November 16, 1969, and January 26, 1970.

20. In addition to interviews, material for events of 1947-1950 has been drawn from Stanley Kerry Hamilton, "Factors Influencing Investment and Production in the Peruvian Mining Industry, 1940-1965," unpub. diss., University of Wisconsin, 1967, pp. 34-38, 98-100.

21. Interview with Robert Koenig, Cerro Corporation, New York, June 14, 1968.

22. Decree Law No. 11357, promulgated May 12, 1950.

23. Interview with Koenig, June 14, 1968.

24. Sheldon P. Wimpfen, "How the Toquepala Project Runs," *Mining Congress Journal*, April 1969, pp. 42-50.

25. Carlos Malpica, *Los dueõs del Perú* (Lima, Ediciones Ensayos Sociales, 1968), pp. 175-181.

26. Interview with Klaus Kursell, SPCC, Lima, August 5, 1968.

27. Interview with Koenig, June 14, 1968.

28. *Cerro Corporation 1967 Annual Report*, pp. 5, 7.

29. For published comments on the revision of Article 56, see *Ingeniero Andino* (Lima), April-June 1968, and the *Peruvian Times*, April 26, 1968, and August 9, 1968.

30. Interview with Nixon Crossley, Marcona Mining Company, Lima, August 14, 1968.

31. See *Peruvian Times*, September 22, 1967; May 10, 1968; and January 17, 1969.

32. *Peruvian Times*, June 21 and 28, 1968.

33. *Peruvian Times*, September 5, 1969; January 9, 1970, February 27, 1970, and April 3, 1970.

34. Decree Law No. 18880.

35. Interview with Koenig, June 21, 1971.

36. *La Prensa*, December 14, 1968, and May 23, 1969.

37. *Peruvian Times*, December 26, 1969; *New York Times*, January 26, 1970.

38. *Peruvian Times*, September 18, 1970; January 29, 1971, and May 21, 1971.

39. "Bargaining, Communication, and Limited War," *Journal of Conflict Resolution*, 1 (1957), 19, 22-23, 32-33.

40. *Peruvian Times*, March 20, 1970.

41. *Forbes*, March 15, 1970, p. 58.

42. *Peruvian Times*, August 21, 1970, and March 26, 1971.

43. Interview with General E.P. Marco Fernández Baca, Petróleos del Perú, Lima, July 5, 1971, and *Peruvian Times*, November 26, 1971, and January 21, 1972.

44. *Peruvian Times*, June 11, 1971, and October 1, 8, and 22, 1971.

45. Interview with Wallace Life, Goodyear del Perú, Lima, July 5, 1971, and *Peruvian Times*, December 17, 1971.

46. *Peruvian Times*, January 7 and 14, 1972.

47. Drawn from quarterly economic reports of the Banco Continental, Lima, for 1971.

48. This arose from confusion over the meaning of the Decree-Law (No. 18999) which ratified Peru's participation in the Andean Pact.

49. *Peruvian Times*, November 5, 12, and 19, 1971, and January 28, 1972.

50. *Peruvian Times*, May 14, 1971, and November 26, 1971.

Chapter Seven, Politics in the Company Town

1. Head of the Department of Welfare.

2. Some relevant comments are found in Richard W. Patch, "An Oil Company Builds a Town," *American Universities Field Staff Reports*, West Coast of South America, vol. 5, no. 2 (March 12, 1958), pp. 6, 12.

3. Note "San Juan: The Company Town in the Desert," *Peruvian Times*, December 24, 1971.

4. On institutions of local Peruvian government see: Wells M. Allred, "System of Government in Peru," *Philippine Journal of Public Administration*, 4 (January 1960), 46-60; William L. Furlong, "Peruvian Local Government: Structures, Functions, and Style," unpub. diss., University of Florida, 1967; and Earl W. Morris, et al., *Coming Down the Mountain: The Social Worlds of Mayobamba* (Ithaca, Department of Anthropology, Cornell University, 1968), pp. 163-174.

5. H.J. Mozans, *Along the Andes and Down the Amazon* (New York, Appleton, 1911), pp. 292-293.

6. Dora Mayer, *The Conduct of the Cerro de Pasco Mining Company* (Lima, Impresa El Progreso, 1913), pp. 6-11.

7. Richard W. Patch, "The Role of A Coastal Hacienda in the Hispanization of Andean Indians," *American Universities Field Staff Reports*, West Coast of South America, vol. 6, no. 2 (March 15, 1959), p. 11.

8. Interview with Carlos Orams, Sociedad Paramonga Ltda., Paramonga, July 15, 1968. Also source for following paragraph.

9. Law No. 16708, published November 15, 1967.

10. Interview with Orams, July 15, 1968. Also source for following paragraph.

11. Interviews with Guillermo Gorbitz, IPC, Lima, July 31, 1967, and June 28, 1968.

12. Interviews with María Neira, IPC, Talara, August 5, 1967, and July 5, 1968. See also Alicia Olaechea García, "Una experiencia de servicio social de grupo con un club infantil en la zona industrial de Talara," unpub. thesis, Escuela de Servicio Social del Perú, Universidad de San Marcos, Lima, 1961, and "Los niños aprenden a mandar," *Noticias de Petróleo* (Lima), 19 (November 1966), 4-5.

13. Interview with William Machie, SPCC, Pueblo Nuevo (then Ciudad Nueva), August 14, 1967.

14. Interviews with: Miguel Custodio, *Junta de Progreso de Cabo Blanco*, Cabo Blanco, August 5, 1967; Froilán Miranda, IPC, August 4, 1967; María Neira, IPC, August 5, 1967. See "Antes subsistian . . . hoy viven," *Noticias de Petróleo* 19 (November 1966), 7-8.

15. For general discussions of the Peruvian labor movement, consult James L. Payne, *Labor and Politics in Peru: The System of Political Bargaining* (New Haven, Yale University Press, 1965), and U.S. Department of Labor, *Labor Law and Practice in Peru* (Washington, D.C., GPO, 1968).

16. Compare these conclusions to those reached by François Bourricaud in *Power and Society in Contemporary Peru* (New York, Praeger, 1970), ch. 3, particularly pp. 93-104. Payne, cited above, regards violence as a systematic feature of a system of "political bargaining" that he perceives in Peruvian labor politics.

17. On the Peruvian church generally, see Luigi Einaudi, Richard Maullin, Alfred Stepan, and Michael Fleet, *Latin American Institutional Development: The Changing Catholic Church* (Santa Monica, The Rand Corporation, 1969), especially pp. 51-55.

18. Compare this finding to those of Edward Dew in his *Politics in the Altiplano: The Dynamics of Change in Rural Peru* (Austin, University of Texas Press, 1969). Dew finds in the Department of Puno a conflict between Indians and mestizo elites that is so intensive that peaceful bargaining becomes almost impossible. L. LaMond Tullis, in *Lord and Peasant in Peru: A Paradigm of Political and Social Change* (Cambridge, Harvard University Press, 1970), attempts to identify factors that underlie successful and unsuccessful peasant revolt in the sierra. Insofar as his concept of "structural bind" (rigidly oppositional elites) would seem to exist in the company towns, one would apparently predict them as ripe for revolution. Yet the managements may be accommodating enough to defuse potential tension, thus avoiding the build-up of the "solidarity" Tullis sees as necessary to revolt.

19. The following discussion is based on several interviews conducted at Cerro de Pasco and Lima in mid-1968. Mayer, *The Conduct of the Cerro de Pasco Mining Company*, discusses some early background on the question (pp. 14-15, 18-19). See also "La nueva Cerro de Pasco," *Ingeniero Andino* (Lima), April-May, 1967, pp. 16-17.

Chapter Eight, Aspects of National Integration

1. J.B. Alberdi, *The Life and Industrial Labors of William Wheelwright in South America* (Boston, A. Williams & Co., 1877).

2. Alberdi, *ibid.*, p. 110.

3. "A Brief History of the Pacific Steam Navigation Company," *Peruvian Times*, December 3, 1965.

4. The leading biography is Watt Stewart, *Henry Meiggs: Yankee Pizarro* (Durham, Duke University Press, 1946). This source is employed for the section on Meiggs except where otherwise indicated.

5. Brian Fawcett, *Railways of the Andes* (London, George Allen & Unwin, 1963), ch. 8. This volume is marvellously entertaining as well as informative.

6. See Fredrick B. Pike, *The Modern History of Peru* (New York, Praeger, 1967), pp. 125-144 ff.

7. *Peruvian Times*, October 11, 1968, and April 9, 1971.

8. Gary Glen Kuhn, "The History of Aeronautics in Latin America," unpub. diss., University of Minnesota, 1965, pp. 126-128, 191-193, 215.

9. Principal sources of data on Faucett's life are articles in the *Peruvian Times*, August 23, 1946, October 1, 1948, and July 19, 1957.

10. For material on the history of the Faucett company, I have relied on the firm's archives in Lima, which were opened to me. Published accounts are found in the *Peruvian Times* of May 5, 1961, October 4, 1968, and September 18, 1970.

11. This and the following paragraph based on U.S. Department of Commerce, *Peru: A Commercial and Industrial Handbook*, by W.E. Dunn (Washington, D.C., GPO, 1925), p. 40.

12. Department of Commerce, *Peru*, pp. 71-72.

13. See Fawcett, *Railways of the Andes*, ch. 9. In her anticompany tract published in 1913, Dora Mayer charged that operating policies of Cerro trains were exploitive. "By way of second-class carriage, a car was added that deserved no better name than that of a hogsty, in which the workmen were huddled together in utter dirtyness and almost without any light." She further said that Cerro had an agreement with the Peruvian Corporation whereby if the La Oroya-Callao track were blocked Cerro ore trains would take precedence over other traffic. As a result, she claims, the town of Tarma was in 1909 "exposed to famine" because following a landslide only Cerro trains were permitted through. Dora Mayer, *The Conduct of the Cerro de Pasco Mining Company* (Lima, Imp. El Progreso, 1913), pp. 12-13.

14. On Harris, see *Peruvian Times*, April 26, 1968.

15. *Peruvian Times*, November 11, 1966. This plane was presented to the Peruvian Air Force Aeronautical Museum in 1966.

16. Matthew Josephson, *Empire of the Air: Juan Trippe and the Struggle for World Airways* (New York, Harcourt, Brace & Co., 1943), pp. 66-67. For a description of later acrimony between the two parent companies, see pp. 180-181.

17. Information on the early growth of Panagra was obtained from the company archives in Lima (now in possession of Braniff Airways). A published document on the subject is Andrew B. Shea, *Panagra: Linking the Americas During 25 Years* (New York, Newcomen Society, 1954).

18. Interview with Bill Peper Nicolas van Meurs, Braniff Airways, Lima, July 12, 1968.

19. U.S. Department of State, *Resources Survey for Latin American Countries* (Washington, D.C., GPO, 1965), p. 58.

20. Department of Commerce, *Peru*, pp. 78-93 ff; *Statistical Abstract of Latin America, 1966* (Los Angeles, University of California Latin American Center, 1967), p. 152.

21. Department of Commerce, *Peru*, p. 90.

22. This and the following paragraph drawn from David P. Werlich, "The Conquest and Settlement of the Peruvian Montaña," unpub. diss., University of Minnesota, 1968, pp. 399-400. See also Antonello Gerbi, *Caminos del Perú* (Lima, Banco de Crédito del Perú, n.d.), p. 75.

23. Department of Commerce, *Peru*, pp. 84, 169.

24. Interview with Paul Boswell, Cerro de Pasco Corporation, Lima, July 30, 1968.

25. *Peruvian Times*, September 15, 1967, and July 19, 1968.

26. This and the following two paragraphs based on examination of LeTourneau literature and articles in the *Peruvian Times*, October 2, 1964, February 28, 1969, and October 9 and 23, 1970.

27. For Belaúnde's concept in his own words, see his book, *Peru's Own Conquest* (Lima, American Studies Press, 1965), pp. 149-178.

28. This and the following discussion of the Tarapoto project is based largely on *Ingeniero Andino* (Lima), September 1965; *Peruvian Times*, March 31, 1967, and June 28, 1968; *New York Times*, August 23, 1970.

29. Interview with G.R. Barlow, Morrison-Knudsen Company, New York, June 11, 1968.

30. See references in note 28 above.

31. Richard W. Patch, "An Oil Company Builds a Town," *American Universities Field Staff Reports*, West Coast of South America, vol. 5, no. 2 (March 12, 1958), p. 17.

32. Data furnished by Industrial Relations Department, SPCC.

33. Interview with Father William Beuth, La Oroya, August 1, 1968.

34. Richard N. Adams, *A Community in the Andes: Problems and Progress in Muquiyauyo* (Seattle, University of Washington Press, 1959), pp. 94-96 and ch. 6 generally.

35. Interview with Carlos Orams, Sociedad Paramonga, Paramonga, July 15, 1968. Richard W. Patch, "The Role of a Coastal Hacienda in the Hispanization of Andean Indians," *American Universities Field Staff Reports*, West Coast of South America, vol. 6, no. 2 (March 15, 1959), p. 4.

36. Eduardo Soler, "Fuentes de migración al complejo agricola-industrial de Paramonga," in Henry F. Dobyns and Mario C. Vasquez, eds., *Migración e integración en el Perú* (Lima, Editorial Estudios Andinos, 1963), pp. 82-87.

37. "The Role of a Coastal Hacienda," pp. 5-7.

38. Department of State, *Resources Survey*, p. 509.

39. Ladislao J. Prazak, "Family Planning & Birth Control in Peru" (San Juan, Peru, reproduced, 1968).

40. SPCC memorandum dated August 10, 1967, "Plan general para el desarrollo de charlas culturales a los padres de familia en Toquepala y Ciudad Nueva."

Index